COUNSELING SECONDARY STUDENTS WITH LEARNING DISABILITIES

A Ready-to-Use Guide to Help Students Prepare for College and Work

MICHAEL KOEHLER ◆ MARYBETH KRAVETS

THE CENTER FOR APPLIED RESEARCH IN EDUCATION
West Nyack, New York 10994

Library of Congress Cataloging in Publication Data

Koehler, Mike, 1938—
     Counseling secondary students with learning disabilities : a ready-
to-use guide to help students prepare for college and work /
Michael Koehler, Marybeth Kravets.
          p.   cm.
     ISBN 0–87628–272–9
     1. Counseling in secondary education—United States—Handbooks,
manuals, etc.   2. Learning disabled youth—Counseling of—United
States—Handbooks, manuals, etc.   I. Kravets, Marybeth.
LB1620.5.K595   1998
373.14—dc21   97–49127
                                                            CIP

© 1998 by Michael Koehler & Marybeth Kravets

Acquisitions Editor: *Connie Kallback*
Production Editor: *Mariann Hutlak*
Formatting/Interior Design: *Dee Coroneos*

Printed in the United States of America

10 9 8 7 6 5 4 3 2 1

ISBN 0-87628-272-9

ATTENTION: CORPORATIONS AND SCHOOLS

The Center for Applied Research in Education books are available at quantity discounts with bulk purchase for educational, business, or sales promotional use. For information, please write to: Prentice Hall Career & Personal Development Special Sales, 240 Frisch Court, Paramus, NJ 07652. Please supply: title of book, ISBN, quantity, how the book will be used, date needed.

THE CENTER FOR APPLIED RESEARCH IN EDUCATION
West Nyack, NY 10994
A Simon & Schuster Company

On the World Wide Web at http://www.phdirect.com

Prentice Hall International (UK) Limited, *London*
Prentice Hall of Australia Pty. Limited, *Sydney*
Prentice Hall Canada, Inc., *Toronto*
Prentice Hall Hispanoamericana, S.A., *Mexico*
Prentice Hall of India Private Limited, *New Delhi*
Prentice Hall of Japan, Inc., *Tokyo*
Simon & Schuster Asia Pte. Ltd., *Singapore*
Editora Prentice Hall do Brasil, Ltda., *Rio de Janeiro*

DEDICATION

This book is dedicated to the many people who have committed themselves to winning the war against learning disabilities. To the millions of students with learning disabilities who wage silent, but fateful battles every day in the face of what could be overpowering obstacles, and to the parents and teachers who stand with them, we extend our appreciation, respect, and continuing support.

ACKNOWLEDGMENTS

The authors would like to acknowledge the following individuals or organizations for giving us permission to reprint materials in this book.

The Association on Higher Education and Disability (AHEAD)

Dr. Pamela Adelman & Debbie Olufs, *Assisting College Students With Learning Disabilities: A Tutor's Manual*

Sheila Anderson, Parent

Loring C. Brinckerhoff, Dr. Joan M. McGuire & Dr.Stan Shaw, *Promoting Postsecondary Education For Students With Learning Disabilities*

Dale S. Brown, LDA/Newsbrief

Clara M. Chaney, LDA/Newsbrief

Chicago School District #299

Deerfield High School, Deerfield, Illinois

Nelle S. Gallagher, LDA/Newsbrief

Richard Lavoie, Riverview School

Learning Disability Association

Learning Disability Association of Ontario, Canada

Learning Opportunities Program, Barat College, Lake Forest, Illinois

Karen M., Parent

Mundelein High School, Mundelein, Illinois

National Information Center for Children and Youth with Disabilities (NICHY)

S. Scott, *Journal of Learning Disabilities*

Southern Illinois University, Carbondale, Illinois

Township High School District #113, Highland Park, Illinois

Imy F. Wax, Parent & Co-author of *The K&W Guide To Colleges For The Learning Disabled,* 4th edition, by Kravets & Wax, RandomHouse/Princeton Review Publishers

United States Department of Education

ABOUT MIKE

Mike Koehler counseled high school students, served in a variety of administrative positions, and has been an adjunct professor of educational administration and supervision since 1974. Currently, he is devoting all his time to writing, teaching at the university level, speaking at conventions, and consulting with schools on teacher supervision, learning disabilities, and the eligibility and recruitment of student athletes. Mike is the author of scores of articles for professional journals, a nationally syndicated radio show, a newspaper column, and the videotape, *The ABCs of Eligibility for the College-Bound Student Athlete,* which is being marketed by the College Board. It currently is in its second edition.

Mike has written twelve books, the most recent being *The Athletic Director's Survival Guide, Advising Student Athletes Through the College Recruitment Process, Building the Total Athlete, The Department Head's Survival Guide, and The Football Coach's Survival Guide,* all with Prentice Hall. He also has written *Leadership Through Collaboration,* released in the fall of 1996 by Eye on Education. He currently is in the planning stages for two more books, one a biography of his grandfather, Jim Thorpe, and is involved in a variety of speaking engagements across the country.

Mike has been married to wife Pat since 1962, has three delightful daughters, Kathleen, Carrie, and Peggy, two fine sons-in-law: Bruce and Dwight, and enjoys time spent with his two grandchildren, Eric Michael and Cassie Jean.

For additional information or to contact Mike for consultation or in-service presentations, write or call:

Mike Koehler
Ideation, Inc.
8246 Voss Rd.
Minocqua, WI 54548
715-358-8802

ABOUT MARYBETH

Marybeth Kravets has been involved in education for over thirty years. She is currently the college consultant at Deerfield High School, a public high school in Deerfield, Illinois, and has been part of the counseling department for nineteen years. She received her A.B. in education from the University of Michigan, Ann Arbor, Michigan, and her M.A. in counseling from Wayne State University, Detroit, Michigan. Kravets is the president of the Illinois Association for College Admission Counseling and a member of many professional organizations; has appeared as a guest on the "NBC Today Show" as well as other television and radio shows; served as a consultant to *Time* magazine in the selection of the 1997 College of the Year and is an advisory board member for Apply Technology, DePaul University, and University of Southern California.

Marybeth has published many articles in journals and magazines including the *National Association for College Admission Counseling Journal; Attention,* the magazine of children and adults with attention deficit disorders; and *Our World,* the magazine for the National Center for Learning Disabilities. She has presented at major national conferences on the understanding of learning disabilities, the transition process for students with learning disabilities from high school to college, and disabilities and the law. Kravets is the co-author of *The K&W Guide to Colleges for the Learning Disabled* by Kravets and Wax, 4th edition, 1997, Random House/Princeton Review Publishers.

Marybeth is married to Alan Kravets and they have four children, Wendy, Mark, Cathy, and Daniel; a son-in-law, Steve; a daughter-in-law, Sara, and three grandchildren who are the loves of her life, Allison, Connor, and David.

For information you may contact Marybeth at:

Deerfield High School
1959 Waukegan Road
Deerfield, Illinois 60015
847-405-8467

ABOUT THIS RESOURCE

Dear Mother—

I started the store several weks. I have growed
considerably I don't lik much like a Boy now-Hows
all the folk did you receive a Box of Books from
Memphis that he promised to send them—Languages.

Your son Tom

Any sensitive mother would be heartbroken to receive such a letter from her teen-aged son. In a world often impressed more by appearances than substance, such a youngster would most likely encounter more than his share of problems in life. Indeed he did. But like so many before him and since, he used his problem not as an obstacle but as a stepping stone to future success. And his mother never lost confidence in the ultimate expression of the genius of her son, Thomas Alva Edison.

Edison was fortunate. Like Albert Einstein, Thomas Jefferson, and perhaps millions of other accomplished Americans who were, and are, learning disabled, he surmounted the assault of ignorance, misunderstanding, and his own wounded self-esteem as a child. Others in our society, however, are less fortunate.

Learning disabilities in this country affect some two million elementary and secondary school students, 10 percent of all college students (students with learning disabilities are among the fastest growing populations in postsecondary schools), and over six million adults, most of whom have average to above-average intelligence, yet they remain among the most misunderstood of all interferences to learning. They are hidden disabilities, subtle but persistent, misunderstood by teachers, parents, and the disabled themselves. Victims of a problem that is suspected to be neurological in origin, persons with learning disabilities may have difficulty with reading, writing, math, oral language, study skills, and social skills.

Problems with social skills, in fact, often signal one or more learning disabilities. The child who is frustrated almost daily by confusing coursework or misinterpreted requests from family and friends often acts out. The inappropriate behavior is the most conspicuous flag the child waves when the learning disability becomes intolerable. Sometimes delinquency results, and those of us who are unfamiliar with the characteristics of learning disabilities focus on the symptoms instead of the causes.

Any delinquent is a new car with a faulty steering mechanism and an unreliable starter. Often, we can't get it moving, and when we do, we worry about the direction it takes. As a result, we question its value. That's at least our first mistake. With a few adjustments and the right road, we usually discover a car with great power and potential stability. The delinquent is also capable of such stability.

According to the National Center for Learning Disabilities (NCLD), 40 percent to 70 percent of juvenile delinquents who allowed themselves to be tested were found to have previously undetected learning disabilities. Interestingly, when they received remedial services for their disabilities, their delinquent behavior virtually disappeared. Their rate of recidivism dropped to only 2 percent. With suitable remedial services and an understanding of their disabilities, their behavior began to reflect their improved self-concepts.

When such disabilities continue to go undetected, however, problems persist into adulthood. It is estimated by the NCLD that 30 percent to 60 percent of all adults with severe literacy problems are suffering from undiagnosed learning disabilities. It is a fact that over 25 percent of high school age children with documented learning disabilities drop out of school. Those of us involved in the field can only guess at the percentage of undetected learning disabilities in the thousands of others who drop out of schools every year. We are certain, for example, that significant numbers of the homeless have undetected learning disabilities.

Because the problem affects an estimated 10 percent to 15 percent of the American population and involves skills that are so critical to success in our society, parents, teachers, professionals in private practice, and other school and college personnel must know all they can about the diagnosis, treatment, and effects of learning disabilties. *Counseling Secondary Students With Learning Disabilities* looks at learning disabilities from a number of different perspectives. It is a must for every parent who has a child with a learning disability or who suspects such a problem. It is a must for teachers and other school and college personnel who must disagnose such problems and assist in their treatment.

One of the book's primary strengths is that it looks at the contexts within which learning disabilities occur. It provides ways not only to identify and treat learning disabilities but to look at the home and school to seek out systemic causes for the behaviors of students with learning disabilities. The child who worries more about constant fighting on the playground than doing social studies homework has a problem. Parents and teachers must look at the child within the context of his or her daily environment in order to identify the specifics of that problem.

To really understand learning disabilites, therefore, we must look at the environment within which they occur. Dyslexia probably wasn't much of a problem to homesteaders on the early frontier. It looms much larger in today's classrooms, particularly for children with learning disabilities who consistently fail to meet the traditional expectations of some teachers or who attend schools each day that are unable to promote their behavioral and educational growth.

Counseling Secondary Students With Learning Disabilities answers the kinds of questions that people are asking every day about the label "learning disabled":

◆ Counselors ask: "How do I help a child with learning disabilities select courses and ultimately apply to college or find a job?"

◆ Teachers ask: "How do I teach a child with learning disabilities?"

◆ Special educators ask: "Can we provide all the services that children with learning disabilities require?"

◆ Administrators ask: "What does the law say, and are we in compliance with it?"

◆ Colleges ask: "Can we be flexible in the admissions process for applicants with learning disabilities?"

◆ The child with learning disabilities asks: "Should I tell people that I have a learning disability?"

◆ Parents ask all the above questions because they wonder most of all: "Will it hurt my child to be labeled learning disabled?"

Counseling Secondary Students With Learning Disabilities addresses all these issues in several ways. First, it defines learning disabilities and discusses the symptoms as well as the processes for identifying them, including the wide range of warning signals for parents and school personnel. Second, it considers the necessary relationships among elementary and secondary schools and colleges and vocational schools. Third, it looks at educational planning in high school, such specifics as the development of Individual Educational Plans (IEP), actual course selection, mainstreaming issues, and the transition from high school to some form of postsecondary education. It looks as well at the world of work and how persons with learning disabilities must deal with employers and co-workers.

Section 6 discusses the needs of teachers in the mainstreamed classroom—in essence, how teachers accommodate the learning styles of students with learning disabilites in order to teach them without sacrificing or "watering down" course content. Section 9 looks at learning disabilities and the law, in effect identifying and discussing the rights of learning-disabled students and focusing on such issues as testing, the filing and release of documents, efforts at reasonable accommodation, the reality of due process, and how to qualify for services in high school and beyond.

Most important, *Counseling Secondary Students With Learning Disabilities* provides a conversational approach to each of these issues, avoiding jargon, and explaining the issues simply and completely. It serves as an introduction to the understanding of learning disabilities as well as a handy reference to keep at home or in school. Although this resource is written primarily for teachers, counselors, and parents, its focus is on children with learning disabilities, youngsters who must learn to understand and live successfully with such interferences. They need our educated help to move beyond coping, and to realize their full potential.

Mike Koehler
Marybeth Kravets

CONTENTS

_____ *Section 2* _____

IDENTIFYING STUDENTS WITH LEARNING DISABILITIES / 39

Section 3

WORKING WITH STUDENTS AND THEIR PARENTS / 79

Section 4

SPECIAL EDUCATION—THE HUB OF ACTIVITY / 115

Section 5

THE COUNSELOR AND OTHER SUPPORT PERSONNEL / 159

Section 6

WORKING WITH CLASSROOM TEACHERS / 191

——————————— *Section 8* ———————————

TRANSITION PLANNING—FOCUS ON CAREERS / 279

———————— *Section 9* ————————

LEARNING DISABILITIES AND THE LAW / 299

Section 10

LD PROGRAMS—THEIR LIKELY AND DESIRABLE FUTURES / 325

UNDERSTANDING LEARNING DISABILITIES

First, a quick story...

Tommy was an all-American kid, sandy-haired, bright-eyed, and active, a high school freshman with a profusion of interests, freckles, and friends. His early goal in high school was to make the swim team, and his greatest fear was the academic monsters that loomed so large to entering freshmen, particularly those who struggled with their grades in junior high.

Tommy's struggle was waged on at least two fronts. On the one hand, he worked hard to compensate for an auditory memory loss. He received help from his junior high school's LD teacher, and he tried hard to take notes during class discussions and review audiotapes afterward. On the other hand, Tommy never scored above 85 on aptitude tests and arrived in high school with achievement scores in the single percentiles. Tommy was battling two relentless opponents simultaneously, and he was hurting from the beating he was taking.

To make matters worse, the Special Education department in Tommy's new high school was reluctant to offer help with his apparent learning disability. His achievement test results were consistent with his tested aptitude. This suggested to school personnel that Tommy was not learning disabled, but that he was just slow, an intellectual straggler in his new school's highly competitive race for grades and for eventual acceptance to the nation's "best" colleges and universities.

Tommy had learned long ago that he would never be a candidate for such a college. His experiences in school and his conversations with his parents and friends had determined the educational road he must travel. His parents had worked hard to accept his limitations and to encourage Tommy to accept them. While many of his classmates were traveling superhighways, therefore, Tommy was negotiating a back road, slowing at each twist and turn and detouring at times because of some of the road's obvious disrepair.

Fortunately, he learned to enjoy the view. In spite of these obstacles, perhaps because of them, Tommy learned to balance academic work with social relationships and the satisfactions of athletics. The Special Education department ultimately decided to work with him to provide periodic assistance with his mainstream placement. Although not a great athlete, he eventually earned spots on the JV swim team and the varsity wrestling team and, after graduation, decided to study early childhood education and to become a preschool teacher.

1

EVOLUTION OF THE TERM

In spite of his limitations, Tommy was a success story. Not all children with learning disabilities or other handicaps are as fortunate. Education is still struggling through the formative stages of working with children with learning disabilities. The term has received so much educational and political attention within the past several years that it suggests a long history of research and practice. All this belies the fact that it has been relatively short-lived. It received the name *learning disability* only in 1960. (Refer to Figure 1.1 for a brief outline of the evolution of the term.)

The phenomenon, however, has received considerable attention. As far back as the early 1800s, scientists researched the brain for possible causes of abnormal behavior and language difficulties. The Gillingham Method, a remedial approach to reading and spelling, was introduced in the 1930s in an attempt to meet the needs of youngsters who exhibited obvious but undefined interferences to their learning. Then, in 1962, Samuel A. Kirk coined the term *learning disability* in his book, *Educating Exceptional Children.*

The term largely replaced such concepts as *brain-injured* and *minimal brain dysfunction* and opened the door to more research and a range of compensatory strategies for persons identified with such disabilities. Then, a few years later, the Children with Specific Learning Disabilities Act was passed, followed a few years later by Title V of the Rehabilitation Act, which provided civil rights legislation for persons with disabilities.

In 1975, the landmark Public Law 94-142 was passed, which provided for a free and appropriate education for all handicapped children ages 3 through 21. It was followed by additional legislation in 1986 that guaranteed the same privilege to preschoolers. Then, in 1990, Public Law 101-476 changed the words "handicapped" to "disabled" and "children" to "individuals" and acknowledged the additional disabilities of autism and traumatic brain injury. It also mandated a transition plan for teenagers with disabilities.

In the same year, 1990, the Americans With Disabilities Act was passed. It protects people with disabilities from discrimination in public accommodations, employment, transportation, and telecommunications. It represents the legislative guarantee that individuals with disabilities will be provided not only an appropriate education but the freedom from discrimination that assures the opportunities promised by the Constitution.

Feel free to reproduce Figure 1.1—and the many other forms and figures throughout this resource for use in meetings with parents, teachers, and students, and during large-group presentations. We hope they will complement your files of information regarding learning disabilities and enable others in your school and community to understand and appreciate their implications for learning.

1.1 — Evolution of Learning Disabilities

1800–1930	Brain research into abnormal behavior, language difficulties.
1930–1960	Gillingham Method — remedial approach to reading and spelling.
1960	Samuel Kirk — coined the term *learning disabilities* to replace terms such as *brain-injured* or *minimal brain dysfunction*.
1969	PL 91-230 — Children With Specific Learning Disabilities Act
1973	Title V of the Rehabilitation Act — civil rights legislation for persons with disabilities.
1973	Section 504 of the Rehabilitation Act of 1973 — nondiscrimination in federal agencies, i.e., "No otherwise qualified person with a disability in the United States…shall, solely on the basis of disability, be denied access to, or the benefits of, or be subjected to discrimination under any program or activity provided by any institution receiving federal financial assistance."
1975	PL 94-142 — Education for All Handicapped Children Act — free and appropriate education to all handicapped children ages 3-21.
1983	PL 98-199 — Education of the Handicapped Act Amendments of 1983 — reauthorized the discretionary programs and established services to facilitate the transition from school to work.
1986	PL 99-457 — Education of the Handicapped Act Amendments of 1986 — mandated services for preschoolers with disabilities.
1988	PL 100-407 — Technology-Related Assistance for Individuals with Disabilities Act — Assisted states in developing comprehensive, consumer-responsible programs of technology-related assistance and extending technology to individuals with disabilities.
1990	PL 101-476 — Individuals With Disabilities Education Act (IDEA) — reauthorization of PL 94-142. Kept the mandates of 94-142 but changed "handicapped" to "disabled" and "children" to "individuals"; included additional disabilities of autism and traumatic brain injury; requires a transition plan for all adolescents with disabilities.
1990	Americans With Disabilities Act — protects individuals with disabling conditions from discriminatory practices in public accommodations, employment, transportation, and telecommunications.

3

DEFINING LD

The nation's sensitivity to the problem of learning disabilities may have outdistanced its understanding of the term. This is both praiseworthy and frustrating. In spite of important educational and social guarantees, which clearly reflect a heightened national sensitivity to the needs of individuals with disabilities, educators and scientists continue to search for answers to the causes and effects of learning disabilities, and to promote ways in schools and communities to enable individuals to compensate for them.

Given the continuing research in the field and an increased social awareness of the problem, future definitions probably will change, but, at this point, two seem to reflect the current understanding of learning disabilities. Perhaps the most obvious is the definition offered in PL 94-142:

> Specific learning disability means a disorder in one or more of the basic psychological processes involved in understanding or in using language, spoken or written, which may manifest itself in an imperfect ability to listen, think, speak, read, write, spell, or to do mathematical calculations. This term includes such conditions as perceptual handicaps, brain injury, minimal brain dysfunction, dyslexia, and developmental aphasia. The term does not include children who have learning problems that are primarily the result of visual, hearing, or motor handicaps, of mental retardation, of emotional disturbance, or of environmental, cultural, or economic disadvantage.

This definition, as reemphasized fifteen years later in Public Law 101-476, the Individuals With Disabilities Education Act, focuses on the learning disability as an interference to spoken or written language and excludes such causal considerations as hearing or sight impairment, physical disability, mental retardation, emotional or environmental factors, and cultural or economic disadvantage. See Figure 1.2 for additional clarification.

A second definition—this one offered by the board of directors of the American Council for Learning Disabilities (ACLD), one of the nation's most powerful forces for understanding and treatment of learning disabilities—provides a clearer understanding of the impact of LD on the individual:

> Specific Learning Disabilities is a chronic condition of presumed neurological origin which selectively interferes with the development, integration, and/or demonstration of verbal and/or nonverbal abilities.

> Specific Learning Disabilities exists as a distinct handicapping condition in the presence of average to superior intelligence, adequate sensory and motor systems, and adequate learning opportunities. The condition varies in its manifestations and in degree of severity. Throughout life the condition can affect self-esteem, education, vocation, socialization, and/or daily living activities.

This definition emphasizes the learning disability as a chronic condition that has a neurological origin, that involves a discrepancy between achievement and intellectual ability, and that can have lifelong effects on individuals personally, educationally, socially, and vocationally. Such definitions promote an understanding of the condition, but they act only as a starting point. Figure 1.3 represents another approach.

1.2—DEFINITION OF LEARNING DISABILITIES

Public Law 101-476—Individuals With Disabilities Education Act

"Children with specific learning disabilities are those children who have a disorder in one or more of the basic psychological processes involved in understanding or in using language, spoken or written, which disorder may manifest itself in imperfect ability to listen, think, speak, read, write, spell, or to do mathematical calculations. These disorders include conditions such as perceptual handicaps, brain injury, minimal brain dysfunction, dyslexia, and developmental aphasia. These terms do not include children who have learning problems which are primarily the result of visual, hearing, or motor handicaps, of mental retardation, of emotional disturbance, or of environmental, cultural, or economic disadvantage."

. . . Is a chronic condition

. . . Has a neurological origin

. . . Interferes with spoken or written language

. . . Discrepancy between achievement and intellectual ability

. . . Not underachievement

. . . Excludes hearing and sight impairment

. . . Excludes physical disabilities

. . . Excludes mental retardation

. . . Excludes emotional or environmental factors

. . . Excludes cultural or economic disadvantages

1.3 — WHO IS THIS CHILD?

Usually   . . . This is an intelligent child who fails at school.

Usually   . . . This is the child who at school age reads "on" for "no," writes 41 for 14, p for q or d for b, and can't remember the sequence of letters that make up a word.

Usually   . . . This is the child who hears the dog barking, the truck honking, but barely hears his mother calling him . . . who hears the scratching of pencils, the sound of the air conditioner and footsteps outside, but does not hear what the teacher says.

Usually   . . . This is the child who forgets names of people, places, things, his own address and telephone number, but does remember the ads on TV.

Usually   . . . This is the child who loses her homework, misplaces her book, doesn't know what day it is, or what year, or what season.

Usually   . . . This is the child with the messy room, the shirttail hanging out, the shoelaces undone, the child who attracts dirt to his person like a magnet.

Usually   . . . This is the child who doesn't look where he's going, who bumps into the door, swings, his lunch box into the nearest leg, who trips on his own feet and doesn't look at the person who is talking to him.

Usually   . . . This is the child who has trouble lining up, who can't keep her hands off the child in front of her . . . who doesn't stop talking, who giggles too much and laughs the loudest.

Usually   . . . This is the child who calls breakfast "lunch" . . . who is confused by "yesterday," "today," and "tomorrow," the child whose timing is always off.

Usually   . . . This is the child who can't tolerate making the smallest mistake . . . who tunes out in mid conversation . . . who is happy one moment and tearful the next.

Usually   . . . This is the child who is reluctant to try anything new, who is frightened by change.

Usually   . . . This is the child who says "I don't care" or "I won't" when he or she really means "I can't" . . . who would rather be called bad than dumb.

Frequently   . . . This is the child who can't picture things in his mind, who can't visualize or remember what he sees.

Frequently   . . . This is the quiet child who bothers nobody in the classroom but does not learn.

Frequently   . . . This is the older child whose language comes out jumbled, who stops and starts in the middle of a sentence or an idea . . . who talks about hospitals, animals, and enemies.

1.3 continued

Frequently	. . . This is the good swimmer . . . who stumbles up the stairs.
Frequently	. . . This is the child who draws the same thing over and over . . . who asks constant questions but doesn't seem interested in the answers.
Frequently	. . . This is the child who can't keep a friend . . . who prefers to play with children younger than herself.
Frequently	. . . This is the child who wants everything done in a certain way . . . who tattletales…who picks on others for every little thing and bosses everyone around.
Frequently	. . . This is the expert strategist in checkers or chess who can't understand a riddle or a joke.
Sometimes	. . . This is the child who lopes through life, slow to get up, slow to move or to think, but quick to play.
Sometimes	. . . This is the child who rushes headlong into his work, is the first one finished and has done all the problems wrong.
Sometimes	. . . This is the child who can add and multiply but not subtract or divide…who can do math in his head but can't write it down.
Sometimes	. . . This is the child who skips words, omits them, or adds them when he is reading aloud.
Sometimes	. . . This is the child who smiles at everyone, greets strangers with open arms, says "hello" to anyone he sees . . . whose good nature leads him into trouble as "the fall guy."
Occasionally	. . . This is the child who tends to feel that life is unfair, who carries a big chip on her shoulder and refuses to try.
Occasionally	. . . This is the child who can understand the *Odyssey* of Homer, but can't read the words "in," "the," or "if."

This may well be a child with a learning disability.

L.D.A.O.
124 Merton Street
3rd Floor
Toronto, Ontario
M4S 2Z2
416-487-4106

CATEGORIZING LEARNING DISABILITIES

Categorization of learning disabilities is also important to help professionals and parents identify problems. See Figure 1.4 for additional information. Learning disabilities tend to manifest themselves in four primary ways:

Input

This is the process for receiving sensory input. Individuals with learning disabilities sometimes misinterpret visual material, such as confusing the letter *b* for the letter *d* or the number 3 for the letter *E*. They often confuse left with right and have difficulty playing catch or shooting a basketball. Their hearing may be similarly affected. They may confuse instructions, misinterpret lecture material, be easily distracted by extraneous sounds, or require that questions be repeated several times before answering.

Examples of input difficulties are:

◆ *Aphasia*—difficulty with the use or the understanding of language

◆ *Auditory discrimination deficit*—difficulty in determining the similarities or differences in sounds

◆ *Dyslexia*—difficulty with reading, often expressed in letter or number reversal

◆ *Dyscalculia*—difficulty grasping mathematical concepts

Integration

This process involves the ability to sequence. Individuals with integration problems have problems putting things in order. They have difficulty with spelling or putting elements in a story in their proper sequence. Often, they grasp only the literal meaning of gestures and words and, as a result, have problems with social cues. Children who misinterpret the written word are just as likely to misinterpret body language and mood. They routinely miss verbal intonation and patented adult "looks" designed to alter behavior.

Examples of integration difficulties are:

◆ *Dyssemia*—difficulty interpreting social cues, such as voice tones, humor, or body gesture

◆ *Reasoning deficits*—difficulty with logical thinking, sequencing, or critical thinking

◆ *Spatial deficits*—difficulty visualizing or understanding dimensions

Memory

This process involves the storing of auditory and visual information. Short-term memory loss in students may require writing instructions or repeating them several times. Long-term memory loss may result in the inability to retrieve normally permanent facts, such as one's telephone number or dog's name.

1.4 — TYPES OF LEARNING DISABILITIES

Dyslexia:	Difficulty with reading: letter or number reversal
Dysgraphia:	Difficulty with handwriting and expressive writing
Dyscalculia:	Difficulty with mathematical concepts
Auditory deficit:	Difficulty receiving information through hearing and processing this information
Visual perception:	Difficulty copying; difficulty with fill-in-the-dot exams; difficulty differentiating between objects
Language deficit:	Difficulty articulating words; difficulty differentiating between past and present; difficulty remembering words
Dyssemia:	Difficulty with signals such as social cues; difficulty reading body language; difficulty differentiating voice tones; difficulty understanding humor or criticisms; difficulty making small talk
Spatial deficit:	Difficulty understanding dimensions
Memory deficit:	Difficulty remembering information or rote facts
Attention deficit:	Difficulty organizing; difficulty staying focused
Reasoning deficit:	Difficulty thinking in a logical order; difficulty with sequencing; difficulty with critical thinking

Examples of memory difficulties are:

◆ *Short-term or long-term memory deficits*—difficulty remembering information or rote facts

◆ *Apraxia*—difficulty remembering how to perform complex muscle movements

Output

This process involves problems with motor and language expression. Individuals with output problems may struggle for the right word or use words incorrectly. They may be unable to play sports or to write legibly.

Examples of output problems are:

◆ *Dysgraphia*—difficulty with handwriting

◆ *Dysnomia*—difficulty in expressing words

MORE ABOUT LEARNING DISABILITIES

Each of these definitions and examples fails to indicate that learning disabilities are often "hidden handicaps," sometimes inappropriately or incorrectly diagnosed and often rejected by others as causes for poor performance. Figures 1.5 and 1.6 offer further insights.

These problems are further complicated in that learning disabilities tend to run in families, require early diagnosis and suitable intervention if their destructive influences are to be minimized, and affect *at least* 10 percent of the United States population.

Because learning disabilities are often hidden, many parents and educators can misinterpret the behaviors of children with learning disabilities and compound a child's problems with poor self-esteem and lack of support. It is important, therefore, that anyone associated with an individual with learning disabilities understand what it is like to be so disabled. Such an understanding promotes adequate diagnosis as well as the support that is so important to the individual.

What Is a Learning Disability?

To understand the world of the individual with learning disabilities, consider the following. Individuals with learning disabilities often find themselves:

◆ Having trouble distinguishing between right and left and getting lost in their own neighborhood.

◆ Having perfect eyesight but seeing letters or words incorrectly or in reverse order.

◆ With an unselective memory that often fails to distinguish between important and useless information.

◆ Experiencing great difficulty making friends and interacting in social situations.

1.5 — EXPLAINING LEARNING DISABILITIES

Individuals with learning disabilities usually have a difficult time taking in, remembering, or expressing information.

The learning process: Information — Memory — Expression

1   Take in information

2. Understand what the information means

3. File the information in appropriate file drawers in your memory

4. Be able to retrieve the information from your memory and remember it

5. Express this information through verbal communication, written communication, or action.

Learning disabilities affect the following areas:

1. Memory

2. Spoken language

3. Written language

4. Arithmetic

5. Reasoning

6. Visual perception

7. Auditory perception

8. Spatial perception

9. Motor coordination

10. Reading

11. Studying

1.6—What a Learning Disability Is

1. Lifelong; permanent; forever

2. Average to above-average IQ

3. Erratic; present on Tuesday but perhaps not Wednesday

4. A gap between true capacity and actual performance

5. Uneven pattern of development

6. Usually affect areas that involve:
      oral expression
      written expression
      reading
      handwriting
      spelling
      mathematics
      reasoning
      social skills

7. Heterogeneous group of disorders

8. Intrinsic; due to factors within the person

- Experiencing anger resulting from almost constant frustration.
- Capable of complex verbal reasoning but unable to spell the simplest word.
- On task Tuesday but completely unfocused on Wednesday.
- Unable to take notes in class because of an inability to process auditory information.
- Being frustrated by multiple-choice exams because of the wide range of choices for each question.
- Fearful of going bowling because of an inability to keep score or of eating out because of an inability to read menus.
- Asking the same question over and over again.
- Feeling lonely, rejected, isolated, and depressed.

Even after such a disability has been diagnosed and a support network has been established, individuals with learning disabilities continue to experience many of the above circumstances because of the subtlety and the chronicity of their problems. Disabilities continue to affect students, for example, in and out of the classroom—influencing their performance on athletic teams and their behavior at parties, and highlighting their inability to do what their friends appear to be doing so easily. Figure 1.7 provides further evidence of what a learning disability "looks like". As such, it is helpful to parents and teachers during the diagnostic process.

What a Learning Disability Is Not

Parents, teachers, and others can be part of the reason that learning disabilities have such profound influence on students. Many of us operate under a range of misconceptions about people with learning disabilities. Such misconceptions promote misunderstandings and inappropriate educational and personal responses to the needs of students. Consider just a few of these misconceptions:

1. due to environmental disadvantages
2. mental retardation
3. an emotional disturbance
4. lack of motivation
5. due to academic disadvantages
6. the result of visual handicap
7. the result of hearing handicap
8. the result of motor handicap
9. due to a cultural disadvantage
10. due to an economic disadvantage

1.7 — LEARNING DISABILITY CHECKLIST

Individuals with a learning disability may exhibit some of the following behaviors:

- Poor organizational skills
- Reversals in writing and reading
- Reduced short-term or long-term memory
- Impulsive behavior
- Difficulty in reading, writing, or spelling
- Poor peer relationships
- Hyperactivity
- Difficulty concentrating
- Poor coordination
- Inability to follow instructions
- Obsession on certain topics
- Inability to read body language
- Frequent frustration
- Difficulty with money concepts
- Difficulty with time concepts
- Difficulty with sequencing
- Forgetfulness
- Omitting or adding words when reading
- Difficulty in completing tasks
- Poor handwriting
- Difficulty with note taking
- Inability to make decision
- Inability to anticipate consequences of actions
- Delayed learning of tasks
- Inattentiveness
- Hesitant speech
- Low self-esteem
- Left-right confusion
- Difficulty with abstract reasoning
- Poor adjustment to environmental changes
- Difficulty setting priorities
- Difficulty learning self-help skills
- Difficulty with pronunciation
- Difficulty learning math facts
- Difficulty studying
- Reacts before thinking
- Restlessness
- Poor social judgment
- Difficulty working with others
- Difficulty completing assignments
- Difficulty answering questions
- Difficulty with athletics
- Difficulty remembering names
- Excessive difficulty learning a foreign language
- Easily distracted by background noise or visual stimulation
- Difficulty recalling common words
- Takes two or three hours longer to read than others
- Verbal skills far exceed abilities to read, spell, or write
- Difficulty listening to a lecture

- Slow processing of information
- Difficulty organizing thoughts on a page
- Inconsistent performance
- Inappropriate behavior
- Difficulty copying from chalkboard
- Inability to finish tests without extra time
- Impulsivity
- Need to solve problems immediately
- Poor sentence structure
- Incorrect grammar
- Poor reasoning
- Inability to persist in sedentary activities
- Transposes numbers
- Difficulty with time management
- Inability to retain abstract concepts
- Difficulty interpreting nonverbal messages

- Difficulty making friends
- Difficulty recognizing changes in tone of voice
- Inflexibility
- Difficulty setting priorities
- Prefers manuscript to cursive writing
- Often uses the upper case when printing
- Weak vocabulary
- Difficulty outlining
- Difficulty using the dictionary, thesaurus, and other resources
- Performs similar tasks differently from day to day
- May learn information presented in one way, but not another
- Inability to tell or understand a joke
- Gets lost easily
- Often has trouble reading maps

FURTHER MISCONCEPTIONS

1. Students with learning disabilities may have problems, but many of them have grown lazy from all the coddling they receive.

   This "pick-yourself-up-by-your-bootstraps" mentality may be appropriate for a cowboy who has just been thrown from a horse, but it falls flat for students with learning disabilities. What may appear lazy to some is usually depression and frustration to others, particularly to the student with the disability. A tougher mental attitude may help students as they battle the assault on their self-concepts and struggle with the development of compensatory strategies, but it does little to lessen the impact of the disability.

   Learning disabilities are substantive interferences in the lives of many students and require understanding and eventual accommodation from parents and teachers. A "come-on-you-can-do-it" pep talk may provide the periodic inspiration students require, but it won't provide the understanding and the knowledgeable help that such youngsters need to compensate for their disabilities.

2. Learning disabilities are caused by poor parenting or dysfunctional home circumstances.

   Learning disabilities are neurological in origin and, although they tend to run in families, particularly among males, they have little to do with parenting. Parenting may be a factor during diagnosis and the eventual acceptance of the reality of the disability, but it has nothing to do with causality.

3. Students with learning disabilities are not "college material." Most teachers favor students who spell correctly, write clearly, and cause few problems in class. Such students make their jobs a whole lot easier and realize the kinds of academic goals that qualify them for additional success in college. They become the prototype of the "college-bound student" and contrast daily with students who struggle through in-class writing assignments and need additional time to complete multiple-choice tests.

   When a student with a learning disability is perceived by teachers or parents as unable to accommodate the demands of a college education, he find himself combating not only the demands of his disability but a self-fulfilling prophecy that works insidiously on his self-perception. We have worked with bright, even gifted, students with learning disabilities who constantly questioned their ability to handle the demands of college. With the proper accommodations and continuing support, they not only survived in college; they prevailed.

   Consider the comments shared by the parents in Figures 1.8 and 1.9. They provide sensitive insights into the courage of both students and parents when confronted with a bleak prognosis for the future. Figure 1.9 is particularly compelling. This parent affirms that, with love and proper intervention, even the severest learning disability need not be an interference to future academic and personal success.

1.8 — Is Anyone Out There Listening?

by Sheila Anderson
Parent of a child with ADD

I cry in the dark consumed with the thought of what the future holds for my child. The comments, "Don't make him more disabled than he is, "He's more like other children than not" come crashing though the black cloud like a bolt of lightning. I have to ask myself for the one millionth time—is he really disabled or am I just making excuses for his lack of effort? After all, that is what I've been told so many times. Would that this were true!

If he were only like other children when he takes three hours to write six sentences on a page with no punctuation. If he were only like other children when his medicine runs out and he is completely out of control. If he were only like other children when he is the only child in the neighborhood who is not invited to the birthday party. If he were only like other children when he can't remember his coat time after time in 10-degree weather. If he were only like other children with a disability one could see, not one most often associated with lack of motivation.

Feelings of panic and anxiousness creep into each day like a thief, stealing those moments of achievement, creating a sense of impending disaster. Will he ever be like other children? Yes and no! He is a wonderfully creative, inquisitive, loving, outgoing, bright child who will find ways to cope with his disability with the help of sensitive, caring individuals along the way. Each time we take a mallet to pound him into that round hole, we chip off a piece of his self-esteem. I challenge those who deal with him not be part of that chipping process, and as his parent, I will never give up on him!

1.9 – A Parent of a Student with Learning Disabilities

Life as a single parent-mother of 6 children, ranging in age from 19–27 was like a "magical mystery tour." Life as the mother of a child who is both "gifted," LD and ADD, was like being on a roller coaster, Ferris wheel, and merry-go-round at the same time.

All through elementary, junior high and high school we had to be "trail blazers." We were not supported by professionals to guide us and we had to rely on our own resources to seek out and identify strategies, philosophies, evaluations and evaluators. We even had to endure a due process hearing and a major United States Education Office of Civil Rights Complaint in order to secure a laptop computer for my son to use to accommodate his severe dysgraphia. What was so tragic was the fact that he was a gifted writer and simply needed the laptop to benefit from spellcheck and grammar check; his words and creativeness were awesome. I was one of two parents who filed a complaint, and it resulted in the resignation of the superintendent, the principal, the vice-principal, the head of guidance, and two special education directors.

We had to gather our self-esteem and confidence and pick up the pieces of his life. We began to work with a new special education teacher and director. We constantly ran up against issues that seemed to stand in the way of progress. My son had never taken any foreign language as he was advised that the available accommodations would not be enough for him to be successful. In place of foreign language he took "technical education" courses such as woodworking, metalwork, and mechanical drawing and he was very successful. My heart said to let him continue with the technical courses because he smiled and was happy, but my intellect said he should try foreign language to make him more admissible to college. I feared that the wrong decision would close doors for his future. He is unsure of where he would like to apply to college as well as what he would like to study. As a mother I look for answers but know that there is no crystal ball to look into the future.

Guiding my son has been a totally unique and different experience than it was with my oldest three children who graduated with class honors. As a mother I try to stay in the background and give my son room to be his own person and develop self-advocacy skills; I try to guide him but not decide for him; I try to give him advice without really knowing what the consequences will be for his future. No matter what, he will always be my son; he will always make me proud; and he will always have my support in any decision he makes for his life. If only all of the individuals he encounters in life could be as accepting and understanding of the challenges and frustrations of living with a hidden disability. However, I am so proud of him and believe in his future and I know that the choice between foreign language and technical education courses will be a small decision in a life full of future decision as long as he continues to have his positive attitude. The future will be his for the taking.

Karen M.
Reprinted from the K & W Guide to Colleges for the Learning Disabled by Kravets & Wax.

4. Learning disabilities can be outgrown. Learning disabilities are a lifetime proposition. Some individuals with learning disabilities have worked so hard to compensate for them and function so successfully in life that they seem to have outgrown or overcome them, but they still experience the same problems as when originally diagnosed. That's another reason why early diagnosis is so critical. The earlier the problem is identified, the sooner students can begin to develop the kinds of compensatory strategies that lessen the impact of the disability.

5. It is unfair to the students themselves to provide "accommodations." If schools and colleges continue to "accommodate" students with learning disabilities, they won't develop the skills and the drive they need to succeed in life.

Such thinking is similar to the "pick-yourself-up-by-your-bootstraps" mentality. Fortunately, it has effectively been overthrown by legislation that requires society to accommodate preschoolers, employers to accommodate employees with learning disabilities, teachers to accommodate mainstreamed students, and universities to accommodate applicants with learning disabilities. Students cannot be denied admission to college on the basis of a learning disability alone.

In every instance, however, such accommodations require written documentation of the disability. Parents and students are advised, therefore, to maintain comprehensive records of diagnoses, multidisciplinary conferences, intervention strategies, and recent test results.

Accommodation is society's way of leveling the playing field for individuals with learning disabilities. It seeks to give them equal opportunity to realize the same kinds of educational and vocational successes available to others. It also provides the opportunity for students to repair the damage done to their self-perceptions. This is an important topic and warrants closer examination.

A Word About Self-Perception

The disability itself is not the only factor that influences how individuals with learning disabilities perceive themselves. Poet Robert Burns wrote long ago about our desire to see ourselves as others see us, suggesting that self-knowledge leads to self-improvement. Certainly, it does, but we must never forget that many adolescents—maybe most—define themselves through the perceptions of others. They often try to become what they see reflected in others' eyes.

Because of their dependency on friends and family, students with learning disabilities tend to have an external locus of control. This is why parents and teachers must assist them to accept responsibility for their own actions and promote an atmosphere of caring by praising their efforts instead of their results. Their helplessness has been learned; they can learn their competence and a sense of independence.

It is important, then, that they see self-worth and competence reflected in the eyes of those closest to them, especially when they don't seem to deserve it. The students who claim to spend hours on homework assignments but continually turn in work with multiple errors are a source of frustration to themselves and to others. Even the most frustrated teachers can be assured that the students are even more frustrated with themselves. Their disabilities are a constant reminder that they are different from others, that their efforts usually fall short of expectations, and that superior accomplishment infrequently rewards hard work. See Figure 1.10 for a detailed listing of other social problems.

Parents, teachers, and others who have frequent and substantive contact with students with learning disabilities can do much to help these students overcome such frustrations. What they must do first is acknowledge and modify their own attitudinal barriers when working with them. Figures 1.11 and 1.12 can help in that regard. Such barriers are often unconscious and can affect students with learning disabilities in insidious and disturbing ways.

What Are Some of the Attitudinal Barriers?

The change process can be very difficult, in persons as well as in organizations. Most people don't fear change itself. Most of us recognize its inevitability, necessity, and—usually—its desirability. What we tend to fear, however, is the need to change ourselves, to adjust our own behavior to new circumstances and to modify the value systems that have sustained us through life. Yet, these are the very kinds of changes that are necessary when working with students with learning disabilities.

The growing body of research about learning disabilities has broad application. It has promoted improvements in the diagnostic process as well as in instructional techniques for the special education classroom. These same techniques have application in the mainstreamed classroom; they are equally appropriate for all students, with or without learning disabilities. In fact, the growing sophistication of special education instruction is doing much to influence the instructional repertoires of all teachers. More of this is highlighted in Section 4 of this book.

As welcome as these insights are to some mainstreamed teachers, they are resisted by others. Much of this resistance is unconscious, an apparently justified commitment to instructional traditions that have served teachers well in the past. Textbooks and lectures, though questioned in much of the literature over the years, have remained the staple of many American classrooms. Such traditions are hard to destroy, particularly when they have provided knowledge for so many students and convenience for so many teachers throughout our history.

The assumed homogeneity of our nation's classrooms, however, has surrendered to the knowledge that, even in "ability-grouped" or tracked classrooms, students bring variable skills, abilities, and learning styles that respond to different types of instruction. We are learning as a profession that no single type of instruction reaches all students with equal effectiveness. Many teachers have accepted this and have tried to incorporate "modality learning" techniques and "learning style" accommodations into their classroom routines.

Others cling to vestiges of "homogeneity" and memories of well-crafted lectures enlightening their students, supplemented with periodic admonitions that "you'd better learn to take good notes, or you won't do well in college." As appropriate as such instruction may be for some students, it is inappropriate for others, particularly for those who have difficulty processing auditory information. It is especially hard when such a processing difficulty results from a learning disability.

1.10 — SOCIAL DEFICITS

- Inability to read body language; difficulty reading nonverbal cues
- Have difficulty interacting with peers or adults
- Exhibit inappropriate behavior
- Unable to describe feelings of frustrations or anger
- Often very compulsive
- Have difficulty making and keeping friends
- Making small talk is very difficult
- Have undeveloped coping skills and are prone to be frustrated easily
- Have low self-esteem
- Often find themselves interrupting conversations
- Find themselves anxious to say something, but not really aware of what the conversation is all about
- May be very concrete and inflexible in social situations
- May be very immature
- Difficulty handling setbacks
- Difficulty being proactive in making friends
- Ill at ease with other people
- Difficulty communicating
- Difficulty working effectively with others
- Difficulty maintaining relationships with family members
- Unable to read facial expressions
- Unable to differentiate between humor and sarcasm
- Respond negatively to criticism
- Easily persuaded
- Often defensive in social situations
- May have a negative self-image
- Disorganized and inattentive
- Do not always see the consequences of their actions
- Difficulty orienting themselves in time and space
- May need special treatment and different family expectations
- Difficulty managing money

1.11 — MISCONCEPTIONS

An individual with learning disabilities must by dumb or lazy.	UNTRUE
Learning disabilities are caused by poor home situations.	UNTRUE
Learning disabilities are the same as mental retardation.	UNTRUE
Learning disabilities will be evident every day.	UNTRUE
Learning disabilities are the same as illiteracy.	UNTRUE
Dyslexia is a disease.	UNTRUE
Learning disabilities can be outgrown.	UNTRUE
Learning disabilities are hidden, therefore do not exist.	UNTRUE
All learning disabilities are alike.	UNTRUE
All individuals with ADD also have learning disabilities.	UNTRUE
All individuals with learning disabilities also are ADD.	UNTRUE
ADD is the result of poor parenting.	UNTRUE
ADD is caused from emotional imbalance	UNTRUE
Preschoolers are not eligible for special services	UNTRUE
Colleges may deny admission because of learning disabilities	UNTRUE
Employers are immune from making accommodations	UNTRUE
Teachers can refuse to provide reasonable accommodations.	UNTRUE
Students can receive accommodations without documentation.	UNTRUE
The terms *learning disabilities* and *dyslexia* are synonymous.	UNTRUE
All students with learning disabilities suffer from brain damage.	UNTRUE
Learning disabilities are contagious.	UNTRUE
Learning disabilities appear overnight.	UNTRUE

1.12 — Attitudinal Barriers

- Use of improper terminology; always emphasize the person first and the disability second, that is, a child with a learning disability and not a learning disabled child.

- Many educated people think that students with learning disabilities are just lazy, unmotivated, and underprepared.

- Many college professors have never taken methods courses on how to teach to individuals who learn differently.

- Some teachers will not be sympathetic to student needs; usually this is because the teacher has had limited exposure to students with learning disabilities.

- Some instructors think that students requesting extra time on exams are being given an unfair advantage.

- "Labels are for jelly jars" and labeling an individual is disabling.

- Some instructors can not understand why a student who cannot spell or read or write grammatically can possibly be college material.

- Professors are often frustrated at having to devise reasonable accommodations to meet student needs, because typically these professors have had little or no guidance in this area.

- Faculty are uncomfortable evaluating students' academic work based on standard criteria if students are unable to meet these criteria because of a learning disability.

- Many people stereotype all individuals with learning disabilities, and do not realize that there are tremendous differences between mild learning disabilities and severe learning disabilities.

- Some believe that individuals with learning disabilities are not fully functional and treat these individuals in a condescending manner.

Attitudinal barriers, then, can result from our own personal value systems regarding hard work and accepted standards of performance, or they may result from our acceptance of time-honored traditions of instruction. Whatever their causes, they can interfere at times with our understanding of the unique needs of students with learning disabilities. Following are some specific examples.

1. Some people think that students with learning disabilities are just lazy, unmotivated, and underprepared.

   Fortunately, many people at this extreme respond positively to information regarding students with learning disabilities. Once they receive information about the realities of learning disabilities, they often change their minds and seek additional information about accommodation strategies.

   To promote an understanding among parents and teachers of how it feels to be unable to visualize and process words, try the exercise contained in Richard Lavoie's video "How Difficult Can This Be." Lavoie instructs the first person to begin a story. After a few sentences, the next person is instructed to continue the first person's story line. Suddenly, Lavoie changes the rules and the third story teller is instructed to continue but not to use any words containing the letter *n*.

   Needless to say, the pace of the activity slows considerably as each subsequent story teller is required to mentally rehearse each word for the letter *n*. Such a sudden deficit is a daily occurrence for many individuals with learning disabilities, who must take time to visualize each word they process. This is just one reason why schools must do all they can to inform mainstreamed teachers about the problems affecting special education students. This is covered in Section 6 of this book.

2. Some people believe that students with learning disabilities are handicapped in all areas of their lives and tend to treat them in a condescending way.

   This response, although it suggests sensitivity to the student, results from inadequate information about the nature of learning disabilities. Though well intentioned, such people damage the self-perceptions of students with learning disabilities as much as those who regard them as lazy. Students with learning disabilities are often extraordinarily capable in areas unaffected by their disabilities. Even in the area of disability, with appropriate compensation, they can be exceptionally capable.

3. Similarly, many people continue to refer to "learning-disabled" students and to allow the term itself to shade all areas of their lives.

   Such labels color individuals with broad strokes, suggesting that the learning disability and the individual are one and the same. Such a term assumes all-encompassing characteristics and ties the student forever to the disability. People are encouraged, therefore, to refer to students or individuals "with learning disabilities"—in essence to acknowledge that the disability is but one aspect of the person.

   Labels are for jelly jars; they are designed to categorize objects, to put things into their proper places. Every time we force a child into his or her "proper place," we scrape off a layer of self-esteem and limit the scope of future opportunity. We must all remember that the child with a learning disability is also the child with a high IQ, the child with remarkable acting ability, the child with athletic talent, the child with unique insight, or the child with an unlimited future if given the right opportunities.

4. Some teachers insist on applying the same standards of academic performance to all students, even those with learning disabilities.

All students, for example, are expected by some teachers to complete tests and quizzes within predetermined periods of time. Such teachers reason that students given extended time for tests enjoy an unfair advantage over other students in class. In many instances, these same teachers establish grading criteria and expect every student to satisfy those criteria in order to receive an A or a B. They are unable to break from the standards that have established themselves so firmly in many of the nation's classrooms.

"Accommodation" is a hard pill for many of them to swallow. Current insights into the teaching-learning process and significant federal legislation, however, are suggesting and mandating changes in this area. Schools are well advised, therefore, to inform teachers of these changes through appropriate in-service training programs and other informational activities.

5. Many schoolteachers and college professors are unfamiliar with improved instructional techniques that can accommodate the needs of individuals who learn differently.

Unfortunately, many resist such knowledge. Many of them are predisposed more to the subject matter of their courses than to instructional methodology anyway. Most have never incorporated methodologies that address different learning styles. Many college professors, for example, seek to impart knowledge, generally by lecturing, and expect students to keep up or fall by the academic wayside. They reason that such a struggle separates the capable from the not-so-capable and guarantees a college graduate who has successfully negotiated the several obstacles that the search for knowledge requires.

Such reasoning may be correct. Academic obstacles are real and necessarily affect everyone's search for knowledge. The reasoning breaks down, however, when all students are expected to overcome the obstacles the same way. Students with learning disabilities suggest only one area that highlights the natural differences that separate all of us. The genuinely gifted among us hurdle such obstacles in their race for knowledge. Others climb each obstacle; some walk around them. Most of us, however, overcome them.

The attitudinal barriers persist for a variety of reasons. Ross and Thibodeau, two special educators from Connecticut, surveyed teachers in twenty area schools to determine the effects of years of experience and class size on their willingness to use compensatory strategies, to modify instructional practices, and to make exceptions in assignments and examinations for mainstreamed special education students. Regarding class size, approximately 50 percent of the teachers with small classes (five to ten students) agreed to use compensatory strategies and modified instruction. Those with larger classes, however, were less willing to make such changes.

Regarding years of experience, the teachers with one to twenty years' experience, in every instance, were more inclined to employ compensatory strategies, modify instruction, and make exceptions on assignments and examinations than the teachers with twenty-one to forty years' experience. This study, which is consistent with others of its kind, suggests that large class size and teachers with more than twenty years' experience militate against the use of adjusted instruction and grading criteria in the mainstreamed classroom.

Certainly, class size is a factor in a range of educational issues, not the least of which is influencing the attitudes of teachers to accommodate the needs of students with learning disabilities. That schools consider this issue when seeking to influence teacher attitudes regarding the accommodation of special education students is critical and is discussed at length in Section 4 of this book.

6. The tendency of people to stereotype all individuals with learning disabilities obscures the differences between mild and severe disabilities.

Learning disabilities exist on a continuum from mild to severe. Some students with auditory memory deficits, for example, can function in mainstreamed classes quite well by taking careful notes. Students with more severe problems may require tape recorders and a copy of lecture notes before class. Mild problems may require only a seat in the front of the class and the guarantee of a nondistracting environment during testing. The severe problem may require extended time on tests, a modified test, and/or access to a word processor.

The severity of any learning disability relates somehow to its cause.

CAUSES OF LEARNING DISABILITIES

Although much research remains to be done in this area, professionals associate learning disabilities with one or a combination of the following causes:

◆ **Maturational Lag**

Children in the same age group sometimes mature at rates slower than everyone else, resulting in an inability to do the expected schoolwork.

◆ **Heredity**

Learning disabilities often run in families. The parents and other family members of students recently diagnosed with learning disabilities often have similar problems. Learning disabilities may be inherited.

◆ Prenatal Problems or Premature Birth

Learning disabilities sometimes result from premature birth or from problems during pregnancy or shortly after birth. Researchers suspect that the use of drugs or alcohol during pregnancy, prolonged labor and lack of oxygen, low weight at birth, or RH factor incompatibility may cause learning disabilities.

◆ Early Childhood Injury

Poor nutrition, toxic substances, head injuries, and child abuse can sometimes be identified as causes of learning disabilities.

◆ Male vs. Female

Learning disabilities are five times more prevalent in males than females, possibly because of slower developmental rates.

◆ Nervous System Disorder

Children with normal sight and hearing sometimes misinterpret the world around them for no other reason than a suspected nervous disorder. Children who are perfectly normal in every other regard may suddenly evidence perceptual problems. This reality suggests two very important considerations. One, parents should not feel guilty if a child is discovered to have a neurological disorder. Learning disabilities are so subtle that some have been attributed to nuances of the English language, its structure and irregular spelling. Spanish- and Italian-speaking countries, for example, have lower rates of learning disabilities.

Blame, therefore, is generally not an issue when a child is discovered with a learning disability. Treatment is. This suggests the second consideration. Early diagnosis is critical if appropriate intervention strategies are to prevent academic and social difficulty. Parents and teachers, therefore, are encouraged to be sensitive to possible signs of learning disabilities in children and to refer the children immediately to the school or an appropriate agency for diagnosis and treatment.

Intervention is critical if adjustments in the learning environment are to help students with learning disabilities develop the compensatory strategies they need for success in the classroom, at home, and in the community. When we discuss the *causes* of learning disabilities, for example, we must consider the context within which they occur. In essence, learning disabilities are a function not only of processing deficits but of the environment within which they occur.

Homesteaders in early America who experienced dyslexia were bothered only marginally by their reading problems. Although reading provided hours of enjoyment around the fireplace, it wasn't critical to settling the American frontier and didn't affect individuals personally, socially, and vocationally to the extent that it does today. When youngsters develop problems with their learning, therefore, it's important to look first at possible organizational causes for behavior.

Consider the reality that when psychologists work with students with learning disabilities, they talk more about nightmares and fights on the playground than they do about classwork. When fights on the playground and misbehavior in study halls become greater concerns than failed compositions or missing homework assignments, parents and teachers must seek contextual clues for student behavior, and they must acknowledge that such students have significant problems.

Certainly, such problems result from student limitations in the classroom and can spill over to the playground, home, and community. The context within which they occur, however, can magnify such problems or help resolve them. Elements of curriculum and instruction, administrative policies regarding student behavior, and the culture and climate of the school and community are critical environmental factors when assessing the causes and impact of learning disabilities in students.

Years ago, we were involved with a school that developed a central referral agency that collected and categorized every referral made by teachers and other professionals in the building. The purpose was to develop some statistics about the total number of referrals received each month, the nature of the interventions of counselors and administrators, composite pictures of highly referred students, and considerations of the kinds of referrals made by teachers throughout the building.

The program had been in operation for less than one year when it became evident to the guidance department and the administration that many of the referrals were being made by teachers who were imposing unrealistic expectations on students and failing to promote positive student behavior in classrooms and corridors. In the words of one of the counselors, "We started this procedure to explore student behavior and have discovered that the school is referring *itself!*"

We wonder how many schools are willing to determine the extent to which they are referring themselves. How many take a critical look at curriculum, instruction, and administrative policy to assess their impact on student behavior? Such an assessment has obvious implications not just for students with learning disabilities but for all students.

Perhaps the most obvious sign is academic failure and, especially in young children, the inability to sequence or reverse "on" for "no," "b" for "d," or "41" for "14." Certainly, letter and number reversal occurs at times in most young children, hence the need to consider a variety of signs when suspecting learning disabilities. Consider the following examples. The child with potential learning disabilities is the child who:

- ◆ Hears scratching at the classroom door and the sounds of the air conditioner but little the teacher is saying.

- ◆ Remembers ads on TV but forgets his telephone number and home address.

- ◆ Loses homework and textbooks and can't tell you what year it is.

- ◆ Rarely establishes eye contact and bumps into the door on the way out of the house.

- ◆ Calls breakfast lunch and attracts dirt like a magnet.

- ◆ Can't line up or keep her hands off the child in front of her, and would rather misbehave than appear dumb.

- ◆ Starts conversations in midsentence and jumbles his words.

- ◆ Constantly asks questions but appears disinterested in the answers.

- Finishes class assignments before everyone else but is invariably wrong.
- Is the best chess player in the house but can't understand a joke.
- Skips words when reading aloud.
- Understands *Hamlet* but can't read "To be or not to be."

Certainly, a single characteristic does not identify a learning disability, but combinations of them should alert parents and teachers to the possibility of a problem and the need to seek diagnosis. With early intervention, children and parents can prevent the personal, educational, and social problems that accompany learning disabilities.

BEING DISABLED IN AN "ABLED" WORLD

The signs of learning disabilities are sometimes obvious, sometimes subtle, but usually persistent (see Figure 1.13).

Persons who avoid diagnosis because they fear the identification of a learning disability are well advised by teachers and other professionals to consider the several people in our history who have overcome learning disabilities to achieve significant success. Following are examples in selected fields:

- In literature: Hans Christian Andersen, Leo Tolstoy, and Agatha Christie.
- In math and science: Albert Einstein, Louis Pasteur, and Charles Darwin.
- In athletics: Jackie Stewart, Bruce Jenner, and Greg Louganis.
- In music and art: Auguste Rodin, John Lennon, George Gershwin, and Leonardo daVinci.
- In politics: Winston Churchill, George Patton, and John F. Kennedy.
- In entertainment: Loretta Young, Whoopi Goldberg, and Walt Disney.

A list like this can do much to dispel some of the family fear associated with the discovery of learning disabilities in a family member. Share the reproducible in Figure 1.14 and 1.15 at large- or small-group meetings, or at other times to help students and parents overcome their initial fear regarding the acceptance of the problem. Other strategies are necessary as well.

THE NEED FOR SENSITIVITY

Parental and professional sensitivity is important if warning signals are to be observed and if diagnostics and treatment are to be provided at appropriate times. Undiagnosed learning disabilities are responsible for a variety of social as well as personal problems. One of the most startling is the suggestion by researchers that large numbers of the homeless are individuals with learning disabilities.

1.13 — What It Is Like to Have a Learning Disability?

- This is a hidden disability and individuals often have to deal with functional limitations and with the frustration of having to prove that the disability actually exists.

- Eyesight might be perfect but letters can still be seen incorrectly or in reverse order.

- Hearing may be perfect but a sentence could still be heard as "bashed the car" instead of "wash the car."

- Some individuals have trouble differentiating between right and left and can lose their sense of direction in their own neighborhood.

- Some may be able to describe a birthday party from many years ago, but have enormous difficulty with current names, dates, and words.

- Walking in a store can be difficult as they may find themselves knocking into merchandise, dropping things, and getting in the way of other people.

- Individuals with learning disabilities often have a memory that is unselective—they have difficulty differentiating between important information to save in memory and information that is basically useless.

- Have a fairly low tolerance for tasks that are repetitive.

- Have a very difficult time making friends, making small talk, and being successful in social situations.

- They often appear to be in a state of continual confusion.

- Parents often receive continuous negative feedback about a child.

- A medical student with learning disabilities could have major difficulties learning subjects that require direct recall of specific terms.

- Writing is very difficult and deteriorates when the individual is tired or hurried.

- Learning disabilities are life disabilities. The same disabilities that interfere with sports, interfere with getting dressed, keeping a room neat, making small talk, and setting the table.

- Students with learning disabilities worry about day-to-day survival and their parents worry about their future.

- Some individuals are talented artists but are unable to place any lettering or writing on their art work.

- Parents are in pain when their children suffer.

- Students with learning disabilities are often angry and frustrated.

- Teachers must learn to make accommodations and develop strategies and techniques that may vary significantly from their norm.

- Has superior verbal reasoning, but cannot spell easy words.

- On task and organized on Tuesday, but unfocused and in a trance on Wednesday.
- Spend many extra hours on assignments, but turn in papers with multiple errors.
- Much more time and effort to do the work than students without learning disabilities.
- Some students are unable to take notes in class because of their deficit in processing auditory information.
- Some students are stymied by multiple-choice exams because there are just too many possibilities for each question.
- Filling in the bubble on exam sheets can be an overwhelming task, because of the difficulties with hand-eye coordination.
- Many individuals are ashamed of their handwriting, because it can look very infantile.
- Sometimes these students appear to have very basic and simple vocabulary because they are uncertain of using more complex words.
- Some individuals are simply not able to copy anything from a chalkboard.
- Some fear going in groups to restaurants because they are unable to read menus.
- Some fear going bowling because of their inability to keep score.
- Depression comes easily because of low self-esteem, frustration, and fear of feeling like a fool.
- Some individuals recall being sent to the corner because they couldn't do the problem.
- Some actually become violently ill if they know they have to perform on command.
- Many convince themselves that once they get to high school the learning disability will be gone…or once they finish high school they'll never need accommodations again…or once they have a job the disability will be fixed.
- Having a lifelong disability can make these individuals feel that everyone will always notice only their weaknesses.
- Students' inability to process information about themselves can result in low self-esteem.
- Often these students have unrealistic quests for perfection, do very little rather than do something that may not be right.
- These students are not successful at cramming, and need to spread out their study time.
- Fear constant failure.
- May often ask the same question over and over.
- Lack self-confidence.
- Often feel lonely, rejected, isolated, and depressed.
- Unable to perceive and react to traditional social expectations.
- Difficulty making eye contact.

1.14—LEARNING DISABILITIES AMONG FAMOUS PEOPLE

A. Woodrow Wilson	The 28th President of the United States
B. Thomas Edison	Invented the electric light bulb
C. Greg Louganis	Olympic Gold Medal winner in diving
D. Cher	Famous female singer
E. Winston Churchill	Past Prime Minister of England
F. Nelson Rockefeller	Past Governor of New York
G. Charles Darwin	Developed the Theory of Evolution
H. Walt Disney	Cartoonist and movie producer
I. Hans Christian Anderson	A Danish author of children's tales
J. Albert Einstein	Famous for his Theory of Relativity
K. Leo Tolstoy	Author of *Anna Karenina*
L. George Gershwin	Musical composer
M. Leonardo De Vinci	Artist, inventor, renaissance man
N. Agatha Christie	Wrote mystery stories
O. F.W.Woolworth	Founder of a chain of 5 & 10 cent stores
P. The Fonz	An actor who played the part of a mechanic
Q. George Patton	Commander in the US army
R. Bruce Jenner	Winner of '76 Olympic Decathlon
S. Tom Cruise	Movie star in *Risky Business*
T. Louis Pasteur	Invented the method to pasteurize milk
U. Jackie Stewart	Race car driver
V. Stephen Cannel	Script writer for television
W. Loretta Young	Had her own TV show named after her
X. William James	Famous American Thinker
Y. John Bon Jovi	Rock star
Z. Auguste Rodin	Created the sculpture "The Thinker"
aa. John F. Kennedy	President assassinated in 1963
bb. Whoopi Goldberg	Comedy actress
cc. John Lennon	One of the Beatles

1.15—Fears in the Workplace

- Will an employer understand and accept a request to give all directions in writing?
- Fear of being given an entry-level test prior to being hired—perhaps unable to read the questions, or write legibly, or understand the questions
- Inability to evaluate how the individual presents in an interview—how the individual dresses, speaks, and responds to questions
- Concern about difficulties processing information
- Employer may perceive the individual with a learning disability as careless, unmotivated, dumb, or lazy
- Inability to spell correctly
- Fear that the deficits will have tremendous impact on performance
- Inability to memorize facts or data or directions
- Fears disability in math may interfere with formulating budgets, completing expense sheets, working on spread sheets or cost analyses.
- Inability to spontaneously adjust behavior
- Concern about difficulty with understanding subtle cues
- Impulsivity may result in inappropriate interruptions
- Deficit in communication
- Difficulty looking people directly in the eye when talking
- Concern about being easily distracted in the work setting
- Inability to understand oral directions and difficulty asking for clarification
- Inability to calculate how many tasks can be done realistically at one time
- Disorganization
- Concern about an employer's ignorance of learning disabilities; many confuse learning disabled with retarded or slow learner
- Concern that employers may be resistant to providing accommodations
- Concern about reversing numbers and letters
- Concern that disclosing a learning disability may result in being treated differently
- Concern about needing to spend enormous time and energy explaining about learning disabilities and convincing employers that there is such a disability that is hidden
- Concern that requests for accommodations may go beyond what is reasonable
- Fear of being fired when learning disability is disclosed
- Fear of having to look for new jobs continuously
- Concern that a learning disability may prevent being hired in higher paying jobs

- Fear of not being able to be an independent adult
- Concern that an employer will not know how to restructure a job to accommodate the specific learning style of the employee
- Fatigues easily
- Involuntary daydreaming
- Difficulty making transitions
- Inability to stay on task
- Difficulty completing assignments
- Frustrates easily
- Need to move around constantly
- Inability to compromise
- Need for self-advocacy skills
- Fear of discrimination
- Concern about inability to always be punctual
- Inability to work cooperatively
- Concern about reacting negatively to stressful situations
- Inability to handle constructive criticism
- Inability to differentiate between humor and sarcasm
- Concern about getting into power struggles
- Poor judgment
- Irritability
- Inability to concentrate on conversations
- Fear of constantly forgetting people's names
- Inability to follow procedure
- May misread or miscopy
- May only be able to explain things orally and not in writing
- Poor coordination
- Short attention span

Statistics also indicate that up to 60 percent of individuals with severe literacy problems have learning disabilities.Studies indicate that, when tested for LD, up to 50 percent of juvenile delinquents have undetected learning disabilities. Their rates of recidivism drop to below 2 percent when they are offered remedial services. A related statistic indicates that up to 60 percent of students in treatment for substance abuse suffer from learning disabilities, many of which are undiagnosed.

Compare these statistics to the fact that only 5 percent of school-aged children receive special education services in our nation's schools, up to 50 percent of these students having learning disabilities. Then consider the studies that indicate that as many as 15 percent may require services. In addition, these numbers don't include students from private or parochial schools, many of which don't have adequate diagnostic or remedial services. The result is significant numbers of students in our nation's schools with undiagnosed learning disabilities.

As alarming, students *with* diagnosed learning disabilities continue to experience problems well beyond the scope of their educational limitations. Approximately 35 percent of students with learning disabilities drop out of school, more than twice the number of their nondisabled classmates. Up to 62 percent of students with learning disabilities in a recent study were not employed one year after graduation from high school, and 31 percent will be arrested within three to five years after graduation.

Finally, the Office of the Inspector General indicated in a recent report that learning disabilities and substance abuse are the two most common interferences to the continued employment and future financial stability of welfare recipients. This is an alarming statement, especially when considered in relation to such disturbing statistics. Refer to Figure 1.16 for a more comprehensive listing of fears in the workplace.

LET'S WRAP IT UP

Learning disabilities are a significant problem in our society. They deny individuals a broad range of educational opportunities and rob them of their self-esteem. They deprive the rest of us of millions of people who, because of undiagnosed disabilities, not only fail to make their full contribution to their homes and communities but often become wards of the state. Such an alarming number of people suffer a "hidden handicap" that takes a subtle but relentless control over their lives.

Our job as parents, teachers, counselors, special educators, and school administrators is to help them identify their problems and develop compensatory strategies that ameliorate the effects of learning disabilities, promote improved self-esteem, and enable them to take control of their futures. Subsequent sections of this book provide the tools for students with learning disabilities, their parents, and the people who work with them to overcome a problem that is much bigger than most Americans realize.

As important, the strategies and instructional techniques that work for the student with learning disabilities work for other students as well. Questioning technique, modality learning, study skills, lesson organization, an awareness of developmental readiness, and a variety of similar considerations are essential when working with students with learning disabilities. They are equally important for all students.

We hope, then, that the remainder of this book helps parents and school personnel improve the quality of education—and of life—for all students, but especially for students with learning disabilities, who require the improved knowledge and increased sensitivity of all of us.

RESOURCES

The following agencies can be helpful in providing further information on identifying and dealing with learning disabilities:

AHEAD   **The Association on Higher Education and Disability**
           P.O. Box 21192
           Columbus, OH 43221

CH.A.D.D. **Children and Adults With Attention Deficit Disorder**
           499 N.W. 70th Avenue
           Suite 101
           Plantation, FL 33317

CLD   **Council for Learning Disabilities**
           P.O. Box 40303
           Overland Park, KS 66204

HEATH   **HEATH Resource Center**
           One Dupont Circle, NW
           Suite 670
           Washington, DC 20036-1193

NCLD   **National Center for Learning Disabilities**
           99 Park Avenue
           New York, NY 10016

NLDA   **National Learning Disabilities Association**
           4156 Library Road
           Pittsburgh, PA 15234

NNLDA   **National Network of LD Adults**
           808 North 82nd Street
           Scottsdale, AZ 85257

           Orton Dyslexia Society
           724 York Road
           Baltimore, MD 21204

RFB   **Recordings for the Blind and Dyslexic**
           20 Roszel Road
           Princeton, NJ 08540

1.16 – A Dictionary of Terms

Accommodations — Modifications made in a student's academic program to meet the educational needs success for.

Americans With Disabilities Act — Prohibits discrimination against an individual who: "Has a physical or mental impairment that substantially limits one or more of such person's major life activities; has a record of such an impairment; or is regarded as having such an impairment."

Annual Goals — Suggestions by special educators of what students should achieve within one year. These goals are part of the annual IEP.

Aphasia — Deficit of the ability to use or understand language.

Assessment — A gathering of information that includes an evaluation, a diagnosis, and recommendations — the final step toward making decisions about the education of a student.

Attention deficit disorder — A neurologically based disorder that manifests itself in three ways: distractibility, impulsivity, and hyperactivity.

Auditory discrimination — Ability to hear similarities and differences in sounds.

Auditory memory — Ability to remember sounds, syllables, and words.

Auditory perception — Ability to interpret and understand what is heard.

Case history — A summary of the student's background, development from birth, and other important information gathered from parents; also includes medical history and school record.

Diagnostic tests — Include a recent history, a life history, an academic history, and IQ tests.

Distractibility — Paying attention to other sounds, sights, and stimuli that occur in the environment rather than the task at hand.

Due Process — Application of law ensuring that an individual's rights are protected.

Dyscalculia — Inability to understand or use mathematical symbols or functions.

Dysgraphia — Inability to write legibly.

Dyslexia — Impairment of the ability to read.

Dysnomia — Deficit in ability to remember words and express words.

Expressive language — communication through writing or speaking.

Federal financial assistance — Includes money, grants, loans, services of federal personnel, or real or personal property or the use of such property.

IDEA — Individuals With Disabilities Education Act reauthorized and updated PL 94-142, the Educational for All Handicapped Children Act.

Individualized Education Plan — A written educational plan developed by a school for each student with a learning disability.

Learning disabilities — Disorders that affect the way an individual learns.

Learning strategies — Skills to help students compensate for deficits.

Mainstreaming — Placing students with learning disabilities into regular classrooms.

Major life activities — Activities that could include caring for oneself; performing manual tasks; seeing; hearing; speaking; breathing; learning; working.

Minimal brain dysfunction — An unspecific term that is used to describe learning disabilities.

Multidisciplinary team — A group of professionals in the school who evaluate a student's disability and prepare an Individualized Educational Plan.

Orton-Gillingham — A multisensory technique that uses visual, auditory, and kinesthetic modalities.

Reasonable accommodation — Academic adjustments to ensure that students receive an equal opportunity to participate.

REI — Regular Education Incentive — A proposal supported by the Office of Special Education and Rehabilitation Services that says students with varied types of learning problems and students who are low learners can be given effective services in mainstream classrooms.

Resource room — An instructional area usually within a school, designed to help students develop skills and strategies to compensate for their disabilities.

Screening — An assessment to determine if a child needs special services.

Section 504 of the Rehabilitation Act — "No other qualified individual with a disability…shall, solely by reason of her or his disability, be excluded from the participation in, be denied the benefits of, or be subjected to discrimination under any program or activity receiving Federal financial assistance…."

Self-advocacy — Ability to effectively describe your disabilities and accommodations needs.

Self-assessment — Ability to identify strengths and weaknesses.

Social perception — The ability to comprehend social situations and understand body cues.

Social skills — Skills needed to understand social situations, and to understand how other people feel.

Undue hardship — Colleges and universities are not required to provide accommodations that would cause undue administrative or financial burdens.

WISC-R — Wechsler Intelligence Scale for Children-Revised — A test measuring intelligence in the areas of language and performance.

IDENTIFYING STUDENTS WITH LEARNING DISABILITIES

First, a quick story . . .

Holly had been in high school for about a month and a half, hardly enough time to decorate the inside of her locker but long enough for her first report card. Grading time was never fun for Holly. Invariably, it embarrassed her, angered her father, frustrated her mother, and provoked veiled threats from her teachers. And it was always the same routine: get a lousy report card, hide it from her parents as long as possible, barely survive the inevitable "discussion" at dinnertime, study harder and longer, and—after the next grading period—get a lousy report card.

What was worse, the longer she stayed in school, the more dramatic seemed the consequences of her poor grades. In elementary school, Holly's parents restricted her television time and required more study in her room after dinner. In junior high school, the consequences imposed by her parents extended beyond home. Invariably, they limited the time she could spend with her friends after school and on weekends. But, now in high school, Holly learned that poor grades extended even further into her future.

Her parents, teachers, and counselor reminded her constantly that poor grades in high school meant a future of struggle, unredeemed by the promise of a college education. Like a condemned person, Holly tried hard to accept an apparently inevitable fate, powerless to oppose it and unable to find anyone to help her change it.

No one seemed willing or, for that matter, able to help Holly redirect her life. Teachers from elementary school to high school made the same mistakes. They obscured her learning problems within the shadows of their own misunderstanding. Each year Holly's parents met with her teachers to discuss her low achievement test results and poor semester grades, and listened to them praise her admirable, if unsuccessful, study habits.

The teacher of Holly's freshman Spanish class even told her parents—in so many words—that she was intellectually incapable of learning the language. Holly's father reacted almost immediately. "Thank heavens she wasn't born in Spain." His remark provoked a somewhat self-conscious smile from the teacher, but he discovered during subsequent interviews with the rest of Holly's teachers that all of them shared the Spanish teacher's assessment of Holly's academic ability—all, that is, but one.

Holly's English teacher regarded her quite differently. He indicated to her parents early in the year that he noticed streaks of insight shining through the misspelling, faulty punctuation, and poor grammar that cracked the foundation of her written work. In fact, he was so impressed by the substance of her ideas that he suggested that she be referred to special education for diagnosis. His reasoning involved one simple principle: How could a young woman with such conceptually sound ideas be so unable to master the fundamentals of written English?

THE NEED FOR EFFECTIVE DIAGNOSIS

Sometimes it's just that simple. When all is said and done, the subtleties of psychological analysis invariably give way to the uncomplicated common sense of concerned people. Such people need not understand the nuances of learning disabilities; they need only look beyond a child's obvious behavior to find reasons for it. Sensitivity to the needs of others is a powerful educational force. It characterizes every successful teacher. Such teachers are invaluable in the early stages of the diagnostic process.

So are parents. We have learned over the years that the daily observations of mothers and their intuitive understanding of the needs of their children are among the earliest indicators in any diagnostic process. Too many school professionals consider parent input intrusive because of its obvious bias. Other professionals invite parent input and regard it as yet another perspective that completes the diagnostic picture.

Parent input is essential if the learning needs of students are to be identified and remedied. The input of sensitive and concerned teachers is also valuable, but it is especially valuable when such teachers recognize and understand the warning signs of learning interferences in their students. Had Holly's early teachers recognized the symptoms of severe language processing deficits, she might have avoided years of unnecessary frustration and an almost constant assault on her self esteem.

Therefore, this section defines effective diagnosis as *a process that promotes the understanding and involvement of parents and teachers, and coordinates their input with the knowledge and experience of trained professionals to develop an informed description of one or more interferences to learning.* The coordinated and carefully analyzed input of a variety of people creates a synergy that maximizes the effectiveness of the entire process. This section provides a description and the materials that can establish such a process in your school.

The list in Figure 2.1, for example, should be included in a larger packet of materials that explains the services provided by the Pupil Personnel program, or it can be discussed separately during an in-service training session devoted to a more generalized discussion of the teaching-learning process. Whatever its use, it should be shared with teachers in order to alert them to the signs of LD. Even a marginal understanding of the checklist is usually enough to break the cycle of frustration for some students, to challenge the well-intentioned but potentially harmful instructional strategies of a few misinformed teachers, and to secure the help from trained professionals such students require to realize their learning potential.

It should be mentioned as well that individual characteristics, even combinations of them, are not determinative. If every youngster who was forgetful or distractible had a learning disability, mainstreamed classrooms would be wastelands. Forgetfulness and distractibility are as descriptive of the "abled" student as they are diagnostic of the youngster with a disability.

The checklist is important, however, because *recurring combinations* of characteristics in a student should alert teachers to possible signs of a learning interference, especially if the student's complementary behavior is contradistinctive. For example, if a student seems conscientious and attentive in class, but his homework is constantly incomplete or missing, and he becomes easily frustrated and fails to complete tests on time, his teacher can reasonably begin to suspect the possibility of a learning problem.

2.1 — Checklist of Warning Signs

Fidgets

Disorganized

Forgetful

Interruptive

Avoidance of tasks requiring sustained mental effort

Distractible

Poor homework completion

Short attention span

Unable to follow instructions

Lack of focus

Lack of follow-through

Frustrates easily

Easily overwhelmed

Poor test taker

Unable to finish tests within traditional time parameters

Often late to class

Difficulty meeting deadlines

Inflexible

Inconsistent in academic performance

Difficulty with new concepts

Problem with immediate memory recall

Difficulty with written expression

Difficulty with spelling

Confuses and reverses words and letters

Inability to read fluently or willingly

Poor self-monitoring

Illegible handwriting

Inability to make and keep friends

Poor social judgment

Difficulty interpreting nonverbal cues

Difficulty working cooperatively

WHAT A LEARNING DISABILITY LOOKS LIKE

Maybe a closer look is in order. Section 1 provided a range of examples of the behaviors of students with learning disabilities. We offer additional examples in this section only because the early identification of learning disabilities is so important. It's important that teachers and others in schools understand, for example, how the warning signs in Figure 2.1 translate into student behavior. In essence, what does a learning disability look like? To answer this question, let's identify behaviors within specific categories.

Figure 2.2 lists these behaviors for teachers and provides descriptive illustrations of the warning signs of potential learning disabilities. It, too, should be shared with teachers early in the year in order to promote a broader understanding of what potential learning disabilities "look like" in certain students. Each of these descriptions also represents a model of the kinds of descriptions teachers must use when writing referrals to the Pupil Personnel program.

INTERPRETING BEHAVIORS

Again, no single behavior, even if repeated often, signals a learning disability. Recurring combinations of them, however, suggest a potential learning interference. Even this interference may not be a disability. Teachers must be careful, therefore, when using the referral form in Figure 2.3, to describe the *behaviors* that require diagnosis rather than to identify specific disabilities or suggest immediate psychological testing.

Figure 2.2 can be helpful in this regard. It lists the kinds of behaviors that suggest a need for qualified personnel to look further into a student's personal background and educational history. The diagnostic process does not begin with immediate testing. It involves the study of scores of documents, a variety of interviews, and the early input of a considerable number of people, the opinions of whom may require the kind of additional information that only testing can provide.

Because many different people are involved in the diagnostic process, information in and about referrals should be shared with all relevant parties. We suggest that schools use referral forms that provide multiple copies—one for the referring teacher, one for an administrative file, and one for the student's counselor. A professional response from the Pupil Personnel program—one that satisfies the needs of the student, the expectations of the teacher, and any and all federal mandates—is impossible without clear communication among all parties.

That's why descriptive referrals from teachers are so important. Classroom teachers who offer opinions when writing referrals reflect a poor understanding of the process and can cause problems when and if parents are consulted to discuss the school's response to the referral. If Pupil Personnel specialists determine during a screening, for example, that the child is intellectually limited but shows no signs of a learning disability, an earlier referral from the teacher stating that the child has a learning disability can promote confusion or unrealistic expectations from parents.

For this reason, schools are well advised to discuss the referral process with teachers early in the school year, using the materials provided in Figures 2.1 and 2.2. Teachers must be encouraged to include descriptions and anecdotes that reveal insights into the student's learning interferences, not to request specific services from special education or to suggest opinions about the student's "problem." Forms such as the one provided in Figure 2.4, promote an understanding of the process and should be shared with the staff during discussions of the referral process.

2.2—What Does a Learning Disability "Look Like"?

Please review the following information in order to identify the kinds of student behaviors in your class that may signal a potential learning disability. Recognize that no single behavior identifies the existence of a disability but that recurring combinations of them may suggest one. If you observe such chronic problems in a particular student, please refer him or her to the Pupil Personnel program by using a Referral for Learning which can be found in your department office. Also, please be sure to identify specific student behaviors on the referral, using descriptions such as those contained in the following information. Actual learning disabilities are difficult to identify; your description of student behaviors will help a great deal in the process. Thanks for your help.

Does this particular student have learning problems:

- *Language Skills*—Seeing a word like "remote" and pronouncing it "motor"? Pronouncing words, especially new words? Following instructions and retelling stories? Spelling a variety of words? Talking in class? Providing summaries to class discussions? Understanding and responding to questions? Talking on the telephone? Taking notes in class? Reading out loud in class? Distinguishing among different sounds? Understanding explanations?

- *Coordination Skills*—Drawing the simplest designs? Using scissors? Writing letters, numbers, or entire words? Tying knots in shoes? Dropping things? Holding a pencil? Throwing a football or a softball? Climbing monkey bars? Buttoning a coat? Using building blocks?

- *Memory Skills*—Remembering the alphabet? Distinguishing among letters and numbers? Remembering the names of relatives and friends? Remembering addresses and phone numbers, even his own? Forgetting days of the week? Constantly forgetting when Columbus discovered America? Spelling? Struggling with math facts and processes? Studying for tests and quizzes? Keeping up with work groups in class? Forgetting the relationship of last week's lesson to this one?

- *Concentration Skills*—Forgetting what she planned to say? Sitting still? Constantly fidgeting? Staying in one place or on one task for any length of time? Making what appear to be silly mistakes? Being easily lured from one task to another? Getting mentally tired early in the day? Getting antsy while waiting for materials to be distributed in class? Handling several simultaneous tasks? Talking before the teacher's instructions are complete? Being unable to budget time in order to complete tasks on schedule?

- *Organization Skills*—Finding his coat? Deciding what to eat for lunch? Indicating what he wants to do first after school? Remembering who he follows in the batting order? Handing work in on time? Developing an outline for a speech? Getting upset when the routine changes? Starting art or other projects and never finishing them? Quitting clubs or sports teams? Starting work on a cooperative project without discussing what needs to be done? Learning left from right?

- *Social Skills*—Being accepted by peers? Constantly fighting on the playground? Hitting friends for no apparent reason? Understanding looks and gestures? Avoiding involvement with groups of students? Making friends? Keeping friends?

THANKS FOR PROVIDING INFORMATION TO THE PUPIL PERSONNEL PROGRAM. REACHING OUT TO STUDENTS WHO NEED HELP WOULD BE IMPOSSIBLE WITHOUT YOUR SPECIAL KNOWLEDGE AND INVOLVEMENT.

2.3 — Referral for Learning Issues

Student _____

Counselor _____

Grade in school _____

Referred by _____

Subject _____

Date of referral _____

★ ★

1. Describe your reason for this referral. Identify your concerns relative to level of academic achievement, learning habits, classroom behavior, attitude toward learning, classroom participation, productive use of time, and follow-through on assignments.

2. What is your assessment of this student's skills, quality of learning, placement in your class, ability to learn, study skills, test-taking skills, organizational skills, time-management skills, ability to follow directions, self-advocacy skills, and attentiveness?

3. What has the student or family done to try to deal with these issues?

4. What have you done to assist the student with these presenting issues?

5. What other insights can you share about the student's learning interferences?

★ ★

COMMENTS:

ROUTING:

_____ Counselor contact parents

_____ Counselor contact student

_____ Counselor contact teacher

_____ Student referred for a screening

_____ Student referred for social work diagnostic

_____ Student referred for academic tutoring

_____ Student referred for Educational Testing

_____ Student referred to Special Education

_____ Consultation with family

_____ Student progress to be monitored

_____ Other interventions:

_____

_____

Copies of disposition to be sent to:

_____ Referring teacher

_____ Administrative file

_____ Counselor

2.4—DESCRIPTIVE INFORMATION ABOUT PRESENTING PROBLEM

Student _____

Referring teacher _____

Class _____   Date _____

Difficulties With language skills:

_____ Word Retrieval   _____ Word recognition   _____ Written text   _____ Reads slowly
_____ Comprehending questions   _____ Poor handwriting   _____ Disorganized phrases
_____ Putting thoughts on paper _____ Drawing conclusions _____ Making inferences
_____ Sounding out familiar words   _____ Abstract concepts   _____ Following directions
_____ Distinguishing among different sounds   _____ Reading comprehension   _____ Oral
reading   _____ Limited Vocabulary   _____ Taking notes   _____ Summarizing   _____ Words
out of sequence   _____ Inappropriate use of words   _____ Poor spelling

Difficulties With Coordinational Skills:

_____ Handwriting   _____ Poor motor coordination   _____ Eye-hand maneuvers
_____ Clumsiness   _____ Holding a pencil/pen   _____ Drawing simple designs
_____ Organizing papers   _____ Holding scissors   _____ Writing letters or numbers
_____ Athletic ability   _____ Dressing neatly   _____ Tying shoes

Difficulties With Memory Skills:

_____ Distinguishing among letters/numbers   _____ Following multiple directions
_____ Remembering phone numbers   _____ Remembering names   _____ Studying for tests
_____ Handing in assignments on time   _____ Remembering days of the week
_____ Remembering key historical events   _____ Remember past lessons
_____ Mathematical computation   _____ Remembering multiplication tables

Difficulties With Concentration Skills:

_____ Distractible   _____ Short attention span   _____ Constantly fidgeting   _____ Hyperactive
_____ Budgeting time   _____ Impulsive   _____ Sticking to a task   _____ Easily frustrated
_____ Handling multiple tasks   _____ Completing tasks   _____ Loses train of thought
_____ Daydreams   _____ Perserverating

Difficulties With Organizational Skills:

_____ Keeping track of assignments   _____ Handing in assignments on time   _____ Punctual
to class _____   Bringing materials to class   _____ Motivated to work   _____ Organizing
ideas _____ Attacking tests   _____ Completing projects   _____ Organized notebooks
_____ Notetaking   _____ Knowing left from right   _____ Planning daily schedule
_____ Study skills   _____ Outlining   _____ Test taking

Difficulties With Social Skills:

_____ Seeking younger friends   _____ Making small talk   _____ Low self-esteem   _____ Making
friends   _____ Understanding humor   _____ Immature   _____ Overreacts   _____ Mood
swings   _____ Very concrete   _____ Dependent   _____ Disruptive   _____ Poor loser
_____ Unable to share   _____ Cannot keep friends   _____ Interrupts   _____ Low level of
frustration   _____ Talkative   _____ Gets off the subject   _____ Gets into fights
_____ Understanding looks and gestures   _____ Blurts out

45

Schools must also be careful to avoid burying referring teachers in an avalanche of paperwork every time they refer a student for diagnosis. The job of Pupil Personnel specialists is to sensitize the staff to the learning needs of certain students and to encourage them to share descriptive information about potential problems. Teachers who make such referrals should be recognized by the Pupil Personnel program and the school's administration as professionals who are willing to go the extra yard to help students.

Teachers should not be punished for their proper performance. Some schools make such a mistake by requiring referring teachers to complete several additional forms in order to provide the information needed by screening committees and other school personnel. Like most organizations, schools are pretty good at "riding their best horses." For example, teachers who are good at lunchroom supervision get it all the time. The hardest working and most dedicated staff members find themselves on more committees, and the best writers among them get to write all the committee reports. Similarly, teachers soon discover that one learning referral can involve hours of additional work. After a few such experiences, even the most dedicated among them begin writing fewer referrals. Our job is not to increase each teacher's already heavy workload, but to encourage as many of them as possible to identify students who may need special help beyond the classroom.

Figure 2.5, the Referral for Behavior Issues, can be very helpful. Teachers who may be unfamiliar with the nuances of learning disabilities can readily identify student behavior that is disruptive or otherwise bothersome in the classroom. Because such behavior can also signal the presence of a learning disability, teachers should be encouraged to use the referral process to alert administrators, counselors, or special educators to the behaviors of certain students.

Admittedly, not as informative as a learning referral, the behavior referral can initiate a similar diagnostic process. To do so, administrators and counselors who deal with behavior referrals must understand the relationship between student misbehavior and learning disabilities. The dean who consistently interprets chronic absenteeism as student misbehavior is much like the teacher who consistently interprets chronic inattention and incomplete work as student laziness.

What makes the diagnosis of a possible learning disability so difficult is that both of these interpretations may be correct. The student referred to the dean for absenteeism may be trying to hold down a very demanding job; the student doing little in class may be nothing more than lazy. If both interpretations *are* correct, then they require a quick meeting with the parents to address the problem. If the interpretations are incorrect, and the students in question are reflecting the chronic frustration of young adults suffering from undiagnosed learning interferences, these problems, too, demand solutions. So what do schools do?

2.5 — REFERRAL FOR BEHAVIOR ISSUES

Student _____ ID# _____

Counselor _____

Year in school _____ Date of incident _____ Date of referral _____

Teacher _____ Class _____ Period/Time _____

Behavioral Issue:

___ Excessive tardiness	___ Disrespectful to adult	___ Weapons
___ Unexcused absences	___ Refuses to follow rules	___ Gang signs
___ Disruptive in class	___ Inappropriate dress	___ Vandalism
___ Interruptions	___ Vile language	___ Gesturing
___ Harassment	___ Argues with peers	___ Noisy in halls
___ Forged passes	___ Argues with teacher	___ Truant
___ Suspicion of drugs	___ Physical threats	___ Lying
___ Suspicion of alcohol use	___ Cheating	___ Tobacco use
___ Disrespectful to peers	___ Refuses to do work	___ Rude

★ ★

Detailed description of the presenting behavioral issue: Include information regarding how often this behavior occurs, how long it lasts, and any other important aspects you feel will be helpful.

Please Describe Any Interventions You Have Tried Prior to Submitting the Referral:

___ Met with the student	___ Assigned additional work
___ Called parent	___ Contacted social worker
___ Called counselor	___ Contacted dean
___ Kept student after class	___ Contacted Case Manager
___ Sent warnings	___ Issued warnings

Referral Request:

___ For documentation only	___ Additional intervention requested
___ Assistance meeting with student	___ Meeting with administrators

Disciplinary Interventions:

___ Meeting with parent(s)	___ Meet with Special Education
___ Conference with student	___ In-school suspension
___ Detention	___ Out-of-school suspension
___ Meet with teacher	___ Recommend expulsion
___ Meet with counselor	___ After-school detention
___ Meet with social worker	___ Saturday detention
___ Study Hall	___ Extra asignments
___ Additional documentation	___ Observation

Student Referred to:

___ Screening	___ Psychologist	___ Counselor
___ Social worker	___ Outside psychiatrist	___ Special Education
___ Dean	___ Drug/alcohol counselor	

Signature _____

Date _____

Copies to: _____ _____ _____

THE SCREENING COMMITTEE:
AN IMPORTANT INITIAL STEP

Screening committees are to a school's referral process what specialists are to a medical diagnosis. They explore the subtleties of individual cases, piece together seemingly unrelated elements, and promote not only an enlightened look at the present but a course of action for the future. After the student has been referred for learning or behavioral reasons, therefore, and if the dean, the counselor, or someone else in Pupil Personnel services or the school's administration feels that the student may require a closer look, the student's situation is referred to a screening committee for further study.

Screening committees vary both in composition and size in many schools, and consist of professionals who are able to provide different but complementary perspectives for committee activities and discussions. Usually, they are composed of a social worker (if the school has one), a counselor, a dean of students, a department head, one or more teachers, and someone from special education. A good screening committee accomplishes a variety of purposes.

Most obviously, it provides expert analyses of a student's background and educational history. Department heads can assess the academic demands and special intellectual requirements of courses within the curriculum; teachers can discuss the different kinds of study habits required for different courses; counselors can relate such academic demands to the developmental milestones of adolescence and their relative cognitive ability to handle such demands; special educators can identify learning discrepancies that signal potential problems; deans can reveal a student's behavioral history in school; and social workers can assess the impact of family history and other developmental factors that affect learning.

Screening committees also provide an in-service training component for all school personnel. Classroom teachers who rotate membership on the committee for a quarter or a semester learn more about learning disabilities and the processes for identifying them. In like manner, deans and department heads broaden their understanding of specific interferences to learning and refine their ability to identify them. Invariably, they use such improved understanding to try to refine a department's curriculum and methods of instruction.

Counselors improve their knowledge of the diagnostic process and of the most recent research regarding learning disabilities. Special educators and social workers are reminded that their work in school is affected by a variety of perspectives and that the curriculum and instructional strategies of teachers may require periodic review in order to satisfy the unique learning needs of all students, not just those referred for diagnosis.

Much of this in-service training occurs incidentally, usually as members of the committee dialogue and share their special expertise with each other. Some of the in-service can be planned, as when the committee seeks to bring in one or more experts to discuss recent developments in the field of learning disabilities. The information used by the committee regarding each student, however, is usually standard and should follow a prescribed format.

The format provided in Figure 2.6 illustrates the kind of information needed by the screening committee to explore all the factors relevant to a particular student's developmental and learning background. It looks at family-related issues, the nature and kind of previous referrals, birth-related issues, the student's medical history, developmental history, and educational history. A close look at all these factors is essential if the committee is to recommend appropriate next steps in order to assure the proper identification and treatment of the student's problem.

BEYOND THE CASE HISTORY

What are the next steps? The case history is a necessary, but only an initial step in determining the existence of a learning disability. If the screening committee feels that elements within the history suggest problems or require further study, the committee will request more information from other persons within the school or from professionals outside the school who may have had contact with the student. Doctors, psychologists, psychiatrists, testing agencies, private social workers, feeder schools—any of these may have detailed information about the student's developmental or learning history.

Figure 2.7 provides a release form the school can give parents to request such information from previous schools or from professionals who have had earlier contact with students. Such a form is necessary to satisfy the confidentiality requirements of federal law and to secure the written permission of parents, some of whom may be reluctant to uncover and share information that identifies their children as something other than "normal."

This written permission enables the school only to secure additional information, not to test the student further or to place her or him in special education. If additional testing is needed, school authorities—usually the screening committee—are expected to meet with parents to explain the reasons for the testing and to secure their permission to do it. Such testing may involve aptitude and achievement testing, reading assessments, psychological inventories, and one or more tests that explore student learning patterns.

In addition to testing, school authorities may also decide to interview teachers and others who have had contact with the student, observe the student in class, and/or secure additional written information about the student from his or her classroom teachers. Figure 2.8 provides a checklist of behaviors that gives additional evidence of the student's unique approach to learning. Symptoms identified by a variety of teachers provide a clear focus on the student's potential problems and help complete a detailed diagnostic picture.

2.6—CASE HISTORY: SAMPLE

- Family members who have exhibited similar difficulties in learning

  Who are these family members?
  What are the types of disabilities?

- Identify any family problems

  Health issues
  Financial issues
  Marital issues
  Sibling issues

- Identify any specialists who have provided services to the student

  Psychologists
  Psychiatrists
  Neurologists
  Speech therapists
  Audiologists
  Ophthalmologists/optometrists
  Surgeons
  Pediatricians
  Social workers
  Counselors
  Allergists

- Birth History

  Age of parents at birth of child
  History of other pregnancies such as miscarriages
  Description of labor
  Status at time of birth
  Birth weight
  Color
  Complications

- Medical History

  Sleep patterns of child
  Allergies

2.6 continued

Family history of illnesses

Medications used

Recurring symptoms that may bother child such as

  Hay fever

  Temperatures

  Nightmares

  Asthma

  Insomnia

  Overactivity

- Past specific problems

  Emotional problems

  Speech problems

  Hearing problems

  Seizures

- Developmental history

  Age child held up head

  Age child turned over

  Age child crawled

  Age child walked

  Age child was toilet trained

  Age child spoke single words, multiple words, sentences

  Child's ability to understand conversation

  Child's ability to interact with peers, siblings, adults

  Child's character

  Coping skills

  Strengths and weaknesses

  Hobbies

  Frustration level

- Educational history

  When was the problem first identified?

  Have there been any interventions?

  Academic strengths and weaknesses

2.7 — RELEASE OF INFORMATION FORM

Date _____

I/We _____

Address _____

Give permission to _____

Address _____

to release or secure information about _____

Social Security # _____

Please provide the following:

____ Medical records	____ Educational records
____ Educational testing	____ Psychoeducational evaluation
____ Social history	____ Reading tests
____ Psychological testing	____ Disciplinary records
____ Psychiatric evaluation	____ Police records
____ Social work documentation	____ Counselor recommendation
____ Testing reports	____ Neurologist report
____ Hospital records	____ Alternative school placement records
____ Interview sessions	____ Observations
____ Other	

Send to the attention of:

Name _____

School _____

Address _____

_____

Telephone _____

Date to be sent by _____

2.8 — SAMPLE OBSERVATION REPORT

Initial Information:

Student name _____ Date _____

Address _____

Social Security # _____

School _____ District _____ Grade _____

Name of observer _____

Title of observer _____

Address_____

Telephone number _____

Reason for referral _____

Class being observed _____ Where _____

Time of day _____ Duration of observation _____

Activity being observed _____ Duration _____

Language being spoken _____

Teacher's identified area of concern and needs of student:

____ Student behavior ____ Attendance ____ Perseveration ____ Learning styles

____ Hearing ____ Vision ____ Speech/language ____ Task completion

____ Academic ____ Processing issues ____ Attention ____ Impulsiveness

What steps should the student be taking? _____

What are the student's strengths? _____

What are the student's weaknesses? _____

Identify problem areas in academic functioning and skills:

____ Reading ____ Motor skills ____ Math ____ Listening ____ Handwriting

____ Written expression ____ Oral expressions ____ Mobility ____ Self direction

____ Maturity ____ Attention ____ Study skills ____ Learning skills

____ Organizational skills ____ Perseverance ____ Motivation ____ Focus

____ Memory ____ Following direction ____ Frustration ____ Impulsivity

Identify characteristics of student behavior:

____ Attentive ____ Inattentive ____ Outgoing ____ Shy

____ Cooperative ____ Disruptive ____ Focused ____ Fidgety

____ Concentrates ____ Distractible ____ Follows direction

____ Confuses directions ____ Calm ____ Hyper ____ Perseverates

____ Retrieves words ____ Stumbles on word retrieval

____ Needs attention ____ Self sufficient ____ Needs assistance

____ Self starter ____ Copies from others ____ Needs repetition

____ Nervous habits ____ Cuts in line ____ Blurts out answers

_____ Irritable   _____ Loud   _____ Overly affectionate   _____ Immature

_____ Childish language   _____ Poor use of time   _____ Messy

_____ Quick recall   _____ Clumsy   _____ Physically immature

_____ Constantly moves leg   _____ Anxious   _____ Fearful   _____ Tense

_____ Poor hygiene   _____ Awkward gait   _____ Glasses

_____ Awkward use of pencil/pen   _____ Disorganized phrases

_____ Reverses letters   _____ Difficulty with conversation

_____ Cries easily   _____ Easily frustrated   _____ Low pain threshold

_____ Poor social skills   _____ Overreaction to noises

Teacher's mode of instruction:

_____ Asks questions   _____ Gives directions   _____ Lectures   _____ Reads

_____ Role models   _____ Provides prompts   _____ Hands on   _____ Group work

How is instruction taken in:

_____ Visually   _____ Hearing   _____ Activity   _____ Touching   _____ Smell

Pace of instruction:

_____ Slow   _____ Moderate   _____ Fast

Location of instruction:

_____ Classroom   _____ Resource center   _____ One-on-one tutorial

_____ Resource room   _____ Quiet area   _____ Library   _____ Gym

_____ Media center   _____ Music room   _____ Audiovisual area

_____ Study center   _____ Cafeteria   _____ Detention area

Description of materials used:

_____ Many items   _____ Few items   _____ Complex   _____ Simple   _____ White

_____ Manufactured   _____ Teacher designed

Types of materials:

_____ Activity sheets   _____ Books   _____ Chalkboard   _____ Computer   _____ Films

_____ VCR   _____ Internet   _____ Recorder   _____ Radio   _____ Television

_____ Interactive video

Time of day for the activity: _____

Sex of teacher: _____ Female   _____ Male

Teacher worked as:

_____ Group leader   _____ Tutor   _____ Instructional aid

_____ Individualized instructor   _____ Student teacher

Teacher provided:

_____ Verbal explanation   _____ Physical activity   _____ Privileges

_____ Honors or awards   _____ Extra credit   _____ Responses

_____ Explanations   _____ Graded papers   _____ Verbal response

CONSIDERING THE CULTURAL COMPONENT

In addition to the characteristics in Figure 2.8, the information in Figure 2.9 can reveal another dimension of the student's educational and personal history. The socio-cultural background of many students, particularly in the inner cities, may be such that the students show signs of significant learning problems in school. Many of them may be exceptionally bright, certainly capable of normal intellectual functioning, but their disadvantaged status in the community has affected their ability or willingness to master fundamentals and to apply themselves to educational tasks in the classroom or at home.

The information in Figure 2.9 can be very helpful in determining the nature of the interferences impeding a particular student's educational growth. Such information is helpful when schools must determine the nature of a student's learning interferences. It's important to recognize that this information is needed not only to deny eligibility for special education services but to focus on the nature of the student's problem and to assist him or her with its resolution.

Poverty has a numbing effect on millions of people each year, and its grip is among our most powerful social forces. Thousands of inner-city teachers, however, reach out each year to youngsters who benefit from their professional skills as well as their personal involvement. The kind of information resulting from the checklist in Figure 2.9 enables such teachers to help these students.

LOOKING AT ATTENTION DEFICIT-HYPERACTIVITY DISORDER (ADHD)

ADHD can be as significant an interference to learning as any problem in the classroom. It has become so prominent in the literature and diagnosed so frequently in some schools that parents and professionals alike are beginning to consider it the "disorder of choice" or "this year's most popular excuse for being the class clown." Such unenlightened reactions are unfortunate.

Don't get us wrong. We realize that some professionals "sell" ADHD diagnoses to today's parents as smoothly as Dr. Quack sold his snake-oil elixir to Old West audiences. Charlatans abound everywhere, preying on the fears of people who have a tough time focusing on reality. We know that some parents would much rather "buy" an ADHD diagnosis than admit to themselves—and others—that Tommy needs continuing doses of Dad's Daily Discipline.

That's simply the way it is, and we're not going to change it. But we *can* accept the other reality; ADHD is real, and it affects thousands of students who suffer daily from the overstimulation and impulsivity it creates. Use the reproducibles in Figures 2.10 and 2.11, therefore, to remind counselors and others in the Pupil Personnel program of its symptoms and the requirements needed for a diagnosis of ADHD. The reproducible can also be used for teachers who may be interested in the topic or who are involved in in-service training activities.

2.9 — SOCIOCULTURAL FACTORS AFFECTING STUDENTS' SCHOOL PROGRESS

Chicago School District #299

A high score on this checklist suggest that there are several factors related to the student's background that are interfering with academic progress. Students with severe discrepancy between ability and achievement resulting from the following intervening factors should not be identified as having a specific learning disability.

1. **Environmental Factors:**

   - Late school entrance
   - Limited experiential background
   - Irregular attendance
   - Transience in elementary school years
   - Adaptation to a culture different from native one
   - Lack of parent involvement in school activities

2. **Language Factors:**

   - Lack of proficiency in English
   - Lack of language development in native language
   - Insufficient exposure to the formal English language
   - Acquisition of basic oral language proficiency in English but inadequate formal or cognitive language proficiency in English

3. **Cultural Factors:**

   - Limited experiences of social interaction with mainstream culture
   - Limited experiences that stimulate growth and fund of knowledge

4. **Economic Factors:**

   - Participation in District's Title I Program
   - Unemployed parents, low income family
   - Physical environment of home is characterized by limited facilities and space

2.10 – CRITERIA USED TO DIAGNOSE ATTENTION DEFICIT HYPERACTIVITY DISORDER (ADHD)

DSM-IV American Psychiatric Association

A. A disturbance that has lasted at least six months and has shown evidence of at least eight of the following criteria:

1) Fidgets or squirms

2) Difficulty staying in a seat

3) Distracted by other noises

4) Difficulty waiting for own turn in games or group activity

5) Blurts out answers to questions

6) Difficulty following through on instructions

7) Difficulty paying attention to tasks

8) Moves from one uncompleted activity to another

9) Difficulty playing quietly

10) May talk abundantly

11) Interrupts others or butts into other children's games

12) Difficulty paying attention to conversation

13) Loses things easily

14) Tremendous risk taker with no thought of consequences

B. Some behaviors were evident prior to the age of seven

C. Some of the impairments are present in two or more settings

D. Significant impairment socially, academically, or occupationally

E. Symptoms do not occur exclusively during the course of a psychotic disorder, and is not more closely identified as another mental disorder

2.11 – DEFINITION OF ATTENTION DEFICIT DISORDER
(CH.A.D.D.)

"The term 'attention deficit disorder' means a disorder in one or more of the basic cognitive processes involved in orienting, focusing, or maintaining attention which results in a marked degree of inattention to academic and social tasks. This disorder may also be manifested in verbal or motor impulsivity and nonredundant activity, such as excessive fidgeting or restlessness. 'A marked degree' is defined as a score exceeding the 97th percentile for the child's chronological and mental age as measured by well-standardized methods of assessing school behavior. Attention deficit disorder must persist over a long period of time (i.e., at least 6 months). When it is observed in children of minority ethnic or cultural backgrounds it must be assessed in relation to other children of the same background and mental age. To qualify as a disabling condition, the inattention must adversely affect school performance as manifested by a significant discrepancy between general mental ability and academic productivity and/or accuracy. The disorder frequently manifests itself in developmentally inappropriate degrees of difficulty in listening to and following directions and in organizing, planning, initiating, sustaining, completing, and verifying academic assignments, which requires reading, written composition, mathematics, spelling, or handwriting."

Professional Group of Attention & Related Disorders (National Headquarters for CH.A.D.D.

- . . . Result of differences in chemistry in part of the brain
- . . . Affects behavior and performance
- . . . Not the result of poor home environment
- . . . May interfere with achievement
- . . . Not caused by low motivation
- . . . Has a negative effect on self-esteem
- . . . Not caused from irresponsibility
- . . . May overlap with learning disabilities
- . . . Not caused by emotional imbalance

THE CASE STUDY EVALUATION

Once the preliminary steps have been completed and the screening committee feels that a full case study evaluation is warranted, the diagnostic process gets into full swing. Figure 2.12 outlines the steps in a comprehensive case study evaluation. Include it in a booklet for everyone in the Pupil Personnel program, for distribution to parents, and for teachers during in-service activities.

Notice that the process starts with a student interview to secure his or her perception of the problem. The child's parents are then interviewed, followed by an analysis of the child's social development, medical history, vision and hearing screening results, and past and current educational performance. It then measures the child's achievement levels in reading, math, and written language; it evaluates the child's learning style and assesses much of the child's learning environment. Finally, it provides—as needed—measurements of other factors, such as intellectual, psychological, and social/emotional functioning.

The full case study evaluation represents art as well as science. Professionals represent different philosophies, employ different approaches, and use different tests to make their diagnoses. Sometimes these differences render contradictory results—not often, but often enough for schools to consider a wide range of opinions before settling on one diagnosis. That's why successful processes combine a range of qualified professionals and share their synergy with parents and teachers to determine the specific problems and intervention strategies for students with diagnosed learning disabilities.

SECURING PARENTAL CONSENT

Parental consent for a case study evaluation should involve documentation of the child's name, birth date, names of parents/guardians, and the date of the original referral and by whom it was made. The form should also indicate the type of evaluation requested and include all the relevant forms and reports that identified the need for the case study.

It should also encourage parents to request additional information and make specific reference to any additional evaluations, such as psychological evaluations and speech and language screenings. Finally, the form should include the parent(s) signatures, giving permission to conduct the evaluation. Feel free to use the reproducible form in Figure 2.13 to inform parents of a case study evaluation and to secure their consent to conduct one.

DEVELOPING A PSYCHOEDUCATIONAL REPORT

Figure 2.14 offers a reproducible of the information contained in a psychoeducational report; it can be included in your department's booklet as a reference for professionals in the program, or it can be used to create a report you can for parents, interested teachers, or others who seek information on the specifics of this type of report.

The sample psychoeducational report provided in Figure 2.15 is also helpful. Perhaps the most important thing to be learned from the sample is that good psychoeducational reports are detailed documents that identify and explain all the relevant aspects of a student's learning processes. They identify the measurements used to make conclusions and explain the results of these measurements clearly and completely.

2.12 – Description of Components of a Case Study Evaluation

United States Department of Education

Comprehensive Case Study Evaluation

- *Interview with child:* Assists the evaluation team to understand the difficulties being experienced from the child's perspective.

- *Consultation with parents:* Provides parents with an opportunity to describe their concerns related to their child's difficulties.

- *Social development study:* Provides the evaluation team with an understanding of the child's in-school and out-of-school functioning by assessing how the environment affects the child's ability to learn.

- *Medical history and current health status:* Information to help the evaluation team determine if any current or past medical difficulties are affecting the child's school performance.

- *Vision/hearing screenings:* Assist the evaluation team in determining visual or auditory problems that would interfere with the testing or school performance of the child.

- *Review of the child's academic history and current educational functioning:* Involves reviewing the child's previous school records and current levels of functioning in the present educational setting.

- *Educational evaluation of learning processes and achievement:* Measures traditional academic skills taught in school, such as reading, math reasoning and calculation, and written language. Additional assessments or observations determine how the child takes in information, understands the information, and expresses answers, and helps the evaluation team determine the best ways for the child to be taught and to learn.

- *Assessment of the child's learning environment:* Helps the evaluation team to determine how the student interacts in the classroom environment and addresses the match between student needs and teaching styles. Physical and environmental factors in the classroom are assessed also to determine their effects on the educational needs of the child.

Speech and Language Case Study Evaluation

- A speech and language evaluation involves select components of a comprehensive case study evaluation.

Specialized Evaluations: Additional components may be recommended depending on the nature of the child's difficulties.

- *Psychological evaluation:* Includes an assessment in the areas of intellectual ability, fine/gross motor coordination, social/emotional development, and learning processes and/or academic achievement.

2.13 – PARENT CONSENT TO CONDUCT
A CASE STUDY EVALUATION

Name of Child _____

Date of Birth of Child _____

Type of Evaluation:

_____ Speech & Language

_____ Comprehensive

_____ Home/Hospital

Date of the Referral _____

Date of Permission Granted _____

I/We _____ acknowledge or _____ do not acknowledge that we have received reports describing the evaluation procedures and records or reports used as the basis for the determination to conduct the evaluation.

I/We _____ request or _____ do not request additional information about the suggested evaluation.

In the event additional evaluations may be needed the high school will notify you to request permission to conduct the evaluations.

I/We _____grant or _____ do not grant permission for
(Name of high school)

_____

to conduct a Case Study Evaluation.

Parent(s)/Guardian signatures

_____

2.14 — PSYCHOEDUCATIONAL REPORT

Name of Psychologist and Address

Cognitive Assessment:

    Name of student _____

    Date of birth _____

    Age at time of testing _____

    Current grade in school _____

    Parents'/guardians' names _____

    Address _____

    Date tested _____

Reason for Referral:

    Referred for testing by _____

    Referred for testing because _____

Observations of Behavior:

    Student's attitude about testing _____

    Student's knowledge of why testing is being done _____

Tests Administered:

    Examples:

    ____ WISC-R/Binet

    ____ WAIS-R

    ____ Detroit

    ____ PIAT-R

    ____ Woodcock Johnson

    ____ Slossen

    ____ Raven Standard Progressive Matrices

Discussion of Test Results and Impressions of Tester:

Summary and Conclusions and Recommendations:

Quantitative Test Results:

2.15—SAMPLE PSYCHOEDUCATIONAL REPORT

Name of Certified Psychologist _____

Address _____

Cognitive Assessment _____

Name _____

Date of birth _____

Age _____

Grade _____

School _____

Parents _____

Address _____

Date tested _____

Reason for Referral

Thomas ("Tom") was referred for testing by his parents, who wanted the results to be included as part of the college admission information packet. This referral specified that only a cognitive assessment was to be conducted at this time.

Tom has a long history of attention difficulties and learning challenges. He has been medicated for the attention problems and has received consistent remediation for learning problems. Tom receives tutorial assistance from the Academic Resource Learning Center at his high school.

Observations of Behavior

Tom is a happy and friendly young adult, who arrived for testing prepared to be productive. He was brought to the testing site by his older sister, as his parents were out of the country on business. He was cooperative and was willing to put forth good efforts. When questioned about the reasons for the testing, Tom felt it had to do with his disorganization and poor homework completion.

Tests Administered

Wechsler Adult Intelligence Scale-Revised (WAIS-R)

Woodcock-Johnson Psychoeducational Battery-Revised, Tests of Cognitive Ability

Discussion of Test Results and Impressions

Tom was given an individual intelligence test, WAIS-R, and a nonverbal test of intellectual functioning to estimate Tom's level of intellectual functioning.

The Verbal Scale score on the WAIS-R was within the Average Range; the Performance Scale within the High Average Range; and a Full Scale score was within the High Average range of intellectual functioning for an individual his age. There was a one point discrepancy between the lower Verbal and higher Performance Scales; this is not statistically significant and actually suggests an even learning pattern. These scores are a valid estimate of Tom's current intellectual functioning; however, this may not be an accurate measure of his full capacity because of the possibility of a learning disability that could be interfering with his functioning to the fullest extent.

On the Verbal Scale, Tom's scores ranged from the 63rd percentile on the Digit Span and Comprehension subtests to the 16th percentile on the Arithmetic subtest. Within this range, he scores at the 50th percentile on Information and Vocabulary and the 37th percentile on Similarities.

On the Information subtest, which assesses ability to integrate information from Tom's general environment and school experience, he displayed average ability in the long-term recall of factual information. He was quite successful on some higher level items, yet unable to answer earlier questions.

The Digit Span subtest determines the ability to attend and measures the immediate memory span in requiring the sequential repetition of digits in both forward and backward modes. Tom retained seven digits forward on two trials and five digits backward on two trials. This indicated that short-term, rote auditory memory for a random sequence of digits was above the expected level.

On the Vocabulary subtest, which is a measure of receptive and expressive elements of language, Tom was able to offer accurate and succinct definitions for words that were familiar to him. Performance was within the average range.

The timed Arithmetic subtest measures the ability to translate word problems presented orally into arithmetical operations and requires the ability to mentally manipulate arithmetic facts. Tom performed below the average range on this task, losing credit for speed of response as well as accuracy. Tom had difficulty doing math in his head.

On the Comprehension subtest, a measure of practical knowledge, judgment, and behavior in applied, hypothetical situations, Tom's responses placed him within the high average range. He showed good impulse control, an awareness of social and moral values, and he seemed to make meaningful, pertinent and emotionally relevant use of facts and relationships which are known to him. This subtest requires verbal reasoning and is predicated on verbal comprehension and verbal expression, but really focuses on relatively concrete social knowledge.

The Similarities subtest is an abstract task of categorical reasoning in which Tom had to determine and verbalize a common factor between two apparently unrelated items. The subtest requires knowledge of symbolic relations, generalization, and the ability to abstract ideas in considering concrete elements. Tom's performance was just in the average range.

Timed tasks on the Performance Scale involving nonverbal concepts were not more challenging for Tom. On the Performance Scale he scored from the 91st percentile on the Block Design subtest to the 25th percentile on the Picture Completion.

Performance on the Picture Completion subtest demonstrates ability to identify the element missing from a common object. Tom has more difficulty noting details of information from a visual format than from details he hears. Nonverbal long-term visual memory is not at the expected level. Variability in performance could be due to fluctuating attention as well as to difficulty in comparing, evaluation, and determining the essential from nonessential details of a visual percept.

The Picture Arrangement subtests measure social awareness with a visual format in the form of sequenced stories. Tom was able to place pictures in order to tell a story when he did not have to express himself verbally. Tom's performance was in the above-average range. Evaluations are made on one's knowledge of social situations but free from the verbal reception and expression constraints imposed in the Comprehension subtest.

The Block Design subtest assesses the ability to analyze and reproduce with both solid color and diagonally colored blocks abstract designs from an illustrated model. This is a nonverbal measure of abstract thought and concept formation. Tom's performance was within the superior range. He worked accurately and quickly, completing all nine designs.

On the Object Assembly subtest, which demands the ability to integrate individual puzzle pieces into a familiar configuration without the structure of a model, Tom was able to work with the visual information of the shapes of the pieces of the puzzles to integrate them appropriately. Tom's score was within the average range.

The Digit Symbol subtest requires one to associate a specific symbol with its corresponding number and integrate that learning as quickly as possible. Tom had no errors on Digit Symbol, suggesting that he was able to discriminate visually between the symbols and, by repeatedly referring back to the guide, he correlated accurately the digits with their corresponding symbols, and demonstrated above-average motor speed on this clerical task.

Please note that when Tom's scores on the WAIS-R are compared with those of his age peers, his performance on the majority of subtests is quite advanced.

In relation to the general results of the WAIS-R, Tom's score and performance were not as even on the Woodcock-Johnson Psychoeducational Battery-Tests of Cognitive Ability.

While measures of language comprehension and expression yielded scores within the average to above-average range, visual processing subtest scores were below the average range.

Short-term auditory memory is superior to long-term memory as measured by the WJ-R.

Summary and Conclusions

Tom is a 16-year-old boy who is currently a junior in high school. He has at least average to high average cognitive ability. His learning disabilities continue to be apparent. His weaknesses are in the areas of speed of visual processing and mathematics. He can work accurately when given ample time to process visual information, including reading, but will most likely have difficulties when put under great pressure. It is recommended that he be given additional time on tests and exams, and helped to understand that some assignments in reading and written work may take him longer than other students. His motivation, good cognitive skills, and appropriate level of courses, should result in success in high school and at a post-secondary institution.

2.15 continued

Quantitative Test Results

Name _____

Date of Birth _____

Date of Evaluation _____

Wechsler Intelligence Scale for Adults-Revised (WAIS-R)

	I.Q.	Percentile
Verbal Scale	109	73
Performance Scale	110	75
Full Scale	110	75

Subtest Scaled Scores

	Verbal	Percentile	# correct
Information	10	50	(12)
Digit Span	11	63	(12)
Vocabulary	10	50	(13)
Arithmetic	7	16	(8)
Comprehension	11	63	(13)
Similarities	9	37	(11)

Mean of Verbal Tests 9.6

	Performance	Percentile	# correct
Picture Completion	8	25	(8)
Picture Arrangement	12	75	(14)
Block Design	14	91	(15)
Object Assembly	10	50	(11)
Digit Symbol	10	50	(10)

Mean of Performance Tests 10.8

Woodcock-Johnson Revised Psychoeducational Battery, Tests of Cognitive Ability

Subtest or Cluster	Standard Score	Percentile Rank
Memory of Names	93	33
Memory of Sentences	104	60
Visual Matching	87	19
Incomplete Words	89	24
Visual Closure	115	84
Picture Vocabulary	116	86
Analysis-Synthesis	105	62
Visual-Auditory Learning	92	29
Memory for Words	119	90
Cross Out	81	10
Sound Blending	119	89

2.15 continued

Woodcock-Johnson Revised Psychoeducational Battery, Tests of Cognitive Ability (continued)

Subtest or Cluster	Standard Score	Percentile Rank
Picture Recognition	97	43
Oral Vocabulary	108	70
Concept Formation	100	50
Spatial Relations	110	75
Listening Comprehension	119	90
Verbal Analogies	109	73
Broad Cognitive Ability-Ext. Scale	102	56
Long-Term Retrieval	92	29
Short-Term Memory	113	81
Processing Speed	82	11
Auditory Processing	105	64
Visual Processing	105	64
Comprehension-Knowledge	112	79
Fluid Reasoning	101	54
Oral Language	113	81

Use this form often with parents, teachers—even students—to explain the process, to provide information about it, and to relieve concerns about the content of evaluations. Students and parents fear such a detailed exploration of aspects of their personalities that are unknown even to them. System theory reminds us that as human beings we seek "steady states," areas of balance in our lives that represent normalcy and that enable us to blend in with everyone around us. Identified or suspected learning disabilities challenge this sense of normalcy.

Use the form in Figure 2.16, therefore, to invite parents and students to meetings to discuss case study evaluations, but be careful when sharing the results with them. Most teenagers struggle daily through the developmental tangle of their own adolescence. They don't need added challenges resulting from insensitive explanations of a problem they fear and are reluctant to accept anyway. (For an explanation of parents' rights in the process, see Figure 2.17, "Sample Procedural Safeguards".)

Hold a preliminary meeting to discuss exactly how you plan to present findings to the family. Such a meeting identifies a protocol for the group to follow and avoids a slapdash approach to a subject that requires open-ended communication. Such a meeting should consider the following:

- ◆ The reasons for the original referral should be reviewed, and the student's symptoms should be discussed in relation to his or her developmental/educational history.

- ◆ Results of tests and interviews should be shared with members of the group so that everyone understands the results before discussing them with the family.

- ◆ Everyone's questions should be answered so that no one in the group is confused about any aspect of the information to be shared with the family.

- ◆ Any and all recommendations to be made to the family should be shared with the group.

- ◆ The rationale behind each recommendation should be explained to the group.

- ◆ The group should provide a question-answer session near the end of the preliminary meeting so that everyone is clear about the issues before meeting with the family.

Such meetings can be held fifteen minutes to half an hour before the meeting with the family. The preliminary meetings need not be lengthy, just long enough to make sure everyone in the group is "on the same diagnostic page." The diagnosis of a learning disability and subsequent recommendations for placement are sensitive issues to the student and his or her family. The whole process can be made much more comfortable for everyone if this preliminary meeting provides a clear focus for the meeting with them.

2.16 – PARENT INVITATION TO ATTEND CONFERENCE TO DISCUSS CASE STUDY EVALUATION

Parent(s) name _____

Date of conference _____ Time _____

Location of conference _____

Purpose of the conference:

____ Review the Case Study Evaluation

____ Determine Eligibility for Special Education Services

____ Develop an Individualized Education Plan (IEP)

____ Determine appropriate placement

____ Review eligibility for continued special education services

____ Review progress of the current IEP

____ Identify continued educational plans and placement needs

Individuals attending the meeting include:

Special Ed Administrator _____   Case Manager _____

Counselor _____   Teacher _____

Social Worker _____   Psychologist _____

Speech Therapist _____   Other _____

If you plan to bring anyone to the meeting, please identify the individual(s) and provide title, relationship, telephone number, and address:

_____

_____

_____

Is a translator or interpreter needed for this conference? _____

If so, please identify the language _____

If the time scheduled for this conference is not convenient, please call the Special Education office to arrange for an alternative time.

Attached is a copy of Parent Rights. Please review this document so that you are familiar with your rights under the law.

PROCEDURAL SAFEGUARDS FOR PARENTS

The red tape that purportedly strangles victims of bureaucracy is often a lifeline for the parents of children with learning disabilities. The problem is, not enough professionals seem willing to throw it. The result is that parents are left to struggle through a morass of fear, misunderstanding, confusion, and professional unconcern. They often are forced to find informational materials and professional advice outside the school.

What a shame—and what a waste of enormous positive energy for the school! The parents of children with learning disabilities are among the most active and energetic in the school system because they are among the best motivated. The problems confronting their children energize them almost daily to explore the school's program for appropriate curricular and instructional experiences for their children. They devote great amounts of time and energy to the study of learning disabilities and to the kinds of solutions their children require.

One result is that they become knowledgeable resources within the community and can serve as valuable allies in the partnership to improve the school's instructional and curricular program. Unfortunately, however, their search for knowledge and the questioning attitude that results often upset some school personnel. At this point, the parents of children with learning disabilities are perceived as adversaries rather than allies in the search for an improved educational program.

The Pupil Personnel program that guards against such an adversarial relationship with parents creates the kind of positive synergy that is needed to satisfy the needs of not only the students in the special education program but most of the students in the school. Parents of children with learning disabilities ask tough questions, not just to criticize the school's program—although that sometimes happens—but to expand the educational opportunities and the delivery of services for their children. Answers to their questions have far-reaching implications for all students.

Because some schools are threatened by their questions, parents and schools sometimes find themselves working at cross-purposes, resulting in an unfortunate waste of energy that affirms the status quo of the school's educational program. We are reminded of the eighteenth-century English proverb, "A blind man will not thank you for a mirror." Schools must guard against such blindness. The self-reflection we require to improve the quality of our educational programs is sometimes found only in the mirrors provided by our most vigorous and forthright critics—our parents and our students.

Share the information in Figure 2.17 with the parents of students with learning disabilities. It outlines the responsibilities of the school and acknowledges the rights of the parents. Topics include the expectation of prior written notice, the right to an independent educational evaluation, the need for parent consent, the handling of complaints, the right to an impartial due process hearing, and the right of accessibility as well as the amendment of records.

The Pupil Personnel program that clarifies these rights and responsibilities early in the relationship with the family helps establish levels of trust with parents that pay significant dividends in the long run. The closer we work together with parents, the better we serve the needs of our students. All schools have benefited from an improved understanding of the learning process provided by research in special education. The parents of students with learning disabilities are often familiar with such research, and ask tough, but good questions.

2.17 – Sample Procedural Safeguards Available to Parents of Children With Disabilities

(Developed by US Department of Education, Office of Special Education Programs and modified by the Illinois State Board of Education to comply with Illinois rules.)

As the parent of a child who is receiving or may be eligible to receive special education services, there are certain rights which are safeguarded by state and federal statutes. A full explanation of rights should be obtained from each individual school district.

Prior Notice to Parents is required:

- When a child has been referred for an initial case study evaluation or reevaluation and the district decides not to conduct the evaluation

- When the district proposes to initiate or change the identification, evaluation, or educational placement of a child or the provision of a free, appropriate public education to a child

- When the district refuses to initiate or change the identification, evaluation, or educational placement of a child or the provision of a free, appropriate public education to a child.

Written notice must be provided at least 10 days prior to the proposed action and must include:

- A full explanation of all of the procedural safeguards available to parents.

- A description of the action proposed or refused by the district/agency, an explanation of why the district/agency proposes or refuses to take the action, and a description of any options the district/agency considered and the reasons why those options were rejected.

- A description of each evaluation procedure, test, record, or report the district/agency uses as a basis for the proposal or refusal.

- A description of any other factors which are relevant to the district/agency's proposal or refusal.

    Notice must be written in language understandable to the general public and provided in the native language or other mode of communication used by the parent, unless it is clearly not feasible to do so.

Parent Consent

- School district must obtain parent consent using state-mandated forms before conducting the initial case study evaluation and any reevaluations and initially placing a child with disabilities in a program providing special education and related services.

- School district may initiate a due process hearing to compel consent for the initial evaluation and initial placement in special education.

- If the hearing officer upholds the district, the district may evaluate or initially provide special education and related services to the child without the parent's consent, subject to the parent's rights to appeal the decision and to have the child remain in his or her present educational placement during the pendency of any administrative or judicial proceeding.

- Except for the initial evaluation and initial placement, consent may not be required as a condition of any benefit to the parent or child.

- If parental consent for reevaluation is not provided within 10 days, the district must request a due process hearing to secure consent.

71

Independent Educational Evaluation

- Parents of a child with disabilities have the right to obtain an independent educational evaluation of the child.

- Parents have the right to an independent educational evaluation at public expense if the parent disagrees with an evaluation obtained by the district. However, the district may initiate a due process hearing to demonstrate that its evaluation is appropriate.

- If evaluation is deemed appropriate, the parent still has a right to an independent educational evaluation, but not at public expense.

- Private evaluations must be considered by the district in any decision.

- Hearing officers' requests for an independent evaluation as part of a hearing must be at public expense.

- Independent evaluation at public expense must use the same criteria as used by the district including the location of the evaluation and the qualifications of the examiner.

Complaint Resolution and Mediation

- Complaints alleging violations of parent and special education student rights can be referred to a local school district representative.

- Complaints can also be referred to the Department of Special Education (in Illinois) for review, investigation and action within 60 days.

- (Illinois') mediation service is designed as a voluntary alternative to the due process hearing as a means of resolving disagreements regarding the appropriateness of special education and related services. There is no cost to the parties.

- Requests regarding rule interpretation or parent/student rights clarification may be referred to the local school district.

Impartial Due Process Hearing

- A parent or a public educational agency may initiate a Level I due process hearing regarding the district's proposal or refusal to initiate or change the identification, evaluation, or educational placement of the child or the provision of a free, appropriate public education to the child.

- A parental request for a hearing must be made, in writing, to the superintendent of the local school district in which the child resides.

- Within 5 school days of receipt of the request for a hearing, the local school district will contact the (Illinois) State Board of Education requesting the appointment of a Level I hearing officer.

- A listing of hearing officers will be sent to the parent and the district. The parties will proceed with the selection procedure, alternately striking names until one name is left, with the parent having the right to strike first.

- The district will inform the parent of any free or low-cost legal assistance if the parent requests the information.

- The (Illinois) State Board of Education will ensure that a final hearing decision is reached and mailed to the parties within 45 days after the receipt of a request for a hearing, unless the hearing officer grants a specific extension of time at the request of either party.

- The decision made in a due process hearing is final, unless a party to the hearing appeals the decision within 30 calendar days after receipt of the decision.

Due Process Hearing Rights

Any party to a hearing has the right to:

- Be accompanied and advised by counsel and by individuals with special knowledge or training with respect to the problems of children with disabilities.

- Present evidence and confront, cross-examine, and compel the attendance of witnesses.

- Prohibit the introduction of any evidence that has not been disclosed to that party at least 5 days before the hearing.

- Obtain a written or electronic verbatim record of the hearing.

- Obtain written findings of fact and decisions.

- Parents have the right to have the child who is the subject of the hearing present at the hearing and to open the hearing to the public.

- Each hearing must be conducted at a time and place which is reasonably convenient to the parents and child involved.

Level I Review

- Any party aggrieved by the findings and decision in the Level I due process hearing may appeal to the (Illinois) State Board of Education for a Level II review.

- If there is an appeal a listing of reviewing officers is mailed to the district superintendent and the parent. The time line and procedure for selecting the reviewing officer is the same as for a Level I Review.

- The impartial reviewing officer will:
  > Examine the entire hearing record
  > Ensure that procedures were consistent with requirements of due process
  > Seek additional evidence if necessary
  > Afford parties the chance for oral or written argument
  > Make an independent decision
  > Give a copy of written findings and the decision to the parties

- Each review involving oral arguments must be conducted at a time and place which is reasonably convenient to the parents and the child involved.

- The (Illinois) State Board of Education will ensure that a final decision is reached in a Level II review and mailed to the parties within 30 days after the receipt of a request for a review unless the reviewing officer grants an extension. The decision made by the reviewing officer is final unless a party brings a civil action.

Civil Review

- Any party aggrieved by the findings and decision made in a Level II appeal has the right to bring a civil action in State and Federal Court.

Child's Status During Proceedings

- During the pendency of any administrative or judicial proceeding, unless the district and the parents of the child agree otherwise, the child involved in the complaint must remain in his/her present educational placement.
- If the hearing involves an application for initial admission to public school, the child, with the consent of the parents, must be placed in the public school program until the completion of all proceedings.

Award of Attorneys' Fees

- In any action or proceeding brought under Part B of the Individuals With Disabilities Education Act (IDEA), the courts may award reasonable attorneys' fees to the parents or guardians of a child with disabilities if they are the prevailing party.

Surrogate Parents

- Each district will make all reasonable attempts to contact the parents of the child. If the parents cannot be identified, or located, or the child is a ward of the State, the district will request the appointment of a surrogate parent by the (Illinois) State Board of Education.

Access to Records

- Each district or public agency will permit parents to inspect and review any educational records relating to their child which are collected, maintained, or used by the district.
- The district will comply with a request to review the education record without unnecessary delay and before any meeting regarding a multidisciplinary conference, individualized education program or hearing relating to the identification, evaluation, or placement of the child and, in no case, more than 15 school days after the request has been made.
- Parents have the right to a response from the participating district/agency to reasonable requests for explanations and interpretations of the records.
- Parents have the right to have a representative of the parent inspect and review records.
- Parents have the right to request that the district/agency provide copies of education records if failure to provide those copies would effectively prevent the parent from exercising his/her right to inspect and review the records at a location where they are normally maintained.
- It is presumed that parents have the authority to inspect and review records relating to the child unless the district/agency has been advised differently.
- Parents can only review information relating to their child.
- Each district/agency will provide parents, on request, a list of the types and locations of education records collected, maintained, or used by the district/agency.

Fees for Searching, Retrieving, and Copying Records

- A participating district/agency may not charge a fee to search for or to retrieve information.

- A fee of not more than $. 35 per page of the record may be charged if the fee does not effectively prevent the parents from exercising their right to inspect and review records.

Record of Access

- Each district/agency will keep a record of parties obtaining access to education records collected, maintained, or used, including the name of the party, the date access was given, and the purpose for which the party is authorized to use the records.

Amendment of Records at Parent's Request

- A parent who believes that information in the education records is inaccurate or misleading or violates the privacy or other rights of the child may request the participating district/agency to amend the record.

- The district/agency will decide whether to amend the information in accordance with the request within 15 school days from the date of receipt of the request. If the agency refuses to amend the information, it will inform the parent of the refusal and advise the parent of the right to a hearing.

- On request, there will be an opportunity for a hearing to challenge information in education records to insure that it is not inaccurate, misleading, or otherwise in violation of the privacy or other rights of the child.

- If the hearing decides that the information is inaccurate, the district/agency will amend the information.

- If the hearing determines that the information is not inaccurate, the district/agency will inform the parent of the right to place in the records it maintains on the child a statement commenting on the information or setting forth any reasons for disagreeing with the decision of the district/agency. If the records of the child or contested portion is disclosed by the district/agency to any party, the explanation must also be disclosed.

SECURING PARENT CONSENT FOR SPECIAL EDUCATION PLACEMENT

If testing reveals that special education placement is necessary to assist with the student's learning interferences, parents should be asked to sign the form in Figure 2.18. It documents that they have been apprised of the specifics about the recommended placement, have acknowledged receipt of relevant information, have been informed that permission to serve the child may be revoked at any time, have the opportunity to request due process hearings, and have or have not agreed to waive a 10-day delay prior to placement. When signed, the form should be filed in the special education department.

LET'S WRAP IT UP

Rather than love our enemies, maybe we should be nicer to our friends and neighbors—especially to those who suffer the chronic effects of learning disabilities. If this is to happen in the nation's schools, teachers, counselors, and administrators must be familiar with the symptoms of learning disabilities and have access to referral processes that result in the diagnosis and treatment of such student interferences to learning.

This section emphasized some of the early signs of learning disabilities, provided sample referral forms, discussed screening procedures and full case study evaluations, explored the most appropriate way to discuss the results with families, discussed the need to share procedural safeguards with parents, and, in general, underscored the importance of working closely with all members of the school community. Figure 2.19 provides a list of important terms that you might want to share with staff members.

The identification of learning disabilities in our students and loved ones is the critical first step in helping them develop the compensatory skills to be successful in school, home, and work. Identifying the problem, however, is only the first step. Getting students and parents to accept the disability and to work cooperatively with school specialists to treat it are difficult next steps.

Most students and many parents are frightened by the suggestion of a learning disability. It represents a mysterious and threatening departure from normalcy that seems to have no visible effect on other aspects of life. Unfortunately, it is easier to deny such a problem than to make the emotional commitment to treat it. Without such a commitment, however, successful treatment is compromised, and varying aspects of the problem persist.

Getting students and their parents to accept the problem and to agree to do something about it, therefore, requires considerable skills on the part of school professionals. It also requires sensitive and informative materials and processes that promote an understanding of the diagnosis and the acceptance of a treatment plan. These are the focuses of the next section.

2.18 – Parent Consent for Special Education Placement

Date _____

Name of child _____

Date of birth _____ Place of birth _____

Name of Parent(s)/guardian _____

_____ I/We approve or _____ disapprove the recommended placement in special education.

_____ I/We acknowledge or _____ do not acknowledge that I/We have been fully apprised of the specifics about the recommendations for placement in Special Education

_____ I/We acknowledge or _____ do not acknowledge that I/We have received copies of all of the conference reports.

_____ I/We acknowledge or _____ do not acknowledge that we have given consent voluntarily to allow for placement in Special Education.

_____ I/We have been informed or _____ have not been informed that our permission to serve this child may be revoked at any time.

_____ I/We have been informed or _____ have not been informed that there will be continual opportunity for comments and input into the IEP of the child.

_____ I/We have received or _____ have not received a copy of the Parents Rights and Responsibilities in writing.

_____ I/We have or _____ have not been given information about how to request a due process hearing.

_____ I/We do or _____ do not give consent for the child to be placed in Special Education.

_____ I/We do or _____ do not agree to waive a 10 day delay prior to the placement into Special Education.

Parent(s)/Guardian Signature _____

Please return this form to: School name

Special Education Department

Address

2.19—DICTIONARY OF TERMS

Case Study Evaluation—Series of multidisciplinary procedures given in an established time frame, designed to provide information about the student, the problems which are or will be affecting educational development, and the recommended interventions and services to assist with these problems.

Comprehensive Case Study Evaluation—An evaluation conducted by a team of professionals; includes an interview with the student and parent/guardian; a social development history; a report of the student's medical history and current health; vision and hearing screenings; a review of the student's academic history and current level of educational functioning; an evaluation of learning processes and level of educational achievement; and an assessment of the student's learning environment.

Speech and Language Case Study Evaluation—An evaluation that includes a hearing screening, a review of the student's medical history and current health, a review of academic history and current educational functioning, a speech and language assessment, and an interview with the student.

Home/Hospital Case Study Evaluation—An evaluation that includes student's physical or health impairment, an estimated length of need for services from the physician, and a review of the student's current educational status and academic needs.

WORKING WITH STUDENTS AND THEIR PARENTS

First, a quick story . . .

Joshua was the best running back in his high school's distinguished football history. He had all the school records for rushing and, during his junior and senior years, heard from hundreds of college football coaches. He was an excellent example of how Mother Nature sometimes grants exceptional gifts in one area when she creates limitations in another. You see, Joshua was a kinesthetic genius, a young man who found his way through a field of would-be tacklers on game days as easily as most of us fall out of bed in the morning.

But he could read only at the third-grade level. Joshua's teachers and counselor suspected mild dyslexia but couldn't be sure. His mother steadfastly refused to have him tested. She, too, suspected a learning interference in his, but refused to believe that it was little more than his disinclination to study anything other than double reverses and play action passes.

The counselor realized that the mother's problem might be a threat to her own self-esteem when she said, "Our family has never had such a problem. Joshua just needs to study harder. I'm working with him every night." The counselor had heard similar comments from a variety of parents. Invariably, they revealed a narcissistic involvement in the child's problem, first, by denying its existence in the family (often incorrectly) and, second, by sacrificing countless hours of their own time in what proved to be a futile attempt to resolve it.

Unable to understand or accept the influence of such a subtle and insidious disability, some parents respond as if hard work alone will somehow make it disappear. Then, once they learn that such disabilities may be hereditary, some of them assuage subconscious guilt by sacrificing their time and energy to the expectation that they can overcome the disability by sheer force of will.

It doesn't work, as Joshua and his parents discovered. The NCAA's bylaw 14.3 (Proposition 48) declared Joshua ineligible for intercollegiate competition at any of the schools that were offering him Division I scholarships. He eventually accepted a scholarship to a junior college in California, became disenchanted by the football program, frustrated by more poor grades, and quit a few weeks into the second semester. He returned home for a short time and then seemingly disappeared.

THE IMPORTANCE OF ACCEPTANCE

One thing is for sure. Wherever Joshua is, his disability has not disappeared. On rare occasions, some adolescents and adults appear to outgrow their disabilities. The appearance of such growth results more from compensatory strategies than from maturational factors. Learning disabilities simply don't go away. As indicated in Section 1, this fact suggests the criticality of early identification and intervention. Had Joshua been tested when the high school originally requested his mother's permission, he might have developed learning strategies that would have improved his academic performance and ultimately qualified him for an intercollegiate football scholarship.

What is more important, he wouldn't have appeared to be a "dumb jock," and he would have achieved levels of academic performance that would have improved his self-esteem and interest in learning. Most of the adults who worked with him in school realized that he was quite intelligent. A young football player doesn't understand several alternative ways to block a "Crossfire Counter Tackle Trap at 6" against either a "Wide Tackle 6" or a "Gap Stack 62" and deserve to be called dumb.

In the kinesthetic world of athletics, Joshua went to the head of the class almost every day, certainly on game days. In the visual world that dominates most classrooms, he struggled just to catch up with everyone. Is it any wonder that he thought of himself as "Joshua the football player" and relegated books, bell-shaped curves, and blackboards to that daily dose of humility everyone called school?

What was needed, then, was a process for getting Joshua and his mother to accept the reality of his apparent disability and to commit to the school's recommendations to treat it. Those of you engaged in special education, counseling, or social work realize that this is easier said than done. The suggestion of a disability to some families is a skeleton they would prefer to hide in the nearest closet. Without an effective process, therefore, and the sensitive and sympathetic involvement of well-trained school professionals, many parents resist treatment and inadvertently allow disabilities to scar their children's lives.

SELF-ESTEEM AND OTHER EMOTIONAL ISSUES

What is especially sad is that many of the children's scars are self-inflicted. Like the protagonists in a Shakespearean tragedy, they are victims of their own tragic flaw, an inability to acknowledge or treat a problem that promises only recurring discomfort or pain. What school professionals must do, then, is engage parents and students in a process that informs them of the disability, relieves their fears, eliminates misconceptions, and provides ongoing exploration not only of treatment strategies but of the immediate and long-range effects of the disability.

This requires a process that involves not only parent and child but counselors, social workers, and special educators. It involves ongoing communication among all parties—certainly routine meetings between the counselor or social worker and the student to discuss the disability in relation to the student's changing educational priorities. Such priorities change and have increasingly significant implications for the future as the child grows older.

In elementary school, the student and his or her parents must consider registration plans and the impact of current courses on the transition to junior high school and secondary school. In high school, the student and parents must discuss registration plans in relation to college admission and the world of work. Each step along the way involves serious discussion of college and vocational planning and selection. It also must address the implications of the disability on such planning. In addition, students with learning disabilities gain or require insights into their personal, social, and educational circumstances as they mature. They require opportunities to simply talk about these experiences and to develop a sophisticated understanding of the disability and the relative success of the compensatory strategies they have learned. They also benefit from encouragement to reflect on their social and educational growth, to recognize their improved self-esteem, and to take a well-earned bow for reacting so courageously to such undeserved adversity in their lives.

SOCIAL ISSUES

Such meetings also provide opportunities for students to discuss and practice the skills that are so difficult for them personally and socially. Figure 3.1 outlines some of these skills and is a reminder for counselors and social workers to provide role playing experiences for students with learning disabilities.

Many schools have social issues classes that address the adjustment needs of students with learning and other disabilities. Such classes are important adjuncts to academic and resource experiences for such students, but they fail to provide the consistent, real-life situations that enable them to practice appropriate behaviors. Counselors and social workers can interact with students to provide the role-playing that results in the practice and, ultimately, the integration of the ability to:

- Read body language and other nonverbal cues.
- Modify behavior as needed in certain social situations.
- Describe one's own feelings.
- Carry on a conversation, including the ability to engage in small talk.
- Know when and how to enter into someone else's conversation.
- Deal successfully with frustration.
- React positively to setbacks.
- Become increasingly independent.
- Establish and pursue realistic educational and personal goals.

Certainly, there are more such behaviors, many which relate specifically to individual students. The important point, however, is that someone in the school, usually counselors and social workers, enable students to practice these behaviors in a supportive environment while they explore the whole question of academic as well as social adjustment. These meetings can also address the issue of stress.

3.1—SOCIAL AND EMOTIONAL GUIDELINES

The following is a list of social and emotional skills students with learning disabilities should work on developing in order to compensate for other areas of deficit.

Social and Emotional Guidelines

- To be able to read body language
- To be successful interacting with peers/adults
- To exhibit appropriate behavior
- To be able to describe feelings
- To not exhibit compulsivity
- To have the ability to make and keep friends
- To have the ability to carry on a conversation
- To be capable of making small talk
- To have the ability to handle frustration
- To develop good coping skills
- To be able to deal with setbacks
- To have a positive self-image
- To be independent
- To know when to enter into a conversation in progress
- To have realistic goals

DEALING WITH STRESS

Students with learning disabilities, particularly if they have only started to develop compensatory strategies, experience almost constant frustration in the classroom. Such frustration leads to stress. Tips on how to reduce stress can help students in the classroom as well as at home and in social situations. Figure 3.2 provides such tips. All that is required, first of all, is access to them, followed by an association with a trusted someone who can explain them, promote their practice, and monitor the student's progress toward them.

Expecting a youngster to "be organized," "make friends," and "be tolerant" without showing him how to do these things is like telling him to master quadratic equations without any instruction. Some students might pull it off, but most will transform an inability to be organized or more tolerant into more frustration and stress. Like the best laid plans of mice and men, our best intentions also can go astray.

Share and discuss the stress test in Figure 3.3 with students with recently diagnosed learning disabilities. It isn't diagnostically sophisticated. Rorschach can rest comfortably. It does, however, break the ice when it becomes obvious that the issue of stress must be discussed with the student and his or her parents. Answers to each question can provoke interesting and valuable discussion with the family.

UNDERSTANDING AND ACCEPTING THE DISABILITY

The most important discussion during the entire process is the one that promotes in the family an eventual understanding and acceptance of the disability. To make this task somewhat easier, counselors, special educators, and social workers are encouraged to use the checklist in Figure 3.4. Although the instructions on the form indicate that the results are to be used by the student, the form can also be used to discuss the student's self-perceptions or to structure an early interview with the family.

The Student Self-Assessment in Figure 3.5 can be used by students individually or by counselors and other school professionals to structure an interview format. Students acknowledge problems in certain areas more readily when they realize their behavior and learning interferences are an open book to someone who has access to substantial information about them. They may delude themselves occasionally, believing they give good answers in class, but the self-deception ends when counselors or special educators show them evidence to the contrary.

Such sharing of information, however, must be done delicately. Anecdotal and testing information is not a mallet for beating sense into intransigent youngsters and their parents. We don't want a butcher when the job requires a brain surgeon. The information, therefore, must be shared slowly and informally, with explanations along the way that comfort rather than threaten. The information should provide light—not heat.

3.2 — STRATEGIES FOR REDUCING STRESS

Being able to develop strategies to reduce stress can make the difference between being successful and not being successful in school and college. The following list of suggestions will help students in reducing stress:

- Students should develop organizational skills
- Students should ask for help as soon as it is needed
- Students should consider taking a reduced course load
- Students should avoid courses in their areas of deficit
- Students should monitor their progress in courses
- Students should see their academic advisor often
- Students should request priority registration
- Students should take time for relaxation
- Students should get plenty of sleep
- Students should always attend all classes
- Students should be aware of all deadlines
- Students should eat correctly
- Students should make friends
- Students should laugh
- Students should find ways to exercise
- Students should not take on more than they can handle
- Students should not obsess about insignificant matters
- Students should learn to plan ahead
- Students should have a positive attitude
- Students should try to be forgiving
- Students should have a healthy outlook on life
- Students should avoid competition
- Students should be tolerant
- Students should set goals they can accomplish
- Students should seek emotional counseling when needed
- Students should not dwell on failures

3.3—ESTIMATING YOUR LEVEL OF STRESS

The following list of questions is about stress. In order to get an idea of how much stress you may be experiencing, please answer each of the questions with a yes or no.

_____ 1. Do you often worry about how you are going to perform in school?

_____ 2. Do you have trouble concentrating on your studies?

_____ 3. Do you go to bed at the same time each night and fall asleep easily?

_____ 4. Do you often get angry with your family over minor things?

_____ 5. Do you overeat?

_____ 6. Do you find that you are not hungry at meal time?

_____ 7. Do you get frustrated over small things?

_____ 8. Do you have trouble managing your time?

_____ 9. Do you overcommit yourself to projects or activities?

_____ 10. Do you often want to stay home from school?

_____ 11. Do you suffer from headaches?

_____ 12. Do you suffer from stomachaches?

_____ 13. Do you find yourself tapping your fingers or swinging your legs?

_____ 14. Do you have difficulty making friends?

_____ 15. Do you feel under pressure to be successful?

_____ 16. Do you like yourself?

_____ 17. Do you feel you are as successful as you could be in school?

_____ 18. Do you find things to do that you enjoy?

_____ 19. Do you find yourself grinding your teeth?

_____ 20. Do you find yourself overreacting to friends?

_____ 21. Do you start something but have trouble finishing it?

To score this Stress Test, add up your "yes" answers. A score of 7 may suggest that you need to talk with someone to develop strategies for reducing stress.

3.4—CHECKLIST FOR UNDERSTANDING YOURSELF

Students who understand themselves and how they function can do a better job planning for their future. The following information can be used as factors that could have an impact on your educational success.

What Do You Know About Your Own Behavior?

	Never	Sometimes	Often
1. Are you good at managing your time?	____	____	____
2. Can you stay focused without distraction?	____	____	____
3. Can you listen and repeat questions?	____	____	____
4. Are you able to formulate good questions?	____	____	____
5. Do you have good study habits?	____	____	____
6. Can you stick to a task for a long time?	____	____	____
7. Are you able to organize yourself?	____	____	____
8. Are you able to stick to a schedule?	____	____	____
9. Are you able to self-advocate?	____	____	____
10. Are you comfortable asking for help?	____	____	____
11. Are you punctual with assignments?	____	____	____
12. Can you take breaks and return to a task?	____	____	____
13. Can you determine time needed for tasks?	____	____	____
14. Do you know when to ask for assistance?	____	____	____
15. Do you know whom to ask for assistance?	____	____	____
16. Are you able to plan ahead?	____	____	____
17. Are you an independent learner?	____	____	____
18. Can you handle setbacks?	____	____	____
19. Can you prioritize tasks?	____	____	____

What Do You Know About Your Own Interpersonal Relationships?

	Never	Sometimes	Often
1. Can you follow the rules?	____	____	____
2. Do you understand about taking turns?	____	____	____
3. Do you have many friends?	____	____	____
4. Are you able to interact with teachers?	____	____	____
5. Do you like to be with groups?	____	____	____
6. Do you prefer to be by yourself?	____	____	____
7. Do you have high self-esteem?	____	____	____
8. Do you find yourself easily distracted?	____	____	____
9. Do you relate well to your family?	____	____	____

	Never	Sometimes	Often
10. Do you relate well to your teachers?	____	____	____
11. Do you have good common sense?	____	____	____
12. Can you carry on a conversation?	____	____	____
13. Are you motivated?	____	____	____
14. Are you competitive?	____	____	____
15. Do you get frustrated easily?	____	____	____

What Do You Know About The Way That You Learn?

	Never	Sometimes	Often
1. Are you able to follow oral directions?	____	____	____
2. Are you able to follow written directions?	____	____	____
3. Can you remember long-term facts?	____	____	____
4. Can you hold on to short-term facts?	____	____	____
5. Can you read difficult materials?	____	____	____
6. Do you read slowly?	____	____	____
7. Do you have trouble understanding texts?	____	____	____
8. Is your handwriting legible?	____	____	____
9. Are you a good test taker?	____	____	____
10. Are basic math skills difficult for you?	____	____	____
11. Do you have trouble taking notes?	____	____	____
12. Is it difficult to put thoughts on paper?	____	____	____
13. Are you disorganized?	____	____	____
14. Do you have trouble with verbal reports?	____	____	____
15. Do you have a short attention span?	____	____	____
16. Can you memorize facts?	____	____	____
17. Are you a procrastinator on homework?	____	____	____
18. Are you bothered by noises?	____	____	____
19. Can you do advanced math?	____	____	____
20. Do you have trouble with spelling?	____	____	____
21. Can you use a computer?	____	____	____
22. Can you outline?	____	____	____
23. Can you take good notes?	____	____	____
24. Can you concentrate in class?	____	____	____
25. Do you miss class frequently?	____	____	____

3.5—Student Self-Assessment

Students benefit from knowing about themselves and having awareness of their academic strengths and limitations. The best way to test your own awareness is to ask questions of yourself, as well as of others who know you well. The following list of questions may be helpful in exploring your own self-awareness.

Student Self-Assessment

- How would your parents describe you?
- How would your best friend describe you?
- How would your teachers describe you?
- What are your best qualities?
- What are your shortcomings?
- Can you define your learning style?
- Can you describe your learning disability?
- What are your academic strengths?
- What are your academic deficits?
- How does your disability affect you academically?
- Do you learn better from certain types of teachers? Which ones? Why?
- What accommodations/services do you feel are necessary for success in school?
- What accommodations/services will you need in college?
- What parts of your high school experiences have been the most enjoyable? Why?
- Where do you want to be in ten years?
- What does success mean to you?
- What would you like to change about yourself?
- What do you like best about yourself?
- What academic subjects do you pursue on your own in order to learn more?
- What would you like to change about your school?
- What do you like best about your school?
- Do you like to read for pleasure?
- How do you get along with your family?
- How do you get along with your friends?
- Do you contribute to class discussions?
- What do you like to do with your leisure time?
- Describe how your learning disability currently affects you.
- Can you articulate what you would like to do after high school? Why?
- If you could change one thing in your life, what would it be?
- Do you take risks? What have you chosen to do because it was new and interesting?
- What adjectives best describe you?
- What majors might you want to pursue in college?
- If you had a year to go anywhere and do whatever you wanted, how would you spend the year?

It must represent the first delicate step in an occasionally indelicate journey that informs the student of the behaviors in Figure 3.6 and eventually enables him or her to integrate them. Again, this is no easy task. Schools are filled with students who are "abled" and who, for whatever reason, fail at self-advocacy, independent learning, and an awareness of deadlines! Our work with students with learning disabilities, then, is among our most challenging job responsibilities.

THE EARLY INTERVIEW

Our jobs are made easier and our students and their parents are more easily convinced of the substance of our recommendations when we use effective interviewing strategies. An interview, no matter what the circumstances, is the organizational equivalent of a complete physical exam. It creates apprehension in the most confident among us, and it delves and probes relentlessly into the most private parts of our lives. It may lead to a more healthy and satisfying life, but no one likes it, so remember the following suggestions when interviewing students and their parents:

1. Arrange a comfortable and informal atmosphere in your office, complete with plants, pictures, family photos, and relaxing decorations. Also be sure to set your desk against a wall, so you can face your guests during interviews and appointments. A desk is an imposing obstacle between you and your guests and suggests power and authority rather than informality and caring. A desk in the middle of the room may be appropriate for the dean's office, but it is deadly for counselors, social workers, and special educators.

2. Greet the student and his or her parent(s) warmly. Offer them a cup of coffee or tea or a can of soda. A dish of candy is also a good idea. Hard candy not only tastes good, but it relieves dry mouth, an occasional interference to relaxed conversation.

3. Smile warmly and frequently. A professional demeanor can include a smile. A warm smile communicates caring and approachability, and it smoothes the way for honest and open dialogue.

4. Eliminate as many potential interferences as possible before the student and his parents arrive. Arrange for all phone calls, except emergencies, to be intercepted by a secretary or answering machine. Also be sure that other interruptions, such as unscheduled visits and questions from office personnel, are anticipated or intercepted. An untimely interruption in an otherwise good interview can destroy effective communication.

5. Establish rapport by matching the voice tone and body gestures of the student and his or her parents. Doing so reflects understanding and establishes a feeling of compatibility and harmony during the interview. People who are in rapport tend to be more honest with each other. For example, if the parents sit down on the edge of their seats obviously nervous about the interview, mirror their behavior by sitting straight in your chair, reflecting an understanding of their sense of urgency. You can settle back in your chair as soon as they do, once you relax them by smiling and speaking informally with them.

3.6—ACCEPTANCE OF A LEARNING DISABILITY

Those of us who work with students with learning disabilities realize what a difficult time many of them have understanding, accepting, advocating, and compensating for their learning differences. Our work with these students must promote the development of the following characteristics.

Student must be able

- To accept the learning disability
- To articulate the learning disability
- To understand strengths and weaknesses
- To describe how the learning disability affects class work in deficit areas
- To be a self-advocate
- To be an independent learner
- To be motivated
- To work longer and harder
- To stay focused on academics
- To work on socialization skills
- To seek assistance when necessary
- To meet often with the counselor
- To work closely with the special education case manager
- To know when to register for SAT/ACT standardized or nonstandardized as appropriate
- To utilize appropriate services/accommodations
- To attend all IEP/MDC conferences
- To research post-secondary options
- To be organized about post-secondary search
- To be aware of deadline dates
- To determine the level of services necessary for success in a college setting
- To be certain testing is current and comprehensive
- To self-identify as a student with learning disabilities
- To practice interviewing techniques
- To understand what questions to ask when visiting colleges
- To be aware of what questions may be asked when visiting college campuses
- To visit college campuses
- To meet with the person on the college campus who is responsible for assisting students with learning disabilities
- To write a personal statement describing the learning disability
- To own the process

This is not to say that we should cross our legs or scratch our heads every time they do. We don't want the focus of the interview to shift to our own behavioral disabilities! We do, however, want to let the student and his or her parents know that we are listening and that we understand their feelings and concerns.

6. Reflect such understanding by paraphrasing significant elements of their conversation. The parent might say, "Frankly, this whole thing confuses us, and it frightens me a little. What does this mean for my son's future?" The good interviewer responds with something like, "Yes, I suspect you're having a tough time understanding the problem—as well as its implications for the future. Something like this can be disturbing. That's why we're here today."

Do not respond with "You shouldn't be frightened; we know what we're doing!" Such a response tells the parents that you simply don't understand their feelings. Once you've given that impression, they will be unable to relate to you throughout the remainder of the interview. Good rapport is a combination of many things, but one of the main ingredients is trust. Earn it by showing that you are listening and that you understand their concerns.

7. Help the student and his or her parents make good decisions by asking presupposition questions:

"What kind of planning went into your decision to…?"

"What information did you use when you decided not to…?"

Such questions presuppose planning and intelligent decision making. If the family is able to answer such questions, students and parents will appreciate your awareness that they *did* plan. If unable to answer such questions, the family will realize the need for planning and intelligent decision making and will be more inclined to hear the information you have on hand to assist with their decision-making process.

8. Keep the meeting relatively short. Forty-five minutes to an hour is an optimal length. If you are unable to cover the major issues in that time, you need to rest and regroup. So does the family. You may need a different plan of attack, and they may need to mentally process your observations and recommendations. Sometimes, parents need time to let the information incubate and to subconsciously talk themselves into agreement.

Schedule a second meeting, if necessary. In the interim, send them a letter that summarizes your first meeting and outlines your primary recommendations. If it is written sensitively, the student and his or her parents will rethink the whole issue and be more likely to accept your recommendations at the second meeting.

9. Finally, once you have established rapport and are prepared to get into the substance of the interview, use the reproducible in Figure 3.7 to structure it. You may not want to ask every question in the figure, but you will find that answers to these questions, either in the initial interview or sometime later, promote the student's understanding of the disability and can lead to careful family planning for the future.

3.7 — STRUCTURING YOUR INTERVIEW

Academic

1. What is your learning disability? Is it in language processing, memorization, math, reading, organization, comprehension? Be able to describe the basis of the disability.

2. How does the learning disability affect you as a student? Does it cause you to have difficulty in certain subjects, tests, oral presentations, reading assignments, memorizing data, completing multiple assignments?

3. What are your major areas of strengths and weaknesses? How do you learn best? Be able to describe what you do better and what is more difficult for you.

4. Do you find that school has become more demanding? How have you acclimated to the heavier load of assignments and expectations in school as you progress from grade to grade?

5. Is your learning affected by your relationship with the teacher? What happens to your learning success in a class where you have a good relationship with the instructor? What happens when the relationship is not good?

6. How do you make use of the resources offered to you? Do you take time to seek help in subjects that are more difficult? Do you work on developing compensatory skills in the areas of deficit?

7. Have you considered your disability in your plans for high school or college? Do you plan on self-disclosing the disability?

8. Are you willing to explore the option of participating in a support program after junior high school or high school? Do you think you will benefit from a structured program or services?

9. What were your initial impressions of your diagnosis of a learning disability and placement in a program? When were you first diagnosed with a learning disability? When were you first tested? When was you last evaluation? When did you first receive special education services? What were these services?

10. Do you feel that the school has been fair in its expectations? Do you think that the requirements have motivated you and allowed you to expand your level of accomplishments?

11. On a scale of 1-10, with 10 being the highest, how would you evaluate your level of disability? Would you consider yourself with a very mild learning disability, a moderate learning disability, or a severe learning disability?

12. What skills have you developed to compensate for your learning disabilities? Have you learned techniques to help you with the areas of weakness? What support services have you received, such as LD Resource, tutoring, individualized classes, remedial classes, speech therapy?

13. What are your plans for after high school? Are these plans realistic?

14. If your plans are to attend college after high school, have you considered the degree of assistance you will need? What degree of support will you want in order to be successful in a college environment?

Personal

1. Are you confused by the fact that you may study very hard but still have difficulty being successful in some areas? Have you been able to sort out the issues relating to why you have difficulty on certain tasks?

2. How do you feel about your level of production? Do you feel as though you are trying hard but not getting as much done as you would like to?

3. Do you find that you often compare yourself to others who may not have a learning disability? Do you find yourself in competition?

4. Have you experienced feelings of frustration? Anxiety? Low self-esteem? How have you dealt with these feelings?

5. How do you explain to others what it feels like to have a learning disability? Can you put this feeling into words?

Parents

1. What are your parents' expectations for your level of learning? Do your parents understand your learning disability? Do your parents understand what areas are more difficult for you?

2. Do your parents have realistic goals for you after high school? Do your parents understand the degree of support you may need in a college setting?

3. What do your parents say to you about your learning disability? Have your parents discussed their own learning strengths and weaknesses?

CONTROLLING TIME

Mother Nature gives us control over our lives, and Father Time takes it away, especially from the learning disabled. Time is always in short supply for the student with learning disabilities. Once the student understands the nature of his or her problem and is committed to do something about it, therefore, share the material in Figure 3.8 to promote discussion of a time schedule. Then use the reproducible in Figure 3.9 to make a weekly schedule.

Notice that the schedule includes school days. Most schools provide either study halls or free time for most students. Much of this time can be wasted without thoughtful preliminary planning. Once the student gets into the habit of developing such a schedule, he or she can do it alone. All that is required is an occasional reminder.

THE IMPORTANCE OF SELF-ADVOCACY

The old adage, "Never bite the hand that feeds you," may be bad advice for the student with learning disabilities. Such students actually may have to bite that hand—if it interferes with their ability to feed themselves. Self-advocacy is essential for people with learning disabilities. Fortunately, the nation's schools are full of caring and competent professionals who are willing to help students develop the skills needed to compensate for their learning disabilities.

Even the most experienced and energetic among them, however, are available only on a limited basis and certainly are unable to anticipate every obstacle that emerges so unpredictably in the paths of their students. Each student, therefore, must develop the ability not only to anticipate problems but to deal with them when they occur. Famed educator Art Costa once said that intelligent people know what to do when they don't know what to do.

Students with learning disabilities must do the same thing. They must understand their disabilities and be familiar with a process that enables them to influence—even control—the factors in school, at home, in the community, and at work that affect them. As Costa suggests, they must know what to do even when the obstacles that confront them are unpredictable and unfamiliar. To develop a successful process, students with learning disabilities should be encouraged and helped to develop the skills listed in Figure 3.10.

They must, first of all, understand and be able to explain their learning disabilities. They must be somewhat familiar with the testing used to identify the disability and be able to identify some of the specific problems that interfere with their performance. Then they must be willing and able to discuss their disabilities with teachers and others in order to receive the accommodations they require for success.

Much of this requires an assertiveness that is unfamiliar to most students and that is inconsistent with the relatively poor self-concepts of students who have experienced one failure after another throughout most of their early schooling. Such a reality suggests the dimensions of the tasks confronting those of us who work with such students. Not only must we help them develop self-advocacy skills but we must help them develop the self-esteem that promotes the use of such skills.

3.8—SCHEDULING YOUR TIME

What should you do to maximize the use of your time?

168 hours in a week:

   63 hours for sleep
   14 hours to eat
   <u>61</u> hours to attend school

Total   138

Which leaves 30 hours of discretionary time

Suggestions for maximizing the hours in a day:

1. Give structure to your week.

2. Identify your routine daily tasks.

3. Use a daily calendar to keep track of assignments, appointments, and important dates.

4. Identify when you should begin on an assignment and estimate how long it will take you to complete it.

5. Set aside blocks of time to do homework, learn new material, work on projects, do research, begin drafts of papers, and study for quizzes or tests.

6. Remember that everyone has different levels for a span of concentration; some people can sit for hours on one project and others will need to break the block up into smaller parts.

7. Identify rewards for yourself for completing tasks.

8. Always keep up with your assignments.

9. Try to preview new materials or assignments ahead of time.

10. Take notes in class and review them as soon as you can after the class.

11. Determine how you learn best; make a recording of a lecture if that helps; study with other students if you learn better by talking and discussing the material; rewrite your notes if you learn by repetition.

12. Have a conversation with your instructor before the class begins, in order to establish accommodations that will help you manage your time more effectively.

13. Ask the instructor for a detailed syllabus of the course.

14. Do not get behind in assignments; work on your assignments every day.

15. Concentrate when you are studying; it is helpful to learn the material in the beginning so that you can use later time to review.

3.9 — WEEKLY SCHEDULE

Hour	Mon.	Tues.	Wed.	Thurs.	Fri.	Sat.	Sun.
7:00 - 8:00							
8:00 - 9:00							
9:00 - 10:00							
10:00 - 11:00							
11:00 - 12:00							
12:00 - 1:00							
1:00 - 2:00							
2:00 - 3:00							
3:00 - 4:00							
4:00 - 5:00							
5:00 - 6:00							
6:00 - 7:00							
7:00 - 8:00							
8:00 - 9:00							
9:00 - 10:00							

3.10—Tips on Being Your Own Self-Advocate

Learning disabilities and attention deficit disorder are hidden disabilities. Therefore, when a student walks into a classroom and takes a seat, it is highly unlikely that the instructor will have any idea about the existence of the disability. Thus, the importance of being your own self-advocate. It is imperative that you be able to identify your limitations and explain to the teacher what you will need in order to compensate. You must be able to articulate your specific needs and it is helpful to practice this as often as possible.

- Be knowledgeable about yourself; understand your disability and be able to describe it; be aware of what could cause you frustration and how to cope with the situation.

- Seek an understanding of the testing used to identify your learning disability; ask the psychologist or case manager or special education teacher to explain the tests and what they identified as learning issues.

- Identify your learning styles; determine how you learn best; know if you are better studying with music or complete silence; know if you learn better in the morning or later in the day.

- Understand strengths/weaknesses; be aware of what subjects will be easier for you and what subjects may cause you more difficulty.

- Understand how you learn; determine if you are a visual learner or an auditory learner.

- Be able to articulate your learning disability; be able to explain your disability so that others will have a better idea of what is difficult for you.

- Understand what interferes with your performance; seek a better understanding of what causes certain tasks to be difficult for you so that you can work on developing compensatory skills.

- Set reasonable goals and expectations; dreams are very healthy, but you must be realistic about your limitations and not set yourself up for an impossible task; it is always rewarding to get all "A's" but this may not be realistic.

- Develop compensatory skills; work on finding strategies and techniques that will assist you with areas of weakness; if you have difficulty taking notes in a class, learn to use a tape recorder; if you have a hard time understanding what you read, perhaps you are eligible to have someone read the material to you.

- Be comfortable with your learning disability; be able to disclose that you have a disability.

- Be willing to discuss your accommodation needs with teachers; practice asking for the necessary accommodations.

- Understand what classroom modifications are necessary for success; know if you need extra time for tests, a quiet place to take your tests, a reader for exams, a computer or calculator to use on exams.

- Develop good coping skills; be able to control your frustrations; get yourself back on track if you are distracted; and understand what makes you agitated and avoid those situations.

- Be willing to seek assistance; know what support services are available and how to access them; do not hesitate to ask for help if you do not understand an assignment or a new concept.

- Be assertive; ask for appropriate accommodations; request a seat in the front of the classroom if that is necessary for your learning.

- Know your rights; know what accommodations and services are identified in your IEP; know when it is appropriate for you to seek advocacy help if an instructor is not allowing you to access necessary modifications; know when you have the right to see your records.

- Set priorities; identify what is most important and get your priorities in order.

- Learn to deal with frustration; develop techniques to help to keep yourself calm and collected.

- Anticipate problems and work to resolve them; identify what might be difficult for you and determine how to compensate and handle these problems.

- Develop a good feeling of self-esteem; develop a belief in your efforts; develop a positive attitude; develop a sense of ownership.

- Attend all IEP/MDC conferences; ask questions; be sure you understand the goals written in your IEP; be a participant in developing these goals.

- Review your records; keep a copy for yourself.

- Be an effective communicator; practice articulating your learning disability; develop a comfort level with disclosing your learning disability.

Simply handing them a reproducible like the one in Figure 3.10, therefore, is only a first tentative step in the right direction. What is required beyond that is a total process of education. Students must know how to translate the items on the figure into behaviors that promote the accommodations they need to function successfully—even when they haven't mastered the behaviors. To give a familiar saying an unfamiliar twist, "Whatever is worth doing is worth doing badly."

Certainly, we'd prefer that students integrate all these behaviors as effectively as possible. That's our goal as we work with them. But they must be encouraged to be self-advocates, even when their skills are poorly developed. Practice and constant encouragement are the keys. The right process, therefore, is critical. This book emphasizes a range of products, only one of which is self-advocacy, but we are just as interested in the processes, time-consuming though they may be, that result in these products.

Students with learning disabilities won't understand their strengths and weaknesses, establish reasonable goals, be comfortable with their learning disabilities, or become assertive without the continuing assistance of knowledgeable school professionals and parents who help them integrate such behaviors. Open dialogue within a process of ongoing meetings is the best answer. Only then will students with learning disabilities find the kind of help they need to become effective self-advocates.

ADDRESSING THE NEEDS OF THE CHILD WITH LEARNING DISABILITIES

In its purest sense, motivation characterizes every person in the school system. We would be hard-pressed to find one student or one teacher who wasn't motivated. All of us have needs, and all of us seek to satisfy them. All of us, therefore, are motivated. In what directions we are motivated, however, is the critical issue for school professionals. Teachers work hard every day to promote a need in students to understand quadratic equations, gerunds and participles, and the geopolitical causes of the Civil War.

Some teachers are successful; others are not. The successful teachers realize that the only way to influence the intrinsic motivation of students is to control the conditions and the circumstances within which students satisfy their needs. In essence, they understand that motivation is not something we do *to* our students, but something we do *for* them. To the extent that we enable the satisfaction of their ego and social needs, we influence students to move in directions we feel are important for them.

Unsuccessful teachers cajole, threaten, and do whatever seems necessary to get students to move in directions which are important *for the teachers*. All math teachers want their students to find unexpected joy, or at least some sense of personal satisfaction in the mastery of quadratic equations. To that extent, they push students in the direction that satisfies their own needs, and fail to influence students to share their interest in math.

They must realize that motivation is like the farmer and the seed. The farmer wants the seed to grow. The satisfaction of the farmer's needs is dependent on such growth. For that to happen, however, he must realize that the predisposition to grow inheres in the seed, not in him. His job, then, is to cultivate, nurture, and remove obstacles to the seed's growth. The same is true when we undertake the responsibility of "motivating" students with learning disabilities.

We must cultivate the circumstances within which such students seek to satisfy their ego and social needs. We must nurture relationships with them. And we must remove and help them remove obstacles to their growth as students and young adults. No one explained this situation better than Abraham Maslow. Undoubtedly, you studied Maslow's paradigm at some time during your college career. Let's review it briefly as it applies to students with learning disabilities.

Figure 3.11 illustrates Maslow's hierarchy and provides a few key words and phrases to explain the relationship of each level to the needs of students with learning disabilities. As you review the figure, remember that unsatisfied needs are motivators. Once a need is satisfied, it no longer motivates. When that happens, the level just above it becomes the next motivator—and so on up the hierarchy.

Physiological

All of us have a continuing need for sustenance. Because the need is so universal, this level on Maslow's hierarchy really fails to distinguish the student with learning disabilities from everyone else in the school.

Security

The security level, however, clearly distinguishes the student with learning disabilities from everyone else in the school. Some classrooms are threatening places for students with learning disabilities. Students with dyslexia are uncomfortable in English classes; dyscalculia causes insecurity in math; auditory deficits provoke discomfort in social studies lectures; and spatial deficits provoke anxiety in geometry classes. The nature and the severity of the disability are often directly proportional to the student's anxiety levels.

Like everyone else, students release anxiety in several ways. They avoid the source of the anxiety by cutting class; they misbehave to camouflage their fear; they tune out class activities and daydream about activities that give them pleasure; or they sit quietly in the back of the class trying desperately to escape the teacher's attention. Such behaviors are easily misinterpreted by the teacher and others in the school, which often results in school responses that only compound the student's problems.

The point is—and this observation is clearly consistent with Maslow's thinking—until students with learning disabilities feel more secure in *all* their classes, they are unable to move up the hierarchy. In other words, until they feel safe, they are unable to feel a sense of belonging, to improve their self-esteem needs, or to actualize the significant potential they may have in other areas.

Our first job, therefore, as school professionals, if we really want to improve the motivations of students with learning disabilities, is to help them feel safe in school. We do this by identifying their disabilities, helping them understand the disabilities, and working with them to reduce stress, to accept their limitations, to acknowledge and capitalize on their strengths, and to realize that who they are as young adults transcends what they may be as learners with disabilities.

3.11 — MASLOW'S HIERARCHY — HOW IT RELATES TO THE STUDENT WITH LEARNING DISABILITIES

Self-Actualization

Students realize their potential

Ego Needs

Accepting who they are with comfort and pride

Social Needs

Having friends and being accepted by their peers

Security Needs

Feeling nonthreatened and comfortable in their environment

Physiological Needs

Being well fed, warm, nurtured, and cared for

Social

Once the students feel secure, they need a sense of belonging. They want to connect socially with others in the school, to be needed by others, to know that the school is theirs, to feel comfortable exchanging ideas, opinions, even sympathy and laughter with others. All of us enjoy being members of a "team," whatever that team may be. We like to have teammates who care about us and work with us to achieve common goals.

Such "teams," unfortunately, range from families to gangs. Both are capable of nurturing—in significantly different ways. The nature of the student's social relationships, therefore, depends very much on how school professionals and parents deal with the student's social needs. If we promote affiliation with classes and other experiences that help students compensate for their disabilities and identify and relate to caring and nurturing people, we provide the circumstances and conditions that promote positive social adjustment.

If we fail to accommodate the needs of students with disabilities, they may seek to satisfy their security as well as their social needs by joining gangs or affiliating with the school's "unsavory elements." We know this happens. We have seen it too often to deny it. Youngsters with poor self-esteem invariably find each other and, just as invariably, behave in ways that make others suffer for their own negative feelings about themselves.

Such behaviors range from making parents' and teachers' lives miserable and verbally or physically abusing schoolmates to running folks off the road with their pick-up trucks or knocking over gas stations. When done with others, all these behaviors satisfy the social needs of youngsters. Our job is to make sure that learning disabilities are adequately identified, then treated in such a way that the social needs of students are satisfied not with pick-up trucks, misbehavior, or gang symbols but with satisfying relationships with parents, school professionals, and classmates.

Ego

Once these social needs have been satisfied, students need to gain a sense of self, to feel comfortable with who they are—not just with how others perceive them but with how they perceive themselves. Ego needs are satisfied when students with learning disabilities can say, "I like myself. I'm OK. I'm comfortable with myself because I tend to handle life pretty well."

At this point it's probably safe to say that many people in our society suffer from an inability to satisfy their ego needs. The behaviors of the young woman speeding by and flashing an unequivocally obscene gesture or the shopper muscling past you in line reveal persons who have not adjusted socially or are somehow threatened. What this suggests to those of us who believe in Maslow's philosophy is that both have failed to satisfy their security or social needs.

We live in an extraordinarily competitive society, one that sometimes promotes obscene gestures and inconsiderate behavior. Unfortunately, we have institutionalized that competitiveness to the degree that we accept it in almost every corner of our lives, certainly in our schools. Parents and students who are confronted with the prospect of a learning disability worry about grades, class rank, levels of classes, "labeling," "watered-down" courses, the reactions of friends, relatives, and classmates, and threats to college admissibility.

A solid sense of self enables us to look beyond these things in order to do what is in our best interests in the long run. You and I know, however, that such a response is very difficult for a great many people. Our work with students with learning disabilities and their parents, therefore, is complicated by a variety of social pressures and expectations. We must recognize them and understand their power as we work with families to identify and accept the disabilities that have such profound influence on the lives of their children.

Perhaps the best way to overcome them is to emphasize during meetings that our work together actually eliminates the basis for most of these fears. Labeling is not the issue that most parents fear, and college admissibility is more likely when the student's learning disability has been accommodated. As important, the experience that promotes in students a willingness to use adversity as a stepping stone to greater personal and educational success provides a lesson in courage and improved self-esteem that positively influences every aspect of the child's life now and in the future.

Self-actualization

At this point, the student needs to self-actualize. All of us need to realize our potential as human beings. Just a brief review of metaphysics reminds us that complete potential is nothing, just as complete actualization is perfection. Neither is attainable for any of us. Perfection may be impossible for us, but we have all actualized varying degrees of our potential. Most of us are also dissatisfied with the thought of our own imperfection, so we work to improve ourselves—in whatever it is that we do well or that gives us pleasure.

Students with unsatisfied ego needs are unable to actualize significant elements of their human potential. They are not only handicapped academically by their learning disabilities but limited personally by their failure to gain a positive sense of who they are. Obviously, the problem is even more pronounced for the student who is confined to the lower levels of Maslow's hierarchy, who never moves beyond the need for belonging or security. Such students are in for a lot of unhappiness in life.

To motivate students with learning disabilities, then, we must satisfy their security, social, and ego needs, and we must not make the mistake of thinking that our attempts to "inspire" them to work harder will ultimately resolve their problems. Too many coaches make a similar mistake with their teams. They believe that motivation is a pregame or a half-time pep talk, and they fail to satisfy the social and ego needs of their athletes. A result is that most of them lose.

The same is true of students with learning disabilities if we fail to understand the essentials of motivation. So, like the successful farmer, let us never forget that the predisposition to grow is in the student, and our jobs are to cultivate the learning environment, nurture productive relationships, and remove obstacles to the student's educational and personal growth. In so doing, we will satisfy our students' ego and social needs and enable them to achieve greater levels of self-actualization.

HELPING PARENTS AND OTHERS WITH
THE DIAGNOSIS

Parents who first learn of any abnormality in their children tend to react very pre-dictably. They resist the diagnosis. And no one can blame them. The diagnosis fright-ens them; they fear the imposition of a "label"; they suspect that the disability might shame members of the family; and they shy away from anything that seems so far beyond their control.

In addition, they are susceptible to reassurances from friends and relatives. In fact, sometimes the most misinformed reassurance is the one that parents are the quickest to believe. "The tests these schools use are almost always wrong." "Don't worry; Josh will outgrow it." "It's the malady of the moment; don't let anyone talk you into something so silly." "The special education department is just creating jobs for teachers." "They said the same thing about my neighbor's son, and he's doing just fine."

Normally, however, parents will accept a diagnosis that is communicated sensi-tively and professionally. Once they accept the reality of the problem, they need help with how to deal with it, especially at home. Figure 3.12 provides general informa-tion and can be used by school professionals as a starting point for discussion about parental behaviors when dealing with their children. Be sure to provide adequate time for discussion of all these items, and encourage parents to contact you should they have questions about any of the behaviors.

Most parents know intuitively how to "be loving and supportive," even to "be accepting of the learning disability," but they often need help "being realistic" or encouraging their children to "be independent," especially when they want so des-perately to help with the treatment of the problem. If you can convince them that the disability will not "go away" and will extend into adulthood, they tend to be more objective and to allow their children to struggle with the adjustments they must make.

Figure 3.13 provides specific information about the stages parents go through after learning about their child's learning disability. The form helps school personnel anticipate parent reactions when dealing with them. It also provides general recom-mendations for parents who want to know more about fostering a sense of indepen-dence in their children.

Figure 3.14 goes several steps further. It provides detailed and candid recom-mendations for dealing with children on a daily basis. This information is the logi-cal follow-up to the more general comments in Figure 3.12. For example, parents acknowledge the importance of "Being involved" and "Guiding their children toward successful experiences" during initial meetings with school personnel. It's also important that they eventually understand the specifics of how to do these things.

3.12 — PARENTAL RESPONSE

Your child's adjustment and acceptance of the diagnosis of a learning disability is dependent on your response to the news. Parents who keep the glass half full rather than half empty, accept the limitations and encourage the areas of strength, and help the child to feel good about himself or herself, will have a better adjusted child who has self-respect and a healthier self-esteem.

Parents should:

- Understand the student's learning disability

- Be supportive

- Be realistic

- Be loving

- Be accepting of the learning disability

- Acknowledge strengths

- Guide toward successful experiences

- Be involved

- Encourage independence in all areas of life including learning

- Teach student to use public transportation when appropriate

- Allow student to be responsible

- Praise positive behavior

- Understand that learning disabilities do not disappear

- Attend IEP/MDC conferences

- Be open to suggestions from the school professionals

- Gather information about post-secondary options

- Investigate the costs of special programs in high school or colleges

- Assist student with understanding the parameters of course selections in high school and college choices

- Give school permission to release documentation to high school or college

3.13 – STEPS FOR PROMOTING PARENTAL UNDERSTANDING AND SUPPORT

If you suspect that your child has a learning disability:

- Contact the school and share your concerns
- The school will follow up
- A screening may take place
- Recommendations will be made
- Testing may be suggested
- If testing indicates a learning disability an IEP will be developed
- The IEP will provide plans to remediate and compensate for the LD

How parents are affected by the diagnosis of a learning disability:

- Some parents deny the diagnosis
- Some parents experience depression and anger
- Some parents experience fear
- Some parents do not understand the diagnosis
- Some parents place blame on a spouse or another family member
- Some parents refuse to allow interventions to occur
- Some parents experience continual sadness

Other parents:

- Accept the diagnosis and look for ways to help
- Look for potential
- Involve the student in successful activities
- Seek an understanding of the disability
- Identify necessary life skills and teach them to the child
- Help with social adjustments
- Provide encouragement, respect, and hope

Suggestions for parents to encourage independence:

- Keep the disability in perspective
- Understand the child's needs
- Celebrate strengths

- Teach everyday living skills
- Involve the student in activities
- Acknowledge strengths
- Develop a structure to the day
- Create a good support system
- Help develop good organizational skills
- Work on time management skills
- Teach good eye contact
- Help the child to understand body language and facial expressions
- Practice casual conversations
- Praise good behavior
- Deal with inappropriate behavior
- Reinforce good judgment
- Make home a noncompetitive environment
- Encourage your child to learn to drive at the appropriate age
- Be sure that the house rules apply to everyone equally
- Be cognizant of times of stress
- Plan for transitions
- Encourage independence
- Never let the learning disability become an excuse

3.14–Pointers for Parents

1. Set aside specific work periods so the child will know that *now* we perform these tasks.

2. Start with short work periods—20 to 30 minutes in length. Increase the time as the child's interest and aptitude increase, and as you gain confidence in your ability as a teacher and gain control of the situation.

3. Learn how to be a teacher, objective and impersonal, during the work period, then go back to being a mother (or father) the rest of the day.

4. Be firm but gentle. Speak slowly, firmly, and clearly, but never with anger or impatience.

5. Use a polite, authoritative voice. Develop confidence in yourself and the child and let your voice carry this confidence to the child during the study periods or when you have assigned the child a task during the day.

6. Insist that the child follow through on each task to its completion, and perform it in exactly the manner you prescribe. Never allow the child to terminate a task unless it is completed.

7. Do not let the child gain control of the situation.

    *   Remember that you are to structure all tasks and give the commands.
    *   The child may use many methods to avoid a given task and try to make minor changes, verbalize, resist, act foolish, giggle or develop aches and pains. Stop these overtures, or if this is impossible, ignore them and work right through them. Remain task oriented.
    *   If the child throws a tantrum, allow the child to blow off steam. Afterward the child will still have to perform the given task.

8. Make commands short, simple and related to the task.

9. Wait until after a command is given, then allow the child time to think it through.

    *   Remember, these children must collect the facts, close the door (so to speak), and correlate the facts before they can perform.

10. Repeat a command only after time for correlation has been given.

11. If you feel the child is ready to perform, but seems unable to pull the action out, say *Now*.

12. If necessary, add tactical stimuli.

    *   Place the child bodily into the task.
    *   Steady the child's hand.

13. Do not give the child a choice unless you intend to abide by the choice.

    *   Do not say, *Come now, shall we do this* or *Let's try this*. Rather say, *Do this now*.
    *   If you give a choice between two tasks make sure the plus value of your preferred task is higher.
    *   Do not use threats or promises. These are proposed actions or events that will take place at a later date and the child has very little, if any, time concept.

14. When the child is working at a table, try to have the table and chair at a height where the child is comfortable and his/her feet are on the floor or stool.

   - Keep the child on the chair during that portion of the work period. Do not allow the child to avoid the task by leaving the table.

   - If, however, the child makes a point of sliding down or off the chair to avoid the material presented, insist that the child carry through and finish the activity at the point where you catch him/her, no matter how uncomfortable the position. Then command the child to sit up and proceed to the next task.

15. Learn to anticipate the child's abortive and resistive moves.

16. Draw the child's eyes into the task repeatedly.

17. If a given task proves too difficult, change to another task and then come back to it. If, after several attempts, the child does not show any comprehension of the task, do not abandon it. Find a simpler approach.

18. Teach the child to relax.

   - Have the child practice sitting, lying, and standing.

   - Massage the child's neck and shoulders during this period or other times when the child seems tense.

   - Use a clock with a prominent second hand or a timer. If you use a clock, have the child be very quiet and relaxed while watching the hand make a revolution. If you use a timer, have the child be very quiet until the bell rings.

   - Begin with very short periods of time (one-half minute to one minute), then gradually increase the time.

19. Use the word *no* sparingly. Do not say *no* unless you intend to carry through and see to it that the child obeys. If you say *no* today, be sure that the same action will bring a *no* with the same repercussions an hour later, tomorrow, or next week.

20. Do not drill.

   - The initial performance is the most important. Never repeat a performance more than 2 or 3 times. If you wish the child to perform more often in one study period, leave the activity, go to another, then return.

   - Add variations.

21. Each parent should work with the child, but not both at the same time except when an extra pair of hands is needed. Even then, all commands for that particular work period should be given by one parent.

22. Mother and Dad...learn to relax.

* *LDA NEWSBRIEF, March/April 1996, P. 16 by Clara M. Chaney.*

This article was originally published in *The Foundations of Learning*, April 1968, and subsequently published by Allegheny County ACLD, 1985.

Again, simply reading about them won't assure the consistency of application parents require to deal successfully with their children. School personnel must meet with parents or provide group experiences for them to enable them to integrate these pointers into their daily behavior. Once they do, they will provide a sense of direction at home that complements the goals and objectives of the special education department and teachers at school.

Note as well that the pointers are also appropriate for mainstreamed teachers. They, too, must complement the behaviors of parents and special education personnel. The advent of special education in this country and the significant progress it has made within the past several years have resulted in new methodologies for classroom teachers that enable them to meet the needs of all students. Many of the pointers in Figure 3.14, for example, are useful with all students, not just those with learning disabilities.

WORKING WITH SIBLINGS

Charlie Brown once said that big sisters are the crabgrass in the lawn of life. The brothers and sisters of children with learning disabilities might say the same thing about them. They demand almost constant attention, never go away, pop up in the least desirable places, and mar the appearance of normalcy in the family. Learning disabilities in families can cause the "abled" children to feel shame, jealousy of the attention received by the disabled siblings, and anger at the increased levels of stress caused by them.

"Abled" children require attention, too. According to the research, the kind of attention they receive will determine, to a large extent, their behavior as adults. Older siblings often become caregivers, to the point of choosing occupations in the helping professions or high-paying jobs in order to provide future support for brothers or sisters with learning disabilities. As such, "abled" siblings tend to be high-achievers. Their success reflects a desire to prove to the world that they are not disabled and to gain attention from their parents.

The immediate relationships of siblings are improved and their future and social emotional growth is promoted if the parents of children with learning disabilities involve all siblings in most diagnostic, treatment, and placement decisions. The children need not make the actual decisions, but their input can be invaluable, especially when describing behaviors their parents rarely see. Who knows the behavior and abilities of children with learning disabilities better than their brothers and sisters?

Such involvement also promotes open communication in the family, and it enables siblings to understand the subtleties of the problem and the occasional special needs of the brother or sister with the disability. Parents should even encourage discussion of the problem during dinner or at other times when the family is together. An honest and candid discussion of the disability and its effects on everyone in the family promotes an understanding of the disability and an acceptance of the sacrifices each person must make to help everyone deal with the problem.

Parents must keep additional considerations in mind when dealing with siblings:

♦ Be emotionally honest with them. Admit that you are upset and scared by the diagnosis, that you are confused at times about how to treat the child with the disability, and that you understand the occasional anger they feel when their brother or sister acts inappropriately. Siblings need to acknowledge and resolve these feelings. If they are disallowed from expressing them behaviorally, they must be encouraged to express them verbally.

Feelings of anger can provoke guilt, and both, if unexpressed, can lead to depression. Much of this can be avoided if siblings are given the opportunity to acknowledge such feelings with their parents and to realize that the feelings are normal. In fact, such a process can lead to an important lesson in life. It's important for all of us to acknowledge our feelings but not necessarily to act on them. The self-discipline that results has significant carry-over value into the rest of their lives. Like their brothers and sisters with disabilities, therefore, siblings can benefit from overcoming the adversity that is thrust upon the family.

♦ Admit to all the children in the family that discipline at times may seem unfair. The child with the learning disability may seem to be "getting off easy," while others in the family are held to a higher standard. This, too, is a lesson in life. The more capable among us generally experience higher levels of expectation.

Parents must be careful, however, to treat "abled" children fairly and have appropriate expectations of them. When compared to their siblings with disabilities, they may seem more mature, but they, too, are experiencing the same developmental milestones of all youngsters their age and deserve understanding and patience.

♦ Recognize everyone in the family for uniqueness. Devise ways for each child to be recognized and to develop a positive self-concept. The more accepting siblings can be of themselves, the more accepting they are of others, especially others with handicaps.

MAINTAINING CONTACT WITH PARENTS

Parental involvement in the identification and treatment of the learning disabilities in their children is encouraged. Parents, particularly mothers, have an intuitive/cognitive understanding of the child's needs that serves as a valuable complement to the professional activities of school personnel. They also play a complementary role at home when they encourage self-esteem and the compensatory skills that minimize the effects of disabilities.

The better the early communication with parents, therefore, the more effective their efforts with their children. The parent who understands his or her child's learning disability and can employ a range of strategies to help the child compensate for the disability performs a valuable role at home. And when the school maintains ongoing communication with parents, their ability to complement the school's efforts is enhanced.

Contact parents frequently, therefore, to:

◆ Provide updates of the child's progress at school.

◆ Meet with parents to discuss ongoing or new strategies.

◆ Encourage parents to ask questions in order to improve their understanding of the child's disability.

◆ Seek assistance whenever the child seems unwilling or unable to work cooperatively with special education personnel.

◆ Promote goal-setting activities at Individual Educational Plan (IEP) sessions or meetings for transitional planning from one school situation to another.

◆ Share additional testing results.

◆ Promote dialogue about course selection during registration times.

◆ Express concern about poor communication/cooperation between the school and the home.

◆ Provide periodic reinforcement for the family to continue with its needed adjustment to the disability.

These kinds of contacts have significant public relations value, too. Appreciative parents become outspoken and enthusiastic proponents of the school system in general and the Pupil Personnel Services specifically. Occasional kind and supportive words from them can garner community support and can promote positive relationships with parents who may become involved with special education at some time in the future. Use the form in Figure 3.15, therefore, to document contacts and to promote communication among everyone at school who calls or meets with parents.

LET'S WRAP IT UP

Students and their parents respond to the diagnosis of a learning disability in several ways. Some sit passively and listen to it; others actively deny it. Few, whether active or passive, accept it without question. For most students, the identification of a learning disability is a blow to their self-esteem, a statement that they are somehow different. None of us likes to be different. The task of working with students with learning disabilities, therefore, involves the continuing reaffirmation that they are worthwhile, accepted, and capable of accomplishing their goals.

Teachers, counselors, social workers, administrators, and parents must accommodate the needs of these children and develop strategies and programs that provide continuing support for them. For these strategies and programs to be successful, school personnel must communicate openly and consistently with students and parents. The synergy that results is a powerful influence on the success of treatment programs for students with learning disabilities.

This section has emphasized the need for parents and school personnel to work together to enable students to defend themselves against the attitudes of the disbelievers, the uneducated, and the assault of their own damaged self-esteem. This is not an easy task and requires the involvement of sensitive and consistent school professionals who want to work closely with students and parents to promote their acceptance of the initial diagnosis, their understanding of the disability, and their continuing efforts to compensate for it.

3.15—Communication Record

Student name _____

Counselor _____ Date _____

Conference with _____

Reason for contact _____

_____

_____

_____

_____

_____

Disposition _____

_____

_____

_____

_____

_____

Follow-up plans _____

_____

_____

_____

_____

Additional comments _____

_____

_____

_____

Send copies to:

____ Special Education

____ Teacher

____ Counselor

____ Psychologist

____ Social Worker

____ Case Manager

Completed by _____

SPECIAL EDUCATION: THE HUB OF ACTIVITY

First, a quick story . . .

Meetings are to the Pupil Personnel specialist what dusting and vacuuming are to the housekeeper. They are housekeeping rituals that demand periodic attention, interfere with other activities, last longer than wanted, sometimes stir up a little dirt, and rarely satisfy anyone. But they get the job done. When they are done well and often enough, no one notices. When done poorly or not at all, the mess is evident to everyone.

Such an organizational necessity provided us with the following experience. We had been asked by a local school to attend a meeting to assess the group's discussion of a student's recently diagnosed learning disability. The purpose of the meeting was to explain the services Larry would receive and to encourage his self-advocacy. Our job was to determine just how well the group accomplished its purpose. The meeting was attended by a counselor, a special educator, two classroom teachers, Larry and both his parents, and a social worker, who facilitated the meeting.

While the counselor and the special educator were encouraging him to share his feelings and concerns with his teachers, Larry's English teacher jumped in with, "Right, Larry, sometimes we have to take the bull by the horns and do things we don't like to do. Hey, you don't have to wrestle the bull to the ground, just get his attention. That way, people will be more inclined to give you the help you need."

Larry smiled blankly at his teacher, then listened as the social worker explained a few specific ways he might approach his teachers. He even gave Larry a list of suggestions, much like the one in Figure 4.1. The materials and the ensuing discussion were successful. Larry was able to express his understanding of the materials by paraphrasing them, even to role-play a couple of them with the social worker.

4.1 — ALTERNATIVE WAYS TO SELF-ADVOCATE

Sometimes students need to provide the instructors with more information about how they learn. Many college professors have never been trained to teach. Therefore, their exposure to students who learn differently may be limited, and they would welcome suggestions on better ways to assist the student in achieving success.

- Practice describing how you learn best; if it would be beneficial for you to review a test after it has been returned, then make an appointment to do this; if having a syllabus of the course in advance is important to helping you be more organized, then request it; provide concrete examples of how you learn.

- If study groups help you to learn the material, ask the instructor to find out who else in the class might be interested in forming a group.

- If you learn better when you sit in the front of the classroom, be sure to arrange to have a seat nearer to the lecturer. Perhaps you will need to ask the instructor to help you by facing the audience when lecturing.

- If you have difficulty remembering assignments or have trouble copying from the chalkboard, ask the instructor for a written list of the assignments.

- If you are unfamiliar with terms or directions, request that they be repeated or explained.

- If you have difficulty organizing math problems on a plain sheet of paper, suggest to the instructor that you be allowed to use lined paper or graph paper to assist you in keeping the problems in columns. If you are required to copy problems from the chalkboard, ask the professor to give carbonized paper to someone else in the class who can copy the problems for both of you.

- If you have difficulty writing quickly or outlining, ask for permission to tape the lecture; look into securing a tape recorder with a numbering system that allows you to jot down the number the recorder was on when you find yourself unclear about what is being stated in the lecture.

- If you have a problem with your handwriting, request to use a computer for in-class assignments or tests.

- If you need more feedback on your term papers or essays, suggest to the instructor that you meet together to allow you to have a more in-depth conversation about your paper.

- If you have difficulty grasping the main point of a lecture, perhaps you could ask the instructor to put more stress on key words.

- If you have major issues with true-false tests, essay tests, or multiple-choice tests, request a modification based on appropriate accommodations.

- If you have difficulty with test-taking strategies, ask the instructor to provide you with study questions that could provide an understanding of the format of a future test.

- If you have difficulty writing or processing your thoughts quickly, arrange with the instructor to have extra time to do the assignment or take the test; if a reader is an appropriate accommodation, be sure that the instructor understands why this is helpful and necessary.

- If you have a language processing deficit and the instructor plans to show a film in class, be sure to request a written version of the tape or an audiovisual version so that you can replay it for yourself.

- Be sure that the instructor knows that you appreciate the support and modifications that are provided.

About a half hour later, the meeting adjourned, Larry and his parents thanked everyone and left, and the special educator and the English teacher adjourned to the hall. After thanking Mr. Moore for coming, the special educator said, "Phil, thanks again for coming; your input was invaluable. Could I make just a brief observation?"

"Certainly," he said, "I have lots of time. You're taking me up on my request for advice, huh?"

"Yeah, I guess I am."

"Fire away."

"Do you remember in the meeting when you suggested to Larry that he take the bull by the horns in order to alert his teachers to any accommodations he might need?"

"Sure," said Mr. Moore, "I wanted him to be more aggressive with me and the rest of his teachers,"

"Good advice," said the special education teacher, "but your metaphor that he take the bull by the horns probably confused him." She continued, "Like most students with learning disabilities, Larry is a very concrete thinker. He will think *literally* about such descriptions and miss your message."

"Do you mean that he actually pictured grabbing a bull by the horns?" asked Mr. Moore.

"Yes, I think he probably did. Other LD kids do the same thing. That's why we have to be so careful about what we say to special needs kids, even to some of the others *without* problems!"

"Wow," said Mr. Moore, shaking his head. "Well, thanks for the help; that's exactly what I need." He then shook our hands and headed down the hall. The special education teacher then informed us that Mr. Moore was one of the best-liked and most effective teachers in the building and that he asks constantly for advice. She admitted that she is generally less candid with others because most aren't as open as he is.

IMPORTANCE OF SPECIAL EDUCATION TECHNIQUES IN ALL INSTRUCTION

Stories like this one illustrate just how far special education has come within the past several years. The research and study that have established it in most schools have also provoked a wide range of considerations for regular classroom teachers. Students with learning and other disabilities learn from teachers who have mastered the techniques and instructional strategies that accommodate the developmental delays and other interferences that hamper them.

In essence, the learning patterns of students with disabilities provoked a corresponding search for specific instructional techniques and processes for teaching them. This search resulted in a body of knowledge that has challenged traditional instructional practices. Much of the research in special education, for example, has affirmed the concept that learning of *all* students is enhanced when their sensory modalities are involved in the learning task. It has challenged lecture as the primary instructional technique in most classrooms.

The research also emphasized the importance of accommodating the developmental milestones of all students, which vary from individual to individual. Many high school freshmen, for example, in spite of superior intelligence, are still concrete thinkers. Because of their intelligence, however, they may be placed in honors or accelerated courses but find themselves unable to handle the high levels of abstraction such courses require. Frustration results, not unlike the frustration of students with learning disabilities.

In this regard, learning research, particularly the studies involving special needs students, has given special educators insights into the learning process that *all* teachers require. A result is that the planning and routine instruction that special education programs provide have outdistanced the professional skills of many, maybe most, regular classroom teachers. The gap separating them must be narrowed by promoting increased interaction among all teachers in the school and using special education personnel as consultants to complement the efforts of mainstreamed teachers.

Such a relationship not only enhances the learning experiences of special needs students, but it promotes improved instruction for *all* students and engages mainstreamed teachers in ongoing learning experiences that are as effective as the most expensive and well-organized in-service training program. This section, therefore, identifies the unique strengths of special education programs and emphasizes the importance of sharing them with regular classroom teachers, parents, and students. In essence, it asserts that children with learning disabilities are only extreme examples of the natural diversity that exists in every classroom.

It also emphasizes the most appropriate ways for such sharing to take place. Increased interaction among all school personnel is desirable not only for informal in-service training to take place but for the creation of the synergy that results in improved services for all students. Therefore, this section also considers teaming and ongoing committee activity as processes for coalescing the skills of school professionals and parents.

DEVELOPING AN ARTICULATION PROCESS WITH FEEDER SCHOOLS

The dictionary indicates that the word "articulate" derives from the Latin *articulare,* "meaning "divided into joints." Implicit within the definition is the notion that the joints cannot remain divided. The success of any system is dependent on the coordination of its different parts. To articulate, then, is to connect the "joints" of language—words and phrases—to promote understanding and to assure the effective operation of the separate but complementary elements within a system.

School systems require effective articulation if they are to assure a consistency of curriculum, instruction, and delivery of services for students, parents, and others in the community. For our purposes in special education, therefore, articulation involves a consistency of processes that promote communication among schools to assure effective diagnosis and treatment for students with special needs. Without such articulation, students often "slip through the cracks" and fail to receive the diagnosis and treatment they require to compensate for their disabilities.

"Process" is the operative word. Art Costa suggested that "Intelligent people know what to do when they don't know what to do." They trust process. It's that simple. When confused about a child's learning interferences, intelligent teachers and counselors tap into a process that engages knowledgeable people in the analysis of the child's learning situation, including his or her strengths and weaknesses.

Similarly, unpredictability and uncertainty often frustrate and confuse children and their parents when moving from one learning situation to another. Even the teachers and Pupil Personnel specialists in feeder schools are often confused about the curriculum and instructional challenges the receiving schools may place on students with special needs. When confused, we must turn to process, in this case an articulation process that coalesces the knowledge of the child, his or her parents, and key people from both schools to determine curriculum decisions, placement, and any additional services the child may require to be successful.

Such a process involves several important steps:

◆ Whenever possible, the professionals from each school should hold a preliminary meeting—without the student or parents—to discuss the unique characteristics of the student's case, the relative cooperation or resistance of the parents, the student's self-advocacy and compensatory skills, and the best thinking of both schools regarding course registration, placement, leveling, and involvement in special programs. Such a preliminary meeting may be logistically inconvenient for many professionals, but it remains desirable for a few reasons.

One, it familiarizes everyone with the specifics of the disability, the best way to approach the student and his or her parents, and the rationale behind the specific recommendations to be made to the family. Two, it guarantees a "united front" among all the professionals in the meeting. Three, it answers the questions that certain school personnel might have regarding the nature of the student's disability and the recommendations to treat it. And four, it assures a uniformity of information and treatment that promotes enlightened input from everyone in the meeting.

This meeting need not be long. It need not even require one group's traveling to the other's school to hold it. Current and future technologies promise a wide range of opportunities for professionals to meet by way of interactive television. Conference telephone calls may involve much the same thing right now. If these technologies are unavailable, however, and if some school professionals simply can't find the time to attend such a meeting, all relevant written materials should be mailed to participants several days prior to the meeting.

Such written materials should include test results, explanations of findings, and the anticipated recommendations of personnel from both schools regarding the student's course selection, placement, and special programs. Figure 4.2 provides a great deal of information that will give personnel from both schools a good understanding of the student's background.

4.2 — STUDENT INFORMATION FORM

Professionals involved in planning for the special needs of students will need all types of information. It is important that the form being used gather detailed data in order to assist the school personnel involved in developing plans for support services, accommodations, or recommendations for the student. Parents should complete this form as accurately as possible.

1. **Specific information about the student**

   Name _____

   Date of birth _____   Current age _____

   Address _____

   Telephone _____   Date _____

   Current school _____   Grade in school _____

   Name of person completing this form _____

   Relationship to the student _____

   Address _____

   Telephone _____

2. **Information about the student's family**

   Mother:

   Mother's name _____

   Birth date _____

   Address _____

   Home telephone _____

   Work telephone _____

   Occupation _____

   High school degree ____ Yes ____ No   Two-year college ____ Yes ____ No

   Four-year college ____ Yes ____ No   Master's Degree ____ Yes ____ No

   Ph.D. ____ Yes ____ No

   Highest degree and in what field _____

   Learning difficulties? ____ Yes ____ No; If yes, please describe:

   _____

   Attention Deficit Disorder? ____ Yes ____ No; If yes, when diagnosed:

   _____

   Any other additional information _____

   _____

   Father:

   Father's name _____

   Birth date _____

Address _____

Home telephone _____

Work telephone _____

Occupation _____

High school degree ____ Yes ____ No   Two-year college ____ Yes ____ No

Four-year college ____ Yes ____ No   Master's Degree ____ Yes ____ No

Ph.D. ____ Yes ____ No

Highest degree and in what field _____

Learning difficulties? ____ Yes ____ No; If yes, please describe:

_____

Attention Deficit Disorder? ____ Yes ____ No; If yes, when diagnosed:

_____

Any other additional information _____

_____

Are parents ____ Married ____ Separated ____ Divorced

If parent(s) are divorced and remarried, please provide information:

    Stepmother's name _____

    Address _____

    Home telephone _____

    Work telephone _____

    Occupation _____

    Date of marriage _____

    Stepfather's name _____

    Address _____

    Home telephone _____

    Work telephone _____

    Occupation _____

    Date of marriage _____

Guardian:

Guardian's name _____

Birth date _____

Address _____

Home telephone _____

Work telephone _____

Occupation _____

High school degree ____ Yes ____ No   Two-year college ____ Yes ____ No

Four-year college ____ Yes ____ No   Master's Degree ____ Yes ____ No

Ph.D. ____ Yes ____ No

Highest degree and in what field _____

Learning difficulties? ____ Yes ____ No; If yes, please describe:

_____

Attention Deficit Disorder? ____ Yes ____ No; If yes, when diagnosed:

_____

Any other additional information _____

_____

Sister/brothers:

Name(s):	_____	_____	_____
Age:	_____	_____	_____
Grade:	_____	_____	_____
Learning issues:	_____	_____	_____
Speech problems:	_____	_____	_____
ADHD:	_____	_____	_____

Other Information about the family:

Has anyone suffered from mental illness? ____ Yes ____ No

   If yes, please explain _____

Has anyone been affected by mental retardation? ____ Yes ____ No

   If yes, please explain _____

Has anyone suffered a serious illness? ____ Yes ____ No

   If yes, please explain _____

Is English the main language spoken in the home? ____ Yes ____ No

   If no, please explain _____

Where else has the family lived as a unit? _____

3. **Information about the student's birth**

Was the mother ill during the pregnancy? ____ Yes ____ No

   If yes, please explain _____

Was it a normal birth? ____ Yes ____ No

   If no, please explain _____

How long was the labor? ____   Was it induced? _____

Was anesthesia used? _____   Was a spinal block used? _____

Caesarean? _____ Breech? _____

Birth weight _____ Length _____ Jaundice? ____ Yes ____ No

Medical attention required such as transfusions, incubator? ____ Yes ____ No

If yes, please explain _____

Breast fed? ____ Yes ____ No For how long _____

4. Student's medical history

Current health status _____

Taking any medications _____ Yes _____ No

If yes, please explain _____

Please list childhood diseases _____

_____

_____

Identify any chronic conditions during childhood _____

Allergies? ____ Yes ____ No

If yes, please identify allergies _____

Surgery? Please identify and give dates _____

_____

Accidents: please identify and give dates _____

_____

Hospitalizations: Please identify and give reason and dates _____

_____

5. Developmental History

Age child rolled over _____ Age child sat alone _____

Age of first words _____ Age crawled _____

Age walked _____ Age weaned from bottle _____

Use a pacifier? ____ Yes ____ No

Age of first words _____ Age using multiple words _____

Age child could reason _____ Age learned to count _____

Age child knew alphabet _____ Age to print name _____

Age learned colors _____ Age ate alone _____

Age tying own shoes _____ Age could color _____

Age could print _____ Age could button clothes _____

Age knew right from left _____ Age could tell time _____

Age child could write in cursive _____

Age child could be a friend _____

6. Educational Background

At what age was the student first identified with a learning issue? _____

How was the learning problem manifested? _____

Was testing done to determine the nature of the learning problem? _____

    If yes, please explain _____

    Identify who conducted the testing _____

    List date(s) of testing   _____   _____   _____   _____

Has the student attended other schools? _____ Yes _____ No

    If yes, please identify what schools and include dates _____

    _____

Did the student receive special services at other schools? _____ Yes _____ No

    If yes, please explain _____

Did the student repeat any grade(s) in school? _____ Yes _____ No

    If yes, please explain _____

What are the student's academic strengths? _____

What are the student's academic weaknesses? _____

* *Part of this material is taken from the Case History Form from the Learning Opportunities Program, Barat College, Lake Forest, IL.*

This information should be gathered and shared at least several days prior to the meeting with the student and his or her parents. A brief review of the materials, including the test results and recommendations, prior to the meeting will promote the understanding of everyone involved in the process and provide the united front that is so important when schools work with families, particularly when they anticipate possible resistance from parents.

◆ The actual meeting should be held in the feeder school setting, where the parents and student are probably most comfortable. This is an important consideration, especially when the student is moving into a new high school setting. Entering freshmen often imagine academic monsters looming large in almost every corner of a high school setting. They need some time and a few informal visiting experiences to realize that such monsters are only imaginary. Comfort is a real factor for them, especially if school personnel plan to discuss particularly sensitive issues.

Although "comfort" may be important for the student and parents, however, it may be an interference for some of the school personnel. Feeder school personnel are often unfamiliar with the programs, curriculum, and instructional characteristics of the receiving school. And rarely do they have the opportunity to visit receiving schools on a regular enough basis to learn more about their programs.

As a result, administrators, special education personnel, and counselors are almost totally dependent on personnel from receiving schools to explain and recommend program placement. Certainly, this is not all bad; some mutual dependency is to be expected. The curricula and methodologies of most schools are constantly evolving, at least we hope they are. The more familiar everyone is with the basic program, however, the better the quality of information parents will receive from the personnel from both schools throughout the school year.*

The meeting with the student and parents also provides the time to explore their concerns and expectations. We suggest that families be asked to complete Figures 4.3 and 4.4 prior to the meeting. They can be used during the meeting to make curricular and placement decisions, then given to the personnel from the receiving school to share with the teachers and counselor who will be working with the student the following year. The personnel from the receiving school may even want to refer to the forms at some future time to discuss the student's current self-perception and future plans.

---

* Deerfield High School in Deerfield, Illinois, conducts two or three annual meetings with all counseling and special education personnel from its several feeder schools to outline changes in curriculum and other aspects of its instructional program. It also uses the meeting to answer questions from feeder school personnel and to renew old acquaintances. The meetings have done much to promote continuity among all the schools in the district.

4.3 — STUDENT'S PERSPECTIVE

It is always helpful to hear students' perspective about their learning issues. Not only does this provide an opportunity for students to put things in their own words, but it also highlights the students' degree of acceptance of the disability. Students should answer these questions in their own words and not be concerned about spelling or punctuation.

1. What is your learning disability? _____
    _____

2. How does your learning disability impact your academics? _____
    _____

3. How do you explain your learning disability to friends? _____
    _____

4. What services are you receiving in school to help you compensate for the learning disability? _____
    _____

5. Why do you think you were tested for learning disabilities? _____
    _____

6. What subject areas are the most difficult for you? _____
    _____

7. What subject areas are the easiest for you? _____
    _____

8. What extracurricular activities do you like to participate in? _____
    _____

9. What special talents do you have? _____
    _____

10. Are you computer literate? _____ Yes _____ No

11. What additional assistance would you like to receive in school?
    _____

12. What are your career goals?
    _____

Part of this material is taken from the Case History Form from the Learning Opportunities Program, Barat College, Lake Forest, IL.

126

4.4 – PARENT'S PERSPECTIVE

All parents have hopes and dreams for their children. Therefore, when a family learns that a child has been diagnosed with a learning disability, the reactions are not always the same. A parent who actively pursue a better understanding of the learning disability and becomes an advocate for the child is more apt to be able to help the child understand and accept the diagnosis. Parents should answer the following questions in an honest and clear fashion. This information will be useful in developing a better understanding of the parents' perspective and their thoughts on impending services and accommodations.

1. Your child's learning issues could be affected by academics, social interactions, and daily routine activities. Please provide your description of your child's learning issue and how it impacts the various parts of the student's life. Be sure to provide information as it relates currently and in the past.

   _____

   _____

   _____

   _____

   _____

2. Some parents seek outside therapy for their child or request social work services in the school setting. Please provide detailed information about your child's clinical treatment, length, reason for seeking the treatment, issues at hand, and the nature of the treatment provided.

   _____

   _____

   _____

   _____

   _____

3. Please describe your views on how the current school can assist your child through services, accommodations, programs, or therapy.

   _____

   _____

   _____

   _____

   _____

4.4 continued

4. Please provide additional information relating to your child's behavior or academic difficulties, or social issues that you feel would be helpful in gaining a better understanding of the student.

_____

_____

_____

_____

Please sign, indicating that you have provided the most accurate information.

Parent(s) signature _____

Date _____

* *Part of this material is taken from the Case History Form from the Learning Opportunities Program, Barat College, Lake Forest, IL.*

After all this information is gathered and discussed and program decisions are made, personnel from both schools should encourage the family to contact them with any additional questions. The meeting should be concluded by providing copies of all forms to the parents and by reviewing specific tasks to be performed by school personnel prior to the student's enrollment in the new school. We like to refer to this as the "I will" list.

The "I will" list contains items such as:

◆ High school counselor: "I will get permission from the chair of foreign language to drop Spanish without grade penalty if Roberta finds that she simply can't handle the course."

◆ Special educator: "I will check with the assistant principal to assure that we can schedule Roberta with Mr. Royer for Freshman English."

◆ Junior high counselor: "I'll talk to Roberta's junior high math teacher to make sure she agrees with our placement recommendations."

Following the meeting, these tasks should be performed and parents and other members of the committee should be notified of their completion. These "I will" items promote consensus building prior to the arrival of the student in the new school setting and avoid future problems. Early communication obviates future arguments. School authorities tend to be much more agreeable when they are elements in an early solution rather than a later problem.

Good articulation among schools, then, like any relationship, is dependent on effective communication. It grows in strength and quality when people talk to one another, help one another, and combine their individual strengths to create a synergy that results in the best possible services for students and their parents. The same is true of articulation *within* schools.

DEVELOPING AN INTERNAL REFERRAL PROCESS

A willingness to communicate is as important to an internal referral process as it is to articulation among schools. It is especially critical for these reasons:

◆ Students with subtle learning disabilities often go undetected during their early schooling. Their developmental delays are not as evident in the early grades as in junior high school and high school.

◆ The diagnostic capabilities of some feeder schools are unsophisticated and, in many, almost nonexistent. It's amazing but true that some schools, given the overwhelming evidence of learning disabilities in the general population, still cling to the notion that *their* children do not get such things.

◆ Some districts, especially poorer ones, are too busy struggling with the maintenance of the regular classroom program to consider the addition of sophisticated special education processes.

◆ The administrators of some feeder districts still disagree philosophically with the notion of "hidden disabilities." A result is their unwillingness to develop diagnostic capability in their schools.

◆ The parents of some elementary school children steadfastly resist suspicions, even diagnoses, of learning disabilities throughout a child's early education. Sometimes these suspicions never get communicated to junior high school or secondary school personnel.

◆ Some parents have instructed junior high school personnel to remove all evidence of the child's learning disability from school records in order to give him or her a "clean start" in high school. Fortunately, a close enough review of the child's cumulative record reveals inconsistencies that ultimately uncover the disability. Without a careful review of the record, however, students in such circumstances are completely dependent on the observational strengths of their teachers and the internal referral processes of the new school.

Considering the Actual Processes

The process starts with someone—a teacher, a parent, or the child himself—recognizing chronic interferences to learning. The process continues with an analysis of the interferences to determine their causes and their impact on the student. As indicated already in this book, many interferences to learning are not disabilities. This section provides additional reproducibles to help Pupil Personnel make such determinations.

Section 2—specifically Figures 2.3 and 2.5—discusses Learning and Behavioral referral forms that enable regular classroom teachers to alert counselors, deans, and other Pupil Personnel specialists to student behaviors that require a closer look. Figure 4.5 provides a form that can be used to secure additional information from all teachers to determine the extent of the problem.

Sometimes, student "problems" result more from the disciplinary procedures or instructional strategies of certain teachers than from student incapacity. Figure 4.5 enables counselors and special educators to determine whether the problem is evidenced in other classrooms as well. Finally, Figure 4.6 provides a composite of the responses from all the student's teachers and provides a "big picture" of the student's learning and behavioral progress in all classes.

This composite is then shared with others in Pupil Personnel to determine if further study is needed. For example, if the composite indicates that the student's learning or behavior is affected only in the English teacher's classroom and that nothing else, including available testing, reveals the same problem, counselors and others can reasonably assume that the student's behavior reflects something other than a learning disability.

In fact, if the English teacher refers other students for similar reasons, he risks self-incrimination! It's not uncommon to route all referrals through a central system that records and categorizes them. The process documents the name of the person making the referral, the reasons for the referral, the time of the referral, and the disposition of the referral, including the name of the person who dealt with it and what he or she did.

4.5 — A REPORT ON STUDENT PROGRESS — REQUEST FOR STUDENT REVIEW

Referral by staff/school personnel

_____ Process through counselor

_____ Process through Special Education

_____ Process through the Dean's Office

_____ Process through Substance Abuse Director

_____ Process through Screening Committee

Report back to _____

Report by _____

Request for information from

_____ Teacher

_____ Counselor

_____ Special Education

_____ Screening Committee

_____ Dean's Office

_____ Psychologist

_____ Social Worker

_____ Substance Abuse Director

_____ Parent

Return information to _____

Return by _____

Student's name _____

Year in school _____ Current date _____

Student's Counselor _____

ACADEMIC REPORT

Teacher submitting report or request _____

Course _____ Period _____

Level of course _____ Current grade _____

Grades on semester assignments _____ _____ _____ _____

Grades on semester tests _____ _____ _____ _____

Describe student's history of homework completion _____

Comment on the quality of the student's homework _____

Identify any work currently outstanding _____

_____

4.5 continued

Identify future assignments pending _____

What advice do you have for the student _____

BEHAVIOR REPORT

Person submitting report or request _____

Describe questionable behavior _____

_____

_____

Comment on other characteristics that provide insight into student behavior such as appearance, attitude, attention span, class participation, peer relationships, motivation, attendance _____

_____

_____

Identify interventions made _____

_____

Provide suggestions for other interventions _____

_____

Additional comments _____

_____

Final outcome of the report/request:

Signature _____

Date _____

Send copies to _____   _____

_____   _____

4.6 – Screening Referral Form

Student name _____ Birth date _____

Referred by _____ Screening date _____

Student's counselor _____ Year in school _____

Identified strengths _____

_____

_____

Identified weaknesses _____

_____

_____

Teacher Comments

    English _____

    Math _____

    Science _____

    Social Studies _____

    Foreign Language _____

    Physical Education _____

    Fine Arts _____

    Applied Arts _____

    Other _____

Prior interventions _____

Instructional accommodations needed and why _____

Screening Committee comments _____

Recommendations _____

Psychoeducational evaluations date _____

Tests to be administered _____

I understand and consent to these recommendations:

_____

Parent signature

Date _____

The body of information that results from the process provides an interesting picture not only of the kinds of student problems being referred but of the teachers and departments making the referrals. The process also documents the actions of counselors, deans, special educators, and others who deal with referrals. As indicated already in this book, the consensus opinion in at least one of these schools was that the school *was referring itself.*

The rigid disciplinary procedures or the inappropriate instructional strategies of some teachers can be discovered as the causes of certain student behaviors. So can the curricular inadequacies or the inflexible policies of entire departments within the school. In effect, the student behaviors being referred serve as much to highlight short-comings in the school as to reflect the discipline or learning problems of students.

Such moments of self-reflection are important for all schools. They are made possible by a system that centralizes all teacher-initiated referrals and provides a look not only at student behavior but the operation of the school itself. Figure 4.7 provides details of the processing of such referrals, including reference to possible intervention strategies.

The process can be included in teacher handbooks, distributed at faculty in-service training sessions, or given to individual teachers or parents to describe the processing of referrals. Interventions range from simple phone calls home to one or more screenings to explore other interferences to learning, including possible learning disabilities.

The Importance of the Classroom Teacher

Classroom teachers are critically important in the school's internal referral process. Without the teacher's specific referral, the process is necessarily limited, even severely handicapped. Occasionally, a conscientious counselor may find the hint of a student's learning disability in inconsistent achievement test results. Such counselors usually explore the issue further by discussing it with the student, the student's parents, and one or more school professionals.

Although disparities in test results can signal possible problems, student learning interferences are most evident in the classroom, where incomplete work, evident frustration during class, poor test results, and garbled writing are observable on a daily basis. With the possible exception of the parents, classroom teachers, therefore, are the most important people in the early diagnosis of student learning disabilities.

This comes as no startling revelation to most of us, but it is a fact that is routinely overlooked in a great many schools. Most schools assume that teachers will make referrals whenever they observe student behaviors that warrant a closer look. Perhaps predictably, misbehavior in the classroom is referred far more often than learning interferences. This is not surprising. Overt misbehavior is far more evident than a subtle learning disability. It is also more disruptive.

This is yet another reason for a central referral system. Most schools require a process that documents the nature of the problems being referred and of the solutions being used. A central referral process enables schools to tally the number of learning referrals it receives from classroom teachers to determine if an in-service training program or some other process is required to promote teacher awareness of the signs of learning disabilities.

4.7 – Process for Teacher-Initiated Referral

Academic/Behavior Progress Report

Referring Faculty Member
- writes progress report or request for intervention
- provides interventions used and those suggested

Send report/request to appropriate chairperson/department
- review report or request

Send report/request to student's counselor
- communicate with referring faculty member
- communicate with parent(s) if appropriate
- communicate with case manager/special education
- identify critical information, interventions, dispositions

Interventions and people involved
- meeting with faculty member and student—discuss plans
- communicate with parents—provide suggestions
- recommend tutoring—complete paperwork
- refer to social worker for diagnostic work-up—parent contact
- refer to screening committee—parent contact
- recommend resource center intervention in academic area

For example, if the school annually receives a significant majority of behavioral referrals and only two or three learning referrals, something is wrong. This is not to suggest that all school populations contain as many potential learning disabilities as misbehavior problems. Certainly, behavior referrals will always outnumber learning referrals, but our experience has been that learning referrals should constitute ten to twenty percent of all referrals from regular classroom teachers. Even if such referrals don't signal a learning disability, they frequently uncover other problems that require the attention of the family and school.

It's important to recognize as well that behavioral referrals often require something other than a disciplinary response from the school's administration. Student misbehavior is often symptomatic of issues far more important than "youthful exuberance." Deans of students and other administrators must be sensitive to signs of problems other than simple misbehavior and be willing to network with other school professionals to find all the possible causes for student behavioral issues.

What Else Does This Suggest? Well, first of all, it suggests the need for periodic in-service training for administrators and mainstreamed teachers to alert them to the signs of possible learning disabilities and to inform them of the processes that are available within the school to refer students and to secure help from learning specialists. The materials in Section 2 provide general information about the signs of learning disabilities. The materials in this section provide information about the processes for responding to such signs.

Figure 4.8 outlines the steps in the evaluation and placement processes, from the submission of the referral to the signing of the Individual Educational Plan (IEP).Every referral does not follow these exact steps—only those that result in special education placement. The outline does, however, inform teachers of what happens after a referral is submitted. If a full case study evaluation is required, Figure 4.9 outlines those steps. As with the other forms in this section, they can be provided separately or included in a booklet that explains the process to teachers, students, and parents.

Notice the several steps involved in the evaluation process prior to actual testing. A full case study evaluation involves a great deal of information and provides a detailed picture of all the factors affecting student learning. Figure 4.10 provides a conference report and a summary of all the steps in the process. It is useful for sharing information with parents and students and for inclusion in special education files for documenting all the steps taken in the process.

Figure 4.11 simply lists the tests that are available to evaluate student achievement, aptitude, and learning patterns. It is appropriate as a ready reference for school psychologists or special education personnel responsible for testing. Finally, Figure 4.12 provides a form that documents the original referral, the reasons for the referral, and its disposition. The form is especially important because it enables the special education department to document its reasons for not conducting a case study evaluation.

4.8—How to Keep Track of the Evaluation and Placement Process

- Referral is received from faculty member or parent and is reviewed by special education department.

- The referral is placed on the screening list and the counselor is notified to gather data and information for the actual screening.

- Screening Committee meets to discuss the referral; they review the data, the referring information, and recommendations are made that could include evaluation.

- A referral letter is sent to the parents identifying the reason for the referral and the recommendations suggested.

- Parents must sign and return the letter giving written consent to proceed with the evaluation.

- The social worker schedules an interview with parents to gather social history information.

- The evaluation is begun once the parents have given permission to proceed and have met with the social worker.

- The student meets several times with the psychologist and/or educational tester to complete the various assessments.

- Once the evaluation is completed, the parents are notified to arrange for a multidisciplinary conference; the conference will include the parents, student, psychologist, educational tester, special education representative, and counselor.

- The Multidisciplinary Conference is held to discuss the results of the evaluation.

- The MDC provides recommendations of special services that are appropriate for the specific needs of the student.

- Parent(s) must give consent to the identified recommendations prior to any services beginning.

- Some recommendations could include adjustments in current classes that might result in reassignment to a different level, different teacher, or different course.

- Class placement recommendations must be acceptable to the parents prior to these changes being instituted.

- Development of the Individualized Educational Plan is a result of the MDC; this plan will include goals for the year based on anticipated outcomes from services and accommodations.

- The parent(s) and the student must sign the IEP indicating their agreement to the recommendations and goals established.

- The plan is implemented and the student's progress is monitored.

4.9 — CASE STUDY EVALUATION

- *Consultation with parents:* Provides parents with an opportunity to describe their concerns related to their child's education.

- *Interview with child:* Assists the evaluation team to understand the difficulties being experienced from the child's perspective.

- *Social development study:* Provides the evaluation team with an understanding of the child's in-school and out-of-school functioning by assessing how the environment affects the child's ability to learn.

- *Medical history and current health status:* Information to help the evaluation team determine if any current or past medical difficulties are affecting the child's school performance.

- *Vision/hearing screenings:* Assist the evaluation team in determining any visual or auditory problems that would interfere with the testing or school performance of the child.

- *Review of the child's academic history and current educational functioning:* Involves reviewing the child's previous school records and current levels of functioning in the present educational setting.

- *Educational evaluation of learning processes and achievement:* Measures traditional academic skills taught in school, such as reading, math reasoning and calculation, and written language. Additional assessments or observations determine how the child takes in information, understands the information, and expresses answers, and helps the evaluation team determine the best ways for the child to be taught.

- *Assessment of the child's learning environment:* Helps the evaluation team determine how the student interacts in the classroom environment and addresses the match between student needs and teaching styles. Physical and environmental factors in the classroom are assessed also to determine their effects on the educational needs of the child.

- *Specialized Evaluations:* Additional components may be recommended depending on the nature of the child's difficulties; a Speech and Language Evaluation involving select components of a comprehensive case study evaluation; Psychological Evaluation: Including an assessment in the areas of intellectual ability, fine/gross motor coordination, social/emotional development, and learning processes and/or academic achievement.

4.10 – REPORT OF THE MULTIDISCIPLINARY CONFERENCE

Student Name _____

Date _____

Psychologist's interaction with the student _____

_____

    Signature of psychologist _____

Interview with parent(s) _____

_____

    Interviewer's signature _____

Information regarding social development _____

_____

    Signature of individual completing this information _____

Information on past medical history _____

Information on current health condition _____

    Signature of individual completing this information _____

Results of the Vision screening: ____ Vision test passed   ____ Vision test failed

                             ____ Needs glasses   ____ Refer to doctor

Results of the Hearing screening: ____ Hearing test passed   ____ Hearing test failed

                             ____ Needs hearing aid   ____ Refer to doctor

    Vision/Hearing Tests completed by _____

Overview of student's past academic performance _____

Overview of student's current academic performance _____

    Academic information completed by _____

Information on the student's learning processes _____

Information on student's level of educational achievement _____

    Learning information completed by _____

Information on the student's environment for learning _____

    Learning environment information completed by _____

Psychological evaluation _____

    Signature of psychologist _____

Speech and language evaluation _____

    Signature of speech pathologist _____

Evaluations from outside evaluators _____

Information about a student with characteristics of learning disabilities _____

_____

Identify any specific behavior noted during the evaluation _____

Identify how behavior relates to academic performance _____

Highlight any effects from environmental factors _____

Highlight any effects from cultural factors _____

Highlight any effects from economic factors _____

Eligibility of student for services under IDEA:

     Student demonstrates one or more disabling condition: _____ Yes _____ No

     The student's disabling condition interferes with educational performance?
     _____ Yes _____ No

     The interference is extreme and requires special education involvement:
     _____ Yes _____ No

Based on these findings, the student _____ is _____ is not eligible for programs or services in special education?

What is the Primary disability _____ Secondary disability _____

Eligibility for services under Section 504 of the Rehabilitation Act of 1973:

The Student _____ does or _____ does not have a physical or mental impairment which substantially limits one or more major life activities, such as caring for one's self, performing manual tasks, walking, seeing, hearing, speaking, breathing, learning and working.

* Parts of this information was secured from the Multidisciplinary Report/Summary of Case Study Components Form, Deerfield High School, Deerfield, Illinois.

4.11 – Some Tests Used to Assess Strengths and Weaknesses

Wechsler Intelligence Scale for Children III: This test is given to children ages 6 through 16 and provides three IQ scores; verbal, performance, and full-scale, yielding information about strengths and weaknesses in language and performance areas.

Wechsler Adult Intelligence Scale-Revised (WAIS-R): The WAIS-R is divided into two parts, a Verbal Scale and a Performance Scale. The Verbal Scale is used to examine word knowledge, auditory memory, general information, problem solving skills, and ability to conceptualize. The Performance Scale assesses nonverbal problem solving skills, spatial visualization, motor development, and visual perception and sequencing. (Ages 16+)

> Verbal Scale IQ
> Performance Scale IQ
> Full Scale IQ

Woodcock-Johnson Psychoeducational Battery-Revised (WJ-R): This test of achievement consists of fifteen subtests that measure various aspects of scholastic achievement in reading, math, written language, knowledge, and skills.

Stanford Binet Intelligence Scale: This Scale is administered to individuals aged 2 through adulthood. Verbal responses are emphasized more than nonverbal responses. Therefore, children tested at age two might score quite differently when tested on another IQ test many years later.

Stanford Diagnostic Achievement Test: This test measures performance in academic subjects such as spelling, grammar, arithmetic, and reading. This test also provides instructional objectives and suggestions for teaching.

Test of Written Language: This is a test used to identify strengths and weaknesses in various areas of writing ability. It can be used to compare students to their peers in written expression.

4.12 – REFERRAL FOR EVALUATION OR REEVALUATION DENIED

TO:

Parent(s) name _____

Current date _____ Date of Referral _____

RE:

Student's name _____

Birth date _____ Social Security number _____

Referred for _____

Referred by _____

Referred because of _____

After a review of the referral the Screening Committee has determined that the request for a Case Study Evaluation has been denied for the following reasons:

_____

_____

Parents are referred to the Parental Procedural Safeguards which are included with this letter. Parents who have further concerns or wish to speak with a professional in the Special Education Department, may contact:

_____

_____

Title _____

Telephone _____

Signature of person submitting letter to parent(s) _____

Copies sent to _____

RESPONSIBILITIES OF THE MULTIDISCIPLINARY TEAM

If the department decides to conduct the evaluation, the results are referred to a multidisciplinary team that discusses information received during interviews, anecdotal or descriptive reports from classroom teachers, vision and hearing screenings, medical history, psychoeducational tests, and any other tests used to assess the student's achievement, aptitude, and learning style.

Figure 4.13 lists many of the questions that are asked by the team. This reproducible is appropriate to introduce new team members to the process and substance of the team's inquiry or to show parents and students the kinds of issues covered by the team. The form is very helpful as a reminder of the kinds of questions to ask to provide the best possible services to students.

If the student requires special education placement, Figure 2.18 informs parents of their rights, identifies the specific placement, and secures written consent from the parents. Figure2.17 offers a detailed explanation of parent rights and expectations. This important information for parents is an expression of good faith from the department and school.

THE IMPORTANCE OF ACCOMMODATIONS

Invariably, the multidisciplinary team identifies a range of accommodations that are needed to enhance the student's learning or in some other way to acknowledge his or her disability. Figure 4.14a and b details and documents several important considerations, including behavior management, changes in graduation criteria, involvement in required standardized tests, and scheduling considerations.

Many parents and a good many teachers are convinced that misbehaving children—no matter what their disabling condition—should receive appropriate punishments. In essence, they should receive the same kinds of punishments other students receive for their misbehavior. It's important, therefore, to provide in-service programming for teachers to explain alternative behavior management plans that are required for students with learning and behavioral disabilities.

If a child is unable to understand the cause-and-effect nature of his actions, punishment serves only to frustrate him further. What is required is an alternative way to enable him to understand the effects of his behavior and to manage it without external control. When teachers fail to understand this, they tend to perceive special education as an unnecessary pot of oil that makes life more comfortable for squeaky wheels. They never experience the incredible patience required to help a child with a learning or behavioral disability understand his actions and develop the internal mechanisms to control them.

Such an in-service training program might also use Figure 4.15 to further detail and discuss the kinds of accommodations some students require to adjust to the normal expectations of most classrooms. When teachers understand the reasons for such accommodations, they are more inclined to provide them. The form should also be used by the special education department to document the accommodations needed by a specific student. It should then be shared with teachers and parents, forwarded to the counselor and case manager for their information, and filed in the special education department for future reference.

4.13 — QUESTIONS ASKED BY THE MULTIDISCIPLINARY TEAM

What is the purpose of the conference?

      _____To determine initial eligibility

      _____To change eligibility

      _____To change student placement

      _____To terminate services

      _____To reevaluate

      _____To have an annual review

What are the primary characteristics?

What are the secondary characteristics?

      _____Speech and language impairment

      _____Behavior/emotional disorder

      _____Physical and health impairment

      _____Learning disability

      _____Visual impairment

      _____Hearing impairment

      _____Traumatic brain injury

      _____Mental impairment

      _____Autism

Does the student need special transportation arrangements?

What classroom accommodations are needed?

What testing accommodations are appropriate?

What is the medical history?

What is the academic history?

What is the current academic functioning?

What is the educational evaluation of the learning processes?

What is the level of educational achievement?

Is there any relevant behavior noted during the observation and if so what is the relationship of this behavior to the student's academic functioning?

Any factors affected by the student's environment, culture, or economic situation?

Does the student have one or more disabling conditions?

Does the student's disabling condition interfere with educational performance?

Is the interference severe enough that the student would need special education intervention?

Is the student eligible for special education program or services?

Does the student have a physical or mental impairment which substantially limits one or more major life activities?

Will the student require special services for attaining transition goals?

Is the student able to understand school rules?

Is the student able to follow school rules?

Does the student need an extended school year?

What criteria must be met for graduation from high school?

Does the student need a special school schedule?

Adapted from forms from Township High School District #113, Highland Park, Illinois

4.14a – ACCOMMODATIONS AND SERVICES IN REGULAR EDUCATION PLACEMENT

Student name _____ Date _____

Identify the accommodations and/or services recommended _____
_____
_____

What special transition services will be necessary to assist the student in pursuing goals in transitioning from high school to postsecondary options?

    This student _____ will _____ will not need special services?

    A Transition Plan _____ has _____ has not been written?

The student _____ will _____ will not be able to understand rules in school.

The student _____ is _____ is not capable of following school rules.

The discipline consequences identified in the school code book _____ are _____ are not appropriate.

If the consequences are not appropriate, then a plan must be developed to ideal with behavior management in case of a violation of school code. An example of this plan can be found on the next page.

The student _____ should _____ should not be required to have an extended school year in order to maintain academic and behavior progress.

What criteria should be used to determine the student's eligibility for graduation from high school?

    _____ regular number of credits required for all students
    _____ a reduced number of credits
    _____ an exemption from courses that impact on the disability
    _____ identified IEP goals
    _____ regular number of credits taken on a pass/fail basis
    _____ other

Should there be accommodations granted for required standardized testing?

    _____ extended time
    _____ excused from the testing
    _____ quiet location to take exam
    _____ reader
    _____ scribe
    _____ tape recorder
    _____ computer
    _____ modification to format
    _____ regular administration

If any specific accommodations must be provided, please provide rationale _____
_____

Should the student be given a shortened school schedule? _____ Yes _____ No

For yes, please provide reasons _____

4.14b — Accommodation Plan for Managing Behavior

Student name _____

Date _____

The student ____ is ____ is not capable of abiding by the discipline policies established for the school district.

 If no, please refer to Goal #____ in the IEP.

The student ____ does ____ does not require that the school's attendance policy be modified to meet the identified needs in the IEP.

Options for providing modifications or strategies could include:

 ____ student provides own self-monitoring
 ____ develop a plan to modify behavior
 ____ student works with professional to work through the problem
 ____ student signs a contract
 ____ student serves an in-school detention
 ____ student serves an out-of-school detention
 ____ student remains in the Dean's Office for a period of time
 ____ student reports to an identified mentor

Behavior concerns identified in the IEP in Goal # ____

 Identify prior behavior that has caused concern _____

 Specify medication being administered _____

 Identify specific conditions or environment that may cause this behavior to be exhibited
 _____

 Specify other behavior that would be acceptable alternatives _____
 _____

 Detail any interventions that have been attempted _____

 Identify plans for any new interventions _____

4.15 – ACCOMMODATIONS SCHEDULE

Student Name _____

Date _____ Grade Level _____

Case Manager _____ Counselor _____

Mainstream Courses			*Special Education Program*	
Course	Teacher		Course	Teacher
1 _____ _____		a _____ _____
2 _____ _____		b _____ _____
3 _____ _____		c _____ _____
4 _____ _____		d _____ _____
5 _____ _____		e _____ _____

Comments:

Accommodations Needed:

____Test modifications
    ____Untimed
    ____Oral
    ____Taped
    ____Reader
    ____Scribe
    ____Edited
    ____Distraction-free room
____Notetakers/notes
____Readers
____Books on tape
____Taping of classes
____Calculators

Comments:

Accommodations Needed:

____Computer
    ____Spellchecker
    ____Grammarchecker
    ____Wordprocessing
____Tutoring
____Learning Resource Center
____Monitoring

____Behavior modification
____Social work intervention
____Study skills assistance
____Reduced course load
____Hand scheduling
____Social skills
____Career counseling
____No support needed
____Termination of services

Student signature _____

Parent signature _____

Case manager signature _____

Counselor signature _____

Other _____

The case manager is then responsible for assuring that the accommodations are provided for the student. Such assurances result from the direct intervention of the case manager and from the self-advocacy of the student. Student self-advocacy is preferable and should represent a primary focus for much of what the case manager does with and for the student throughout the school year. The case manager also has several other responsibilities, all of which are detailed in Figure 4.16.

Such a reproducible should be included in the special education department handbook, provided to parents during and after orientation and planning meetings, included with materials given to students, and used for faculty in-service training programs. It's important that teachers realize the responsibilities of case managers and understand the degree of interdependency that characterizes their professional relationship with them.

Neither the classroom teacher nor the case manager can provide all the help a student needs to develop coping strategies, self-advocacy skills, appropriate study strategies, improved self-esteem, an understanding of the nature of his or her disability, or any of the other responsibilities listed in Figure 4.16. Everyone involved in the process, therefore, requires a periodic reminder that regular classroom teachers, counselors, special education personnel, deans of students, and parents must work closely with one another to assure the proper adjustment of students with learning disabilities.

TEAMING AS ONE OF THE ANSWERS

When these people regard themselves as members of a team, students with learning disabilities find consistency in every corner of their lives. In essence, special education personnel are not the only people that encourage their self-advocacy or help them develop the compensatory skills they require to improve their learning. Every adult in their lives can help enhance their self-esteem, understand the effects of their behavior, and improve their organizational skills.

Shared purpose among school personnel is essential if students with learning disabilities are to realize their full potential. It is most possible when special education personnel, counselors, social workers, deans of students, and classroom teachers work closely to coordinate their efforts and to share their special knowledge about individual students. Teaming is one of the best ways to accomplish such close cooperation.

One school, for example, divides counselors, representatives of special education, social workers, and deans of students into two teams. The teams include classroom teachers who rotate membership on a quarterly basis. One team, the Basic Services Team, is responsible for up to 80 percent of the student body and deals with issues affecting the "normally adjusting" student.

This team discusses such things as curricular issues, increased stress on students, college admissibility, and a few inevitable behavioral problems. The other team, the Extended Services Team, deals with students with serious adjustmental problems: learning and behavioral disabilities, dysfunctional families, addictive behavior, and extreme discipline cases.

4.16 – ROLE OF THE SPECIAL EDUCATION CASE MANAGER

In many school systems students with learning disabilities are assigned to a special education case manager who monitors the student and provides appropriate remediation, compensatory skills strategies, and advocacy. The role of the case manager can be pivotal in assisting students to understand their disability, articulate their needs, and become independent learners. The role of the case manager is to:

- Assist students with understanding their learning disability
- Help students to identify strengths and weaknesses
- Assist students in developing compensatory skills
- Teach the skills necessary to meet the student's IEP goals
- Assist students in developing self-advocacy skills
- Work with students on developing good coping strategies
- Assist students in developing problem-solving skills
- Help students develop organizational skills
- Assist students with study strategies
- Help students to understand how to manage their time
- Assist students with developing strategies for note taking
- Work with students on the acceptance of their learning disability
- Work with students on self-esteem issues
- Assist students with understanding how to identify priorities
- Assist students with social issues
- Provide recommendations for appropriate high school curriculum
- Identify areas in which the students could benefit from remediation
- Provide content tutoring
- Assist students with skills to stay focused and on task
- Be sure that the psychoeducational testing is up to date
- Encourage students to register for ACT/SAT either standardized or nonstandardized (if appropriate)
- Help students to articulate what services are being utilized and what services will be needed to be successful in college or at work
- Help students to work on becoming independent learners
- Help students understand the connection between their learning disability and relationships with peers, teachers, family and friends
- Assist students with understanding their rights according to ADA and #504
- Be involved in planning for the students' post–high school options
- Encourage students to be motivated
- Facilitate communication with teachers and parents
- Monitor the students' progress

The teams meet twice a week and routinely discuss individual students who come to the attention of one or more team members. The dean of students, for example, may seek advice on a student with a sudden increase in behavioral referrals. A counselor may discuss an otherwise good student who suddenly fails two or more courses. And the social worker may want to update the team on the status of a student recently recommended for a series of diagnostic interviews.

Because the teams meet regularly, the members enjoy productive working relationships and an esprit de corps that results in considerable positive synergy during discussions. The group's decisions invariably reflect this synergy, incorporating the combined knowledge of the different disciplines represented on the team. Rarely does any one of these disciplines determine the group's ultimate decision. Almost always, decisions emerge from everyone's combined input.

This is one of the clear advantages of teaming. Teams build upon the ideas of individual members, unlike committees, which tend to consider sometimes conflicting opinions in order to choose the best one. Committee members tend to share their opinions and then decide mutually on the best one. Team members build upon each other's thinking and *create* a best idea.

Certainly, this is not always the case, but it is true often enough for us to recommend teaming to many of the schools with which we consult. Networking among the various disciplines represented in most schools provides a breadth of knowledge that is essential to good decision making. When these decisions are made by teams that coalesce the best thinking of knowledgeable people, students and parents receive the best services schools can provide.

INDIVIDUALIZED EDUCATIONAL PLANS (IEPS)

Well-conceived Individual Educational Plans (IEPs) bring services to life. The diagnostic services and processes of special education programs open the door to a wide variety of treatments and services for students with learning disabilities. Well-conceived IEPs turn on the lights and guide everyone through the sometimes confusing passageways that lead to the realization of important goals.

Well-written IEPs are statements of objectives, treatment and behavioral targets that include their own measurements of success. For example, if the treatment plan for a child with learning disabilities includes the development of self-advocacy skills, the IEP short-term objective might read something like this:

> "Martha will provide evidence of self-advocacy or discuss experiences in which she self-advocated at least ten times during the first semester of the coming school year. She will discuss these experiences with Mr. Adler, who will record them for discussion with Martha and her parents at her annual review."

Other objectives regarding homework completion, study skills, behavioral adjustments, reading comprehension, and the like should be developed similarly, providing not only statements of intent but measurements for determining the realization of the objective. Good IEPs provide evidence of progress, proof that special services are meeting the needs of the student.

Well-written IEPs, therefore, must include the following:

♦ Statements of the student's current performance academically, socially, vocationally, and behaviorally. Such statements should also refer to the student's ability to self-help, to improve language skills, and to develop compensatory strategies in sensory and motor areas.

♦ Statements of yearly goals and the specific objectives designed to realize them. If, for example, the goal is to improve reading comprehension, the objective might be to improve the student's reading comprehension score on the California Test of Basic Skills by at least one grade level by the end of the following school year. The relative ambition of the standards for measuring the success of the objective to be determined by the group developing the IEP and the extent of the student's disability.

♦ Specific mention of the services to be provided to contribute to the realization of the objectives. In essence, these services, both regular and special education, are the solutions that will lead to the realization of the objectives and annual goals. This section of the IEP also identifies the dates for the start and the termination of such services.

♦ A statement of the extent of the student's involvement in regular education classes. Mainstreaming is a very important consideration during discussions of the student's total educational program. Decisions should be included in statements of IEPs.

♦ Finally, statements of Transition Services are now required for students who are fourteen or older. Such statements address transitional issues regarding "life after school." Specifics might include college, employment, vocational schools, apprenticeships, the armed forces, or any of several other options in the "real world." Whenever possible, the services of other agencies should be included in the statements.

Guidelines for Developing IEPs

In the best of all educational worlds, every student in school would have a whole set of IEPs to guide his or her learning activities. Unfortunately, this doesn't happen for all students, but it does for students with learning disabilities. It happens best when the IEPs are developed carefully and comprehensively. Figure 4.17 provides some guidelines for the development of IEPs. Share them routinely with special education and other school personnel to remind them of the right way and the wrong way to write IEPs.

Figure 4.18 provides a format for the development of IEPs. Notice that it provides for all relevant information, including current performance levels as well as statements of long-range goals and short-term objectives. Again, an important consideration involves the input of everyone in attendance at the IEP meeting.

4.17 – Writing IEPs: The Right Way and the Wrong Way

Following are some suggestions as you consider the development of effective IEPs. These suggestion are not determinative, just some thoughts to keep in mind when you work with parents and students to develop IEPs.

The A List

Accept only:

Measure the student's progress from one year to the next.

Documents and statements that specify clear classroom activities.

Statements that include parental expectations and desires.

Objectives that include high expectations of the student's levels of achievement and behavior.

Activities that provide clear accommodations for the student.

Statements that are measurable and that specify usable skills.

A process that includes everyone's input during the meeting.

Statements that are written in clear and understandable language

Statements that promote involvement in the school and community for the student.

The F List

Avoid statements that fail to:

Realistic appraisals of the student's capabilities during the year.

List specified goals from one year to the next.

Indicate the student's current performance.

Contain an element of measurable accountability.

Specify what the student will do and relate only to what teachers will do.

Identify the specific services the student is to receive.

Relate to the student's academic or personal/behavioral experiences in school.

4.18 – INDIVIDUALIZED EDUCATIONAL PROGRAM

Disability Requiring Special Education

Date to be implemented _____

Anticipated duration _____

Number of pages in IEP _____

Primary _____

Secondary _____

Secondary _____

Secondary _____

Purpose of IEP Meeting

New/Initial IEP	IEP Update	IEP Update	IEP Update	Annual Review	Other
_____	_____	_____	_____	_____	_____
_____					
Date	Date	Date	Date	Date	Date

Student Name _____

Address _____

Birth Date _____

District of Residence _____

School of Attendance _____

Parents/Guardian _____

Reevaluation Due Date _____

Primary Language of Parent _____

Primary Language of Student _____

Medication(s) for student _____

Vision Screening: Date _____ Passed ____ Failed ____

Hearing Screening: Date _____ Passed ____ Failed ____

Educational Team
Members Implementing IEP
Name/Title

_____

_____

_____

_____

_____

_____

_____

Current Performance Levels   Goal

ATTENDANCE: (Primary responsibility for attendance belongs with parents/guardians)   _____

COGNITIVE: (Information from the most recent Case Study Evaluation   _____

ACADEMIC: (Describe strengths and challenges)   _____

BEHAVIORAL: (Describe strengths and behaviors of concern—intensity, frequency, duration, setting)   _____

SOCIAL/EMOTIONAL: (Describe strengths and challenges)   _____

Goals and Objectives

Student Name _____

ANNUAL GOAL _____

_____

SHORT-TERM OBJECTIVES: (Condition and behavior) Date: _____

Criteria for Mastery	*Evaluation Schedule*	*Evaluation Procedures*
____ % of accuracy	____ monthly	____ test ____ log
____ # of trials	____ quarterly	____ charting
____ Other	____ grade period	____ Observation
	____ Other:____	____ Other

EXTENT OF OBJECTIVES MET/DATE/COMMENTS/INITIALS:

SHORT-TERM OBJECTIVES: (Condition and behavior) Date: _____

Criteria for Mastery	*Evaluation Schedule*	*Evaluation Procedures*
____ % of accuracy	____ monthly	____ test ____ log
____ # of trials	____ quarterly	____ charting
____ Other	____ grade period	____ Observation
	____ Other:____	____ Other

EXTENT OF OBJECTIVES MET/DATE/COMMENTS/INITIALS:

Form from Mundelein High School, Mundelein, Illinois

Prepackaged goals developed by special education personnel may or may not address most parental concerns. IEPs are most successful when they result from a team effort, and good teams include parent input. They also include input from counselors and other professionals who may have legitimate involvement in the educational and personal life of the student.

LET'S WRAP IT UP

The development of well-written IEPs brings the process of diagnosing and treating students with learning disabilities full cycle. The IEP identifies current performance levels and outlines the goals and objectives for the following school year, at which time additional IEPs are developed to promote continued improvement in the student's personal and academic growth.

The process is completed when the student transfers to another situation or terminates services in the department. Figure 4.19 provides a form that accommodates either. While he or she is in the department, however, progress should be continual and periodic assessments of performance levels must be made to assure such progress.

Schools must also realize that the special education department is no longer a new kid on the block, subject to close scrutiny and periodic battles to find a place in the school's pecking order. Special education departments are now well established and have, in fact, earned a place of respect on the school hierarchy. Their special expertise is a valuable asset to any school program and, whenever possible, should be shared with other departments and individuals within the school.

Emphasized in this section, therefore, is the use of special educators as consultants for mainstreamed teachers. We also emphasized the need for special education to organize in-service training programs for other departments in the school. The research and grass roots study that characterizes special education's growing body of knowledge must be shared with others in schools to maximize the learning experiences of all students, not just those students who need it and currently benefit from it the most.

4.19 — TERMINATION OF SERVICES

Student name _____

Birth date _____ Grade in school _____

Parent/Guardian name _____

Address _____

Date _____

Date of most recent evaluation _____

Area of Primary disability _____

Area of Secondary disability _____

Is this student currently eligible to receive special education services?

_____ Yes _____No

I/We request termination of all special education services:

Signature of parent/guardian _____

I/We _____ have _____ have not received a copy of the most recent MDC report?

I/We _____ have _____ have not received a copy of Parent/Student rights?

Parent/Guardian signature _____

Date _____

Special Education Director/Designee signature _____

Date _____

THE COUNSELOR AND OTHER SUPPORT PERSONNEL

First, a quick story . . .

Ralph had been a high school counselor for more than 25 years and was among the best-liked people in the building. Everyone liked him—students, parents, fellow teachers, and administrators, primarily because he did his job so well. Administrators appreciate someone like that—so do parents and students. Personal charisma also had something to do with his success—but not much. Ralph studied his craft and was open to experience. He depended on knowledge, not charm, to influence the lives of his students and parents.

In fact, Ralph indicated often that school professionals who rely on charisma do more harm than good in education. They depend on personality to attract people rather than on well-integrated philosophies to help them. Fortunately, Ralph had both. Students and parents liked his humor and spontaneity, and they knew that his decisions and advice were rooted in knowledge and practical experience. Ralph was right much more often than he was wrong.

Even when parents disagreed with him, they acknowledged his reputation for good advice and thought long and hard about his recommendations. Many even came to accept his philosophy, which was rooted in one fundamental principle—a quote from Bruce Barton, which Ralph kept framed on his office wall: "If you have anything really valuable to contribute to the world, it will come through the expression of your own personality, that single spark of divinity that sets you off and makes you different from every other living creature."

All of Ralph's counselees had such personalities, but one in particular comes to mind. Danny entered high school disadvantaged by an 89 IQ and a learning history riddled with interferences, none of which were diagnosed as specific learning disabilities. Danny's IQ and tested achievement were too low to permit a diagnosis of LD. In fact, he was such a hard worker, his grades were better than anyone expected of him. When no one in high school gave Danny much of a chance, Ralph met with him at least once a week to give him the boost he needed to battle the rigors of a new school.

Even Danny's parents worried about his future, in spite of Ralph's claims that he was going to be "just fine." Danny was just fine. He took a less challenging curriculum than most students, but he worked hard and, with Ralph's help, realized his "single spark of divinity" through commitment, a love of gardening, and a growing acceptance of himself as a person. Danny's willingness to work hard and his love of gardening eventually resulted in a degree in ornamental horticulture from a nearby community college.

Following his high school graduation ceremonies, Danny marched with his classmates from the auditorium and searched the audience for his parents—and for Ralph. All three were standing nearby smiling proudly as Danny approached. His smile and the firm grip of his handshake were all they needed to share the significance of the moment. The power of self-confidence and personal satisfaction, like that spark of divinity, is always understated.

SEEING YOUR STUDENTS AS STARS

Ralph's philosophy always reminds us of nights on the patio watching stars emerge against the backdrop of a darkening sky. The stars in the lower sky are obscured by a still-bright horizon and are hard to see, especially when you try to look right at them. In fact, the harder you try, the less distinct they appear. When you don't look directly at them, however, they suggest themselves, peripherally, seemingly brighter than before. The experience suggests a simple truism: The good that dots our skies—and our lives—is much more evident to all of us when we don't try so desperately to see it.

Stars shine. That's what they do; it's part of their nature. So do children, even when disabilities and disadvantages try to obscure their sparks of divinity. The counselor who realizes this and deals with students accordingly is a powerful influence in the lives of children, especially those who are disadvantaged or have learning disabilities. Inevitably, all children shine. They shine brightest when they have people like Ralph in their lives.

THE COUNSELOR AND STUDENT SELF-ESTEEM

Self-esteem is a caring companion—with big muscles. It picks us up when we fall, soothes us when we hurt, and keeps us directed when everyone else is faltering. It is not a gift but a reward. It must be earned. The accomplishment of self-esteem involves a lot of hard work and self-denial. We must respect ourselves before self-esteem is possible. While we work to achieve it, however, we can accept all the help and support we can find along the way.

Children—especially children with learning disabilities—need as much of this help as they can find. The love and support of parents and friends are the foundation on which children and adolescents build a lifetime of nurturing relationships, self-confidence, and personal courage. Without such courage and self-confidence, students with learning disabilities are unable to develop the compensatory strategies that ultimately overcome their limitations and result in generous doses of self-esteem.

Before counselors can help promote such self-esteem, they must know as much as possible about the student. Like you and me, students are what they value and what they expect and want from life. Unrealistic expectations and values lead to frustration and disappointment and an environment that thwarts rather than strengthens self-esteem. Use Figure 5.1, therefore, to secure information from parents about their own as well as their child's feelings about school.

Notice that it assesses the parents' feelings before it seeks any other kind of information. Parent and, later, student feelings must be explored and discussed before the other items on the survey have relevance to them. The more honest the discussion of their feelings, the less reserved they will be when discussing the kind of help they need to assure their child's smooth transition into a new school situation.

5.1 – Student Readiness Assessment for Parents

Student name _____

Parent(s) name _____

Counselor _____

Case Manager _____

Date _____

1. As your student begins to plan for life after his/her current school, as parents you feel:

    ____ Excited   ____ Uneasy

    ____ Scared   ____ Ready to go

    ____ Worried   ____ In charge

    ____ Confident   ____ Concerned

    ____ Out of the loop ____ Motivated

    ____ Educated   ____ Prepared

    ____ Other: (Describe) _____

    _____

2. Your student's academic record will:

    ____ Allow for many choices that are acceptable to you and your student

    ____ Require the student to plan carefully to provide several choices

    ____ Be strong in high school or college preparatory courses

    ____ Include mostly courses from the Special Education curriculum

    ____ Prepare my student for the academic rigor in a high school or college and university setting

    ____ Prepare my student for a transition program with limited academic rigor and more emphasis on life survival skills

3. Your student's strengths are _____

    _____

4. Your student's weaknesses are _____

    _____

5. The reason your student is receiving special education services is _____

    _____

6. Your student has completed the following school activities:

    Check as many as apply

    ____ Meeting(s) with counselor and case manager regarding post-secondary plans

_____ Individual conference with counselor
_____ Conference with Career Counselor
_____ Had conversations with representatives from various colleges
_____ Had conversations with representatives from various careers
_____ Completed college search
_____ Completed career search
_____ Conversed with parents about post-secondary plans

7. You feel your student may need help with: (check as many as apply)

_____ Getting started
_____ Understanding what steps need to be taken
_____ Knowing how to use the various resources
_____ Understanding class rank, GPA, Test scores
_____ Understanding how academic success relates to college future
_____ Planning for high school courses
_____ Registering for ACT/SAT
_____ Requesting accommodations for ACT/SAT
_____ Identifying interests and aptitude
_____ Being prepared
_____ Financial aid
_____ Understanding the role of the parents
_____ Understanding the differences between high school and college
_____ Becoming a self-advocate
_____ Being comfortable interviewing
_____ Knowing what to look for in a campus visit
_____ Being realistic about options
_____ Being able to prioritize criteria necessary to select the appropriate post-secondary options
_____ Being able to complete the application process

8. You, as a parent, would like some help with:

_____ Understanding why your student is receiving special education services
_____ Understanding your student's strengths and weaknesses
_____ Identifying appropriate options for life after high school
_____ Identifying criteria for researching appropriate colleges
_____ Understanding the accommodations necessary for continued success in a college setting
_____ Understanding the timeline for post-secondary planning

9. My concern as it relates to my student's plans for life after high school _____
_____
_____

10. My student has already made specific decisions about after high school.
The plans are _____
_____

THE COUNSELOR'S ROLE

The information in Figure 5.2 can also be shared with parents to inform them of the scope of the counselor's role regarding their child's learning disability and general behavior. The form identifies the counselor's educational, personal, emotional, social, and vocational responsibilities to the student and establishes the nature and scope of the parent-counselor-student relationship. This relationship involves areas specifically related to special education.

The Individual Education Plan (IEP)

The counselor's role is generally secondary to the roles of special education personnel. Normally, special education case workers suggest the behavioral and educational goals of students, then discuss them with the family and any others who attend the IEP session. Others in attendance may include the counselor, one or more mainstreamed teachers, and a social worker.

Because of their unique relationships with the student, these others may suggest valuable adjuncts to the goal statements suggested by special education personnel. Such synergistic input results not only in detailed and complete goal statements but the enhanced commitment of everyone who is involved with the student. The teacher who suggests, "Megan rarely completes a test during our class period" is the teacher who is likely to provide extended time on tests and to work closely with special education to establish alternatives to traditional methods of student evaluation.

And the counselor who establishes relationships with students may be able to suggest goal statements that are consistent with each student's levels of emotional and social development. A suggested goal for next fall's IEP, for example, may be "to have Megan discuss her educational needs at least monthly with her English and social studies teachers." The counselor may realize that, although the goal is worthwhile, Megan is emotionally unable to assume such a responsibility.

At that point in the meeting, the counselor may suggest that she meet with Megan at least twice a month to role-play such meetings so that Megan might integrate the strategies needed to self-advocate effectively. At this point, the IEP contains a goal directed toward self-advocacy, an acknowledgment of Megan's level of emotional development, and the involvement of a school professional whom Megan trusts and respects.

Counselors invariably give valuable input to the development of goals that promote the student's general adjustment and that accommodate his or her developmental ability to accomplish them. Although generally reactive in IEP meetings, counselors should be encouraged to contribute regularly as the educational plan is discussed. Unfortunately, this is not the case in some schools. Either the special education department assumes full responsibility for the development of IEP goals, or counselors perceive IEP meetings as routine tasks to be tolerated passively. Such perceptions destroy program synergy and result in perfunctory meetings that may satisfy state and federal mandates but that do little to help students with learning disabilities grow personally and educationally.

5.2 — ROLE OF THE COUNSELOR

- Begin where the client is
- Assist student in assessing academic proficiency
- Assess readiness
- Be an advocate for the student
- Assist student in developing self-advocacy skills
- Guide the student in developing a four year academic plan
- Understand the learning disability
- Understand the level of severity of the learning disability
- Understand the Individual Educational Plan
- Be available for multidisciplinary conferences
- Offer emotional and social counseling
- Assist with building self-esteem
- Assist student in understanding the differences between services and accommodations in high school and college
- Assist student with assessing potential
- Assist student with interviewing techniques
- Provide guidance in the search for appropriate post-secondary options
- Career awareness
- Identify student's expectations
- Provide guidance in developing decision-making skills
- Maintain contact with parents

Multidisciplinary Conferences (MDC)

The same is true of multidisciplinary conferences, which also are reflected in the counselor's role. By definition, the MDC seeks opinions from a range of people: school officials, parents, and outside professionals. Without such opinion, much of which is extremely diverse, the school is unable to create a reasonable picture of the child's educational and personal needs and to develop a program that responds to them.

Annual Reviews

The annual review takes an important look back. It is a retrospective of the past year; it highlights successes and identifies additional areas of need. It is a time to discuss unaccomplished goals and to replace or modify them. It represents the time when planning activities for the student have come full cycle, when progress is documented and continuing needs are explored. A good annual review provides the substance for IEP goals and suggests a sense of direction for the following school year.

The counselor's input at such a meeting is essential. For this reason, counselors must provide a composite of the student's activities and growth during the year. The information contained in forms like Figure 5.3 explains student progress and identifies counseling goals that may relate to future IEP goals. A file of such forms also enables the counselor to review observations from previous meetings and to reexplore future counseling goals in order to assure continuity from session to session.

A quick review of Figure 5.2 reveals the scope of the counselor's responsibilities within the special education department. Counselors are key figures in the treatment plan that enables students to overcome the limitations of their disabilities. That's why it's important for special education and counseling departments to meet regularly to discuss concerns and related issues.

Teams of special educators, counselors, social workers, and deans that meet regularly do much to assure ongoing communication among Pupil Personnel specialists and to deliver relevant and appropriate services to all students and parents. The job of each specialist is complemented by the mutual support received from other professionals in the school.

WORKING TOGETHER TO PROMOTE PLANNING

Mutual support is guaranteed when counselors and special education case managers plan collaboratively to create a clear picture of each student's special situation. Figure 5.4 contains general information and details areas of need for students with learning disabilities. When both persons, in consultation with each other or separately, provide information within appropriate categories, the result is a composite of the child and his or her needs that influences the present and future development of all educational and personal goals.

5.3 – INDIVIDUAL COUNSELING PROGRESS REPORT

Student name _____

Date _____ Student ID# _____

Birth date _____ Sex _____

Counselor _____

What was the purpose of the meeting? _____
_____

What issues were discussed in the meeting? _____
_____

What was the student's emotional state? _____
_____

Did the student willingly provide information? _____
_____

Were there issues that the student was reluctant or unwilling to disclose? _____
_____

What were the main concerns of the student? _____
_____

Did the meeting provide a better identification of the presenting issues? _____
_____

How did the meeting contribute to the assessment of the major issues? _____
_____

Did this meeting result in a reassessment of the presenting issues? _____
_____

What are the plans for topics to cover in future meetings? _____
_____

What is the date of the next scheduled meeting? _____
_____

5.4—COLLABORATIVE PLANNING FORM FOR COUNSELOR AND CASE MANAGER

Student name _____

Address _____

Date _____ Phone _____

Description of disability _____
_____

When diagnosed _____

Last diagnostic testing date _____ Next date _____

Intelligence test data: (include name of test, date administered, subtest scores, and subscale scores) _____
_____
_____

Achievement Test Data: (include name of test, standard scores, and grade level equivalents)
_____
_____

Major problem area _____

Current GPA _____ Current Class Rank _____

PLAN Score _____ untimed _____ timed _____ Accommodation _____

PSAT Score _____ untimed _____ timed _____ Accommodation _____

ACT Score _____ untimed _____ timed _____ Accommodation _____

SAT Score _____ untimed _____ timed _____ Accommodation _____

Abilities in the following areas:

Memory _____

Attention _____

Time management _____

Organization _____

Study skills _____

Self-advocacy _____

Special help received:

Tutoring _____

LD Resource _____

Remedial Reading _____

Study Skills _____

Other _____

Strategies used to compensate for learning disability _____

_____

_____

Strategies used to compensate for any deficits in the following areas:

Reading _____

Writing _____

Spelling _____

Math _____

Note taking _____

Listening _____

Short-term memory _____

Long-term memory _____

Test taking _____

Oral presentations _____

Auditory processing _____

Student's strengths and weaknesses _____

_____

_____

Medication being used _____

Which services are appropriate:

Untimed tests _____   Extended time tests_____

Taped texts _____   Learning Resource _____

Tutoring _____   Notetakers _____

Scribe _____   Proctor _____

Distraction-free environment _____   Reduced course load _____

Study skills assistance _____   Counseling_____

Social Work _____   Computers for exams _____

Calculators for exam _____   Time management help _____

Proofreading _____   Reader _____

Additional information _____

_____

_____

_____

The form provides an initial description of the child's disability, relevant diagnostic testing information, class rank, aptitude and achievement test results, and specific information regarding the child's general educational and behavioral needs. It also identifies appropriate services for the child and includes additional information that completes the picture of the child's school and personal situation.

The form enables the special educator and the counselor to review relevant information for each student before meetings with parents, other Pupil Personnel specialists, the student, teachers, even people like college admissions officials or recruiters from the armed forces. The form is especially appropriate when meeting with parents and/or the child to discuss registration decisions for the following school year.

It's important to note that this aspect of academic planning also requires the collaborative involvement of both the counselor and one or more persons from special education. The school is well advised to promote one or more days of meetings among personnel from both the counseling and the special education departments to discuss the registration plans of the students they have in common.

Figure 5.5 promotes such collaboration and includes the signatures of the student, his or her parents, special education department, and the counselor. Notice as well that it also includes signatures from department heads to approve the student's registration for one or more courses for which he may not have prerequisites.

DEVELOPING A MULTIYEAR EDUCATIONAL PLAN

The information in Figure 5.4 is essential if the student's registration process is to go smoothly. Accommodations must be made, and specific teachers must be identified and ultimately selected if the student is to be successful in certain courses. Additional information is provided in Figure 5.5. Finally, what is required is a multiyear plan that lists the specific courses that will satisfy the school's graduation requirements, promote academic success for the child, satisfy his or her special interests, and accommodate future plans such as college, work, or the military.

Figure 5.6 provides this. It should be completed early in the freshman year and should involve all relevant school professionals to provide the information the student and his or her parents require to make informed decisions. As indicated on the form, this is a *tentative* worksheet. It will change, sometimes considerably, as the student moves through school, but it provides an important road map for the student and his or her parents to negotiate the changing and often confusing journey through high school to college or work.

COMPLETING THE MULTIYEAR WORKSHEET

The process for completing this worksheet requires a closer look. Schools should organize a specific period of time, usually a week to a week and a half, to provide departmental information for students, to organize meetings with counselors, to enable phone calls or meetings with parents, and to secure signatures from the student, his or her parents, the counselor, and all relevant others, such as special educators.

5.5—Academic Planning Form

Student name _____

Date _____ Student ID# _____

Counselor _____ Case Manager _____

Registration suggestions and teaching strategies for school year _____

Course	Level	Faculty	Teaching strategies	Accommodations
English	Regular	Jones	Course syllabus	Spellchecker
Spanish	Lower	Smith	Repetition of words	Tape recorder
Geometry	Lower	Brown	Graph paper	Extended time
Biology	Regular	Lee	Lab Partner	Note taker
Reading	Regular	Stone	Large print	Books on tape

Suggestions for specific courses to be scheduled in the morning _____
_____
_____

Suggestions for specific courses to be scheduled in the afternoon _____
_____
_____

Other comments _____
_____
_____
_____
_____

Signatures:

    Student _____

    Parent(s) _____

    Counselor _____

    Special Education _____

    Department Chairperson _____

        Department _____

    Faculty _____

    Faculty _____

5.6—TENTATIVE FOUR-YEAR CURRICULUM PLANNING WORKSHEET

Student name _____

Date _____

School Year _____

Subject Area	Year	Course	Prerequisite	Yrs. Required for graduation
Applied Arts				1/2
Business				1/2
English				4
Computers				1/2
Consumer Economics				1/2
Fine Arts				1
Foreign Lang.				0
Health				1/2
Math				3
Physical Ed				3-1/2
Science				2
Social Studies				3
Special Education				As needed

Total 25

Counselor signature _____

Special Education signature _____

Student signature _____

Parent(s) signature _____

Following are a few suggestions:

1. Organize a schedule of large-group meetings for all freshmen. The groups should consist of approximately thirty to forty students—large enough to share necessary information and to permit discussion and some individual help. Early meetings should involve a sharing of information from each department in the school. These meetings should focus on graduation requirements, course prerequisites, college admissions requirements, and decisions involving departmental approval.

   This also is a time for departments to "sell" their offerings and to secure enrollment for successive school years. For this reason, schools must guard against a sharing of misinformation and/or promises that departments are unable to deliver. Counselors should be on hand for each of these presentations in order to assure appropriate "pitches" from department heads and others who provide the information.

   In communities with a significant percentage of college-bound students, for example, some departments may be inclined to tell students that certain or most of their courses are essential, even required, for college admission. This may or may not be true. Other departments may promise easy ways to satisfy graduation requirements or suggest other temptations that are irresistible to many young students.

2. Provide follow-up meetings with counselors to discuss the school's graduation requirements, college admissions requirements, and information about the world of work, including specific reference to vocational opportunities during and beyond high school. Because college requirements vary from school to school, this aspect of planning should involve general information. This process is discussed in Section 7.

3. Following these meetings, provide time for each student to select sequences of courses for his or her entire high school career. Such sequences should include specific graduation requirements, prerequisites for vocational and other courses, identification of special education courses, and college admissions requirements.

4. Copies of worksheets should then be shared with parents. Parents should be invited to call or to meet with the counselor, special education personnel, and/or department representatives to secure additional information or to discuss decisions.

5. Finally, the signed copies of worksheets should be returned to the counselor and, as appropriate, given to other school personnel for filing and future reference. Students, parents, and counselors will want to refer to them in the course of the year when families give serious consideration to specific colleges or universities and when registration decisions must be made for subsequent school years.

When this process is completed and just prior to the registration process, a letter should be mailed to parents informing them of recommendations from the counselor and special education department, Figure 5.7. The letter should list the recommendations, invite the parents to call or schedule a meeting, and ask them to approve or modify the recommendations by returning the letter or by calling the counselor.

5.7 – Registration Information Letter to Parents

Date _____   Re _____
                                   Birth date _____

Dear (Parent(s)/Guardian) _____

This letter is written to inform you of the academic recommendations suggested for your child
_____ for the academic
                               name of student

year of _____ at _____.
         school year   name of school

These recommendations were made by a team of professionals consisting of your child's counselor _____
                               name of counselor

and case manager and/or representatives from the Special Education Department

_____
          names of individuals from the Special Ed Department

These courses and varying levels were selected with careful consideration of your child's academic needs, graduation requirements, and strengths and weaknesses. Please review the recommendations with your child. If you have any questions please call _____
                                                                        counselor

at _____.
        telephone number

You are welcome to request a meeting if you feel you would like to discuss these recommendations. Please call with any questions or requests by _____. If you approve the
                                                           date

recommended courses, please sign this form and return it to the following address

_____.

Course	Level	# of Semesters
English II	Regular	2
Geometry I	Lower	2
Spanish I	Lower	2
Biology I	Regular	2
Physical Education	Regular	1
Traffic Safety	Regular	1
Health	Regular	1
Theater I	Regular	1
Learning Center	Lower	2

Parent(s) Signature _____

Date _____

THE COUNSELOR AND THE TRANSITION PLAN

Charles C. Noble once said, "We must have long-range goals to keep us from being frustrated by short-range failures." Few comments are more appropriate for the student with learning disabilities or for the parents and school personnel who work with them. Optimists believe that failures are opportunities for future growth, and, in the right circumstances, they're right. It's not quite that simple, however, for children with learning disabilities. Their short-range failures are so recurrent that long-range goals have little meaning for them.

That's all the more reason why long-range goals must have meaning for the rest of us. We know that, with the proper help, children with learning disabilities will learn to cope with their problems and overcome their recurring short-range frustrations. Proper help involves helping them focus on long-range goals and providing the support they require to realize that their short-term failures are stepping stones to future success.

The reproducible in Figure 5.8 helps promote such a focus. Use it to encourage counselees with learning disabilities to consider their future plans. Notice that the second question encourages them to "shoot for the moon," while the final question forces them to consider the kind of help they'll need to shoot so high. The other topics range from relatively immediate plans to longer-range considerations. This reproducible enables counselors and special educators to encourage students to aim high but to be realistic regarding their expectations for the future.

Figure 5.8 can be used several times throughout the student's high school career. It provides a focus that warrants continued discussion. Counselors will want to be in a position to influence the student who has either grandiose or inadequate plans for his or her future. Grandiosity involves the inability to stop, inadequacy the inability to start. Both lead to failure. A recurring focus on the issues identified in Figure 5.8 helps avoid such failure.

Similarly, Figure 5.9 provides the focus students, parents, and school officials require to provide the transitional planning that is not only mandated by the federal government but so essential for students graduating from high school. The form identifies the persons involved in the transitional planning as well as the nature of their involvement. It also focuses on the nature of assistance the student may require with employment, postsecondary education or training, living arrangements, and recreation and leisure.

The final page identifies the services the student may require in his or her senior year to realize postsecondary goals. Extensive help with several of these areas requires the involvement of a range of people inside and outside the school. In essence, a good transitional plan acknowledges and depends on the synergy created when school and community professionals coalesce their knowledge and expertise to assist students with learning disabilities.

5.8—Plans Beyond High School

Student name _____

Date _____ Year in school _____

Counselor _____

Please complete this questionnaire to assist you in exploring your short- and long-term goals as you plan for life after high school. If more space is needed, please use the back of the form or add additional pages of your own. Please write or print carefully or you may answer the questions using a computer and attach your answers to this form. When it is completed please return it to your counselor in the Guidance Office.

When do you plan to graduate from high school? _____

_____

How do you plan to spend the summer following your graduation from high school?

_____

_____

What are your current plans following your graduation from high school? Do you think you will want to continue your education in a postsecondary institution or do you plan to work, join the military, travel, or another option? _____

_____

_____

_____

If your plans include continuing your education in a postsecondary institution, do you envision yourself attending a two-year college, four-year college, trade school or specialty school?

_____

_____

If your plans include college, why do you want to go to college? _____

_____

_____

If you plan on attending college, what major do you think you want to study?_____

_____

_____

What kind of assistance do you need in exploring your options for college? _____

_____

_____

5.8 continued

Is there a job or career that you dream about pursuing? _____
_____
_____

What do you envision yourself doing five years after graduation from high school?
_____
_____

What do you envision yourself doing ten years after graduation from high school?
_____
_____

What major accomplishments would you like to fulfill within twenty-five years of your graduation from high school? _____
_____
_____

What are your greatest concerns as you begin to make these short- and long-term goals?
_____
_____
_____

5.9 — TRANSITION PLANNING GUIDE

I. General Information

   A.   Personal Identifiers

      1. Name: Last _____ First _____ 2. Sex: M   F

      3. DOB: Mo   /Day   Year   4. ID#_____

      5. Disability Category — (Check one): S/PMH__   TMH__   EMH__
           LD__   BD__   EH__   PH/C__   HH__   VI__   OHI__   SP/L__
           DEAF__   DB__   Other (Describe) _____

      6. Parent/Guardian _____   Secondary Reference _____
           Address _____   Address _____
                      _____   _____
           Phone _____   Phone _____

   B.   Secondary School Experience

      1. Name of School _____   2. School District _____

      3. Type of School (Check one): Regular High School ___   Special School ___
           Other (Describe)_____

      4. Program Placement (R=>40% Reg. Ed; S=>60% Sp. Ed): ___: ___: ___: ___:

   C.   Projected Date of School Exit: _____

   D.   Consumer, School, and Nonschool Participants in Transition Planning:
       Slash (/) if contacted regarding transition planning, (x) if involved in transition
       planning, and circle (O) if in attendance at formal transition plan meeting.

      Date of Transition Planning Meeting

      1. Consumer
            ___a. Student
            ___b. Parent (s)/ Guardian

      2. School (or participants)
            ___a. Special Education Teacher(s)
            ___b. Special Ed Administrator
            ___c. Vocational Education Teacher(s)
            ___d. Vocational Ed Administrator
            ___e. Regular Education Teacher(s)
            ___f. Regular Ed Administrator
            ___g. Psychologist
            ___h. Social Worker

Date of Transition Planning Meeting

    ___i. Prevocational Coordinator

    ___j. Guidance Counselor

    ___k. Other (Describe) _____

                    _____

                    _____

3. Nonschool (or participants)

    ___a. DORS Counselor/VAC

    ___b. JTPA Representative

    ___c. Employment Service Provider

    ___d. Community College Rep

    ___e. Community Living Skills Training
          Program Representative

    ___f. Residential Services Provider

    ___g. Adult Services Case Coordinator

    ___h. Other (Describe) _____

                    _____

                    _____

II. Desired Post-School Outcomes: (Recommended to be done in conjunction with "personal futures planning" activity.)

Date of Transition Planning Meeting

A. Employment (Check one):

    ___1. None due to Expected Enrollment
         in Postsecondary Ed.

    ___2. Competitive Employment
         (No Need for Support)

    ___3. Competitive Employment
         (Time-Limited Support)

    ___4. Supported Employment
         (Infrequent Support)

    ___5. Supported Employment (Daily Support)

    ___6. Other (Describe) _____

                    _____

                    _____

B. Postsecondary Ed or Training (Check one):

    ___1. None Due to Expected Postsecondary
         Employment

    ___2. Community College or University
         (No Need for Support)

Date of Transition Planning Meeting

___3. Community College or University (Needs Support)

___4. Technical/Trade School (No Need for Support)

___5. Technical/Trade School (Needs Support)

___6. Adult Ed Class(es) (No Need for Support)

___7. Adult Ed Class(es) (Needs Support)

___8. Adult Education Class(es) (Special Class)

___9. Other (Describe) _____
_____
_____

C. Residential (1) For Immediate
             (2) For Long Term

___1. With Parents or Relatives

___2. Independent Living (No Need for Support)

___3. Independent Living (Time-Limited Support)

___4. Independent Living (Ongoing, but Infrequent Support)

___5. Independent Living (Daily Support)

___6. Group Home Living (Supervision)

___7. Group Home Living (Supervision and Training)

___8. Group Home Living (Skilled Nursing)

___9. Other (Describe) _____
_____
_____

D. Recreation and Leisure (Check one):

___1. No Assistance Required for Person to Participate in Community Recreation and Leisure Activities

___2. Time-Limited Support Needed for Person to Participate in Community Recreation and Leisure Activities

___3. Ongoing, Infrequent Support Needed for Person to Participate in Community Recreation and Leisure Activities

Date of Transition Planning Meeting

___4. Ongoing, Daily Support Needed for
Person to Participate in Community
Recreation and Leisure Activities

___5. Other (Describe) _____
_____
_____

Comments (Date all entries):

Content of this form is advisory. Not binding on the IEP process.

**III. Activities or Services Needed (SN) in Next Year to attain desired Post-School
Outcomes: Check all that apply. Circle services provided. Date Annual Review.**

Services Needed	SN Date _____ ___ Service Description & responsible party	Timeline begin/end	SN Date _____ ___ Service Description & responsible party	Timeline begin/end
A. Vocational Education				
B. Career Counseling/ Guidance				
C. Career/Voc. Ed Class(es)				
D. Community Work Experience(s)				
E. Job Placement				
F. Post-Employment Support				
G. Academic Training				
H. Domestic Skills Training				
I. Community Skills Training				
J. Social Skills Instruction				
K. Self-Advocacy Training				
L. Rec/Leisure Instruction				

Illinois Transition Project, Southern Illinois University, Carbondale, Illinois

The Role of the College Counselor

That includes professionals like college counselors. Many schools are unable to hire college counselors because of size or money limitations. Some simply don't need them because of the composition of their student bodies. Schools that do hire them generally benefit from the knowledge and experience college counselors share with students and parents during the search, application, and admissions processes.

Their knowledge includes not only the specifics of the admissions requirements of a variety of schools but a general understanding of the schools' cultures, ethnic mixes, and special programs, such as LD services. They also know and correspond frequently with admissions directors, many of whom are responsive to special requests and considerations regarding the admission of students with special circumstances.

This benefit alone often makes them invaluable to college-bound seniors—particularly seniors with learning disabilities. All students can benefit from the intervention of someone who can encourage admissions officers to consider extenuating circumstances that may not be evident on transcripts. College counselors also provide a wide range of other services. Figure 5.10 lists them. Use the reproducible as part of your college counselor's job description, as one page in the special education handbook, as a handout for parents, or as information for teachers during in-services and other meetings throughout the school year.

A quick glance at the list of responsibilities reveals involvement in everything from an understanding of legal requirements to the ability to engage in role-playing activities with students applying to college. College counselors can also attend IEP sessions, multidisciplinary conferences, and annual reviews to answer questions and provide information about the college selection and admissions processes.

The Role of the Career Counselor

Career counselors provide much the same service. They, too, attend varying meetings with students, parents, and special education professionals to provide information about the world of work and to answer questions about specific careers or jobs. In addition, they help students assess their interests and aptitudes, explore a wide range of vocations, practice interviewing strategies, the rights of individuals with disabilities, and develop résumés.

The list of responsibilities in Figure 5.11 is self-explanatory and underscores the contributions career counselors make not only to students with learning disabilities but to the entire student body. If schools are unable to include the role of career counselor in their Pupil Personnel programs, they must assure that someone in the school, probably the counselor(s), is delivering the service to all students, but especially to students with learning disabilities. Such students must be aware of their rights before entering the world of work.

MORE ABOUT SELF-ADVOCACY

A knowledge of their rights is essential if students with learning disabilities are to make the transition from adolescent dependency in school to fully independent living as adults. Perhaps more important, they must develop self-advocacy skills while in school to assure the services and accommodations they require to realize academic and personal success. Figure 5.12 explains the reasons for self-advocacy and suggests some specifics that students must learn to become effective self-advocates.

Counselors and others should distribute and discuss Figure 5.12 during counseling sessions to promote the knowledge and skills for students to become effective self-advocates. The reproducible is also appropriate for parents during IEP meetings or annual reviews, for inclusion as a reference in special education and counseling handbooks, and for teachers during meetings and in-service training sessions.

To paraphrase America's great novelist, Willa Cather: "No one can build security upon the willingness of others." The assistance of friends and family, as indicated already in this book, is essential for the development of self-respect and self-esteem. Self-advocacy, however, like any form of independence, requires a willingness to stand up for one's self. The counselor who helps students with learning disabilities achieve such independence gives them a source of strength for the rest of their lives.

Self-Advocacy and the College-Bound Student

Although we will provide much more about postsecondary decision making later in this book, the counselor's role during the college selection and application processes deserves some preliminary mention now. Students with learning disabilities and their parents have a great deal to think about and do before college decisions can be made. Much of what they have to do must be done well before graduation.

Students must have developed effective study skills, strategies for self-advocacy, an awareness of the demands of independent living, an understanding of their disabilities, and a knowledge of their vocational preferences—in addition to the social and personal as well as educational expectations of college campuses. The task of preparation for college, as well as the world of work, is ongoing throughout high school. Fortunately, counselors and special educators focus on most of these issues anyway, irrespective of future college decisions.

The expectation of college, however, underscores their importance for students with learning disabilities. On that basis, share the reproducible in Figure 5.13 periodically with students and their parents to remind them of your mutual responsibilities. The reproducible also is appropriate for inclusion in counseling and special education handbooks and for distribution during in-service and other faculty meetings.

For most students with learning disabilities—even for their parents—the thought of going to college is threatening, especially as the selection and application processes approach. Even those students with grandiose expectations during their freshman year begin to have second thoughts early in their senior year. That's why all students with learning disabilities need continuing reminders that their counselor is available to help them—and that they must develop a range of compensatory skills if they are to be successful.

Such reminders need not be threatening. The student who already worries about his or her learning aptitude doesn't need someone throwing the "C" word around like a hand grenade. Such occasional threats may be marginally motivating to some students, but they are immobilizing to most. College must not be a threat that looms menacingly around every corner but a goal in each student's life that represents another step toward independence and self-fulfillment.

5.10 — ROLE OF THE COLLEGE COUNSELOR

- Be familiar with the laws protecting students with learning disabilities
- Be familiar with documentation for identifying learning disabilities
- Understand the student's strengths and weaknesses
- Be knowledgeable about programs/services in colleges/universities
- Be familiar with transition programs after high school
- Attend annual IEP conferences
- Attend multidisciplinary conferences
- Develop a list of questions for students to ask colleges about services/programs
- Develop a list of questions that colleges may ask students
- Assist students with articulating their learning disabilities
- Role-play college interviews
- Check for student acceptance of learning disability
- Assist students in prioritizing criteria for college search
- Provide reality check
- Assist with utilization of resources

5.11 — ROLE OF THE CAREER COUNSELOR

- Assist student in assessing interests

- Assist student with correlating interests, majors and careers

- Provide reality check for areas of interest versus areas of strengths and weaknesses

- Instruct student on ways to explore and research careers

- Provide opportunities for job shadowing

- Identify appropriate books and resources

- Assist student in developing a résumé

- Provide assistance in interviewing techniques

- Role-play interviewing situations

- Assist student in understanding the rights of individuals with disabilities in the world of work

- Develop strategies for compensating for deficits in the work world

- Attend IEP sessions, Multidisciplinary Staffings, and Annual Reviews, as appropriate, to answer questions and provide information about the world of work.

5.12 — Self-Advocacy

Why is self-advocacy important?

- It is the critical link between being dependent and independent.
- It allows students to be in control of their own lives.
- It provides the necessary ability to explain the services and accommodations required to compensate for deficits.
- It is often an educational tool for instructors.
- It allows students to communicate assertively.
- It results in credibility.
- It helps to establish a good working relationship.
- It illustrates confidence.
- It is the key to empowerment.
- It encourages students to assume responsibility.

How do students become effective self-advocates?

- Students need to know themselves and what they must do to be successful.
- Students must understand their own strengths and challenges in order to be able to explain these to others.
- Students must be aware of their own responsibilities.
- Students must be the ones to ask for services.
- Students must be in control of their environment.
- Students must be the experts on their disability needs.
- Students must understand the process for accessing services.
- Students must be comfortable requesting services and accommodations.
- Students must request the necessary accommodations before any problems arise.
- Students must be able to articulate their needs.
- Students must be able to explain their needs in simple terms and in a nondemanding manner.
- Students must be able to provide suggestions and examples of how they learn best.
- Students must know who can assist them with resolving problem situations.
- Students must provide appropriate and updated information and testing.
- Students need to be independent and responsible for their own lives.
- Students must be in charge of their own future.

5.13 – STUDENTS' RESPONSIBILITIES IN PREPARING FOR COLLEGE

1. Students must understand their learning disability
   - know the primary disability
   - know how it impacts on daily living
   - know when it was diagnosed and why

2. Students must be able to articulate their strengths and weaknesses
   - be able to describe what courses are easier
   - be able to describe what courses are more difficult
   - be able to explain the compensatory skills learned

3. Students should be able to describe services being used
   - be able to explain what help they are receiving
   - be able to identify the accommodations being used
   - be able to provide explanations to instructors about the accommodations that have been successful

4. Students should be able to describe services needed in college
   - be able to approach instructors to ask for services
   - be able to understand when services need to be in place

5. Students must be sure their psychoeducational testing is current
   - review when the last evaluation was done
   - make sure that testing is current within the last three years
   - make sure that they have the results from the assessments that are required by the college they will be attending

6. Students should request copies of all testing to take to college
   - ask for several copies of the current testing
   - have parents (or student if over 18) release the testing to the appropriate individual on the college campus

7. Students should identify the service provider on campus
   - schedule an appointment with the service provider
   - review accommodations being received and verify that necessary accommodations will be in place when college begins

8. Students should develop good time-management skills
   - practice being in charge of own assignments
   - learn how to make a time chart to use in college
   - learn how to determine how much time must be allotted for various assignments

9. Students should develop good organizational skills
   - develop a system for keeping notes in order
   - develop a strategy for staying current with assignment
   - develop an approach to handling multiple assignments

10. Students should develop good note-taking skills
    - take a study strategy course in high school
    - practice taking notes and taping at the same time to use for review
    - seek help in learning how to identify the key topics in the lectures

11. Students should develop test-taking strategies
    - practice taking multiple-choice exams
    - practice writing for essay exams
    - learn how to allocate time effectively

12. Students should learn how to access library resources
    - learn how to use the Internet
    - learn how to use the library computer system
    - learn how to use the reference section

13. Students should develop good social skills
    - work on making small conversation
    - learn to understand body language
    - understand what it means to be a good friend

14. Students should have a good sense of realistic career goals
    - explore career options
    - talk to individuals in careers of interest
    - take an interest inventory assessment

15. Students should be knowledgeable about their legal rights
    - ask for a copy of student rights
    - ask for an explanation of grievance procedures
    - be aware of what is considered a "reasonable" accommodation

16. Students should be sure to register on time for the ACT/SAT
    - keep track of the deadline dates for each test
    - secure the special applications for nonstandardized tests
    - be sure that the necessary records have been submitted

17. Students should explore college options
    - write for information
    - read the college catalogs
    - talk with the high school guidance/college counselor

18. Students should visit college and meet with the support staff
    - visit colleges with appropriate support programs
    - have an informational meeting with support staff
    - have an informational meeting with admissions

19. Students should verify the level of available services
    - ask specifically about necessary services/accommodations
    - inquire about the process of accessing services
    - inquire about any limitations on amount of services

20. Students should be comfortable with their disability
    - be proud of accomplishments
    - be willing to disclose the disability
    - be patient with uninformed individuals

21. Students should be sure of their desire to attend college
    - understand reasons for going to college
    - test degree of motivation
    - be accepting of the fact that it may take longer than four years

THE EVOLUTION OF AN EGGHEAD

When college is perceived by students as a positive goal, it offers inspiration rather than desperation and becomes motivational to even the most intransigent or anxious student. Consider the story of a young man who exhibited such inspiration. Craig entered high school with a learning disability that had escaped diagnosis in elementary school. His problems with auditory discrimination and organizational skills, however, were so pronounced that his mother and new teachers in high school recommended diagnostic testing.

The testing resulted in a diagnosis and placement in special education. In spite of the special education program's apparent inability to help him to the extent that he needed, Craig managed to develop a range of compensatory skills so comprehensive that he eventually enrolled in the most challenging mainstreamed courses he could find. You see, Craig was disabled, but he also was characteristically bright, like many students with learning disabilities.

Craig did well in high school—much better in his junior and senior years than in his undergraduate years. His freshman and sophomore years presented not only unexpected academic challenges but the inevitable social and personal obstacles that confront high school freshmen. As a result, Craig's cumulative grade point average and class rank as he approached graduation failed to reflect the significant progress he had made in high school. Fortunately, his counselor's recommendation alerted admissions officers to Craig's situation, and he was admitted to a reputable college on the east coast.

Craig's progress in college was amazing. What was most amazing was his evident love of learning. Although grades were important to him, they were secondary to the intellectual pleasure he derived from studying history. During return visits to high school, he invariably found time to meet with his counselor to share his love of history and to revive, if only for the moment, the good times they had enjoyed together years earlier.

After each visit, Craig's counselor smiled as he acknowledged what he came to call "the evolution of an egghead." Squinting through the haze of his disability for a glimpse of what might be his personal identity, Craig was discovering himself to be an intellectual. His love of learning for its own sake, even his almost professorial bearing were not the fantasies of a child trapped in a hopeless situation. They were real, and they affirmed the power of maturing self-confidence and the unconditional faith his mother and counselor had in Craig.

They also affirmed the promises his counselor had made during Craig's first few years in high school. His counselor had noted that students with learning disabilities not only are emotionally stronger than most people because of their sensitivity to the needs of others, but also are more creative and more verbally skilled due to their compensation for problems with language. Craig was all of these. He eventually earned a masters' degree in history, graduated with honors, and became a member of a "think tank" for a major east coast company.

The adolescent who once struggled with social interaction and the demands of formal education is now an honors graduate, an expert in nuclear history, and currently is directly supporting the U.S. Army's attempts to implement the START Treaty.

LET'S WRAP IT UP

Unfortunately, not every child with learning disabilities is a Craig. In fact, only a relative few realize Craig's personal, educational, and vocational success. In that regard, he is a unique young man. Washington Irving once wrote: "Great minds have purposes; others merely wishes." Craig had, and has, a purpose in life—to find pleasure in reading, writing, and thinking—regardless of the obstacles that occasionally get in his way. His self-confidence sustains such a purpose.

During adolescence, there is little "self" in self-confidence. Craig learned, as we all do, that self-confidence is an engine that someone else designed and that many others fuel. Its power—for that matter, its very existence—depends on those others in our lives who influence our self-perceptions and promote our belief in ourselves. Only when such belief is accomplished does self-confidence become self-sustaining.

High school counselors, then, have a responsibility to all their counselees, but especially to those with learning disabilities. Consider these statistics. Recent studies indicate that 1 child in every 430 can expect to be a doctor; 1 in every 350 can expect to be a lawyer; 1 in every 100 can expect to be a teacher—and 1 in every 5 can expect to be an illiterate. Children with learning disabilities often become illiterates. Many, like Craig, are capable of being doctors.

Conscientious counselors who work closely with parents and teachers help children with learning disabilities realize their full potential, if not to be doctors, at least to go as far as their intellectual capabilities will take them. The counselor who praises effort rather than results, gives youngsters faith in themselves, and provides an atmosphere of caring helps create a strength in students with learning disabilities that is far more powerful than the obstacle they struggle to overcome.

We have discovered over the years that an honest belief in others unleashes forces in them so powerful that they surprise even themselves by the scope of their accomplishments. Fortunately, believing in others involves no special skills or training—just the willingness to acknowledge the hidden strengths we all possess. We're reminded of the children's book about the little engine who said, "I think I can; I think I can."

We're pretty sure that somewhere in that little engine's background was someone who said, "I think you can, too."

WORKING WITH CLASSROOOM TEACHERS

First, a quick story . . .

The first semester was coming to an end. George, a PE teacher with twenty-some year's experience, was talking with a group of coaches in the lunchroom:

"I have the worst freshman class I've ever had. And I've got another semester with them."

"Gettin' tired of the freshmen, huh?" asked a friend. "Energetic little creatures, aren't they?"

"That's not it," said George. "A regular class wouldn't bother me, but I'm loaded with BD kids, and it's my last class of the day."

"Yeah, I've got one, too," said Fred, "sophomores, end of the day, too."

"Bad year, huh?" said one of the coaches.

"It wouldn't have to be," said George. "Special Ed told me they offer all their BD classes early in the day so the juniors and seniors can leave school early to work. I think they just want to get the kids out of the building."

"Or," offered Fred, "into our afternoon classes. The underclassmen don't have jobs, so we get them. I have twelve of them in my eighth-period class. The whole class is only thirty-one kids."

"Yeah," said George, "I've got ten. By the end of ninth period I'm ready to strangle someone. No one told me how to deal with these kids, and no one helps."

"Me either," said Fred, "all I do is scream at people all period."

MEETING SPECIAL NEEDS

How often do schools leave regular classroom teachers dangling? Scheduling oversights? Nonexistent professional growth opportunities? Insufficient support? An apparent ignorance of the problems confronting them? The desire to include special education students in the general mainstream of school instruction makes a lot of sense. Students with diagnosed learning and/or behavioral problems need continuing contact with the "regular" world. Their lives are disrupted enough as it is.

School administrators must remember, however, that the regular world was, and still is, the cause of many of their problems. Teachers who are unfamiliar with strategies for meeting the special needs of students with learning disabilities fail to help them develop the compensatory strategies such students require to realize educational and personal success. As George indicated often to his school's administration, "You're identifying these kids as special needs students, but no one's telling us how to meet their special needs. We end up being special needs teachers."

How, then, do schools meet these special needs of classroom teachers? And how do schools wrestle with the concept of "full inclusion?" How do they "normalize" the experiences of students with learning disabilities in mainstreamed classes but continue to provide the programs and accommodations such students require to satisfy their special needs? More pointedly, how do they fight the insidious temptation to simply save money by "including" students with learning disabilities in regular classrooms to avoid the costs of special education programs and personnel? In essence, how do they assure that a change in student placement results from a change in student need, not from a philosophical shift in educational thinking?

CONSIDERING THE PROS AND CONS OF INCLUSION

First of all, what is "inclusion?" The Learning Disability Association of America defines inclusion as ". . . a popular policy/practice in which all students with disabilities, regardless of the nature or the severity of the disability and the need for related services, receive their total education within the regular education classroom in their home school." The term grew out of the 1986 publication, *Educating Students With Learning Problems: A Shared Responsibility*, written by Madeline Wills, the Assistant Secretary for Special Education and Rehabilitative Service, the U.S. Department of Education.

Wills' publication introduced the more general term, *regular education initiative* (REI), which focused on providing a regular classroom education for children with mild learning disabilities. Supporters of the concept argued that placement in special education classes isolated students from the mainstream of the school and negatively affected their social, emotional, and behavioral growth. Placement in regular classrooms, they reasoned, would make them feel less different and would promote positive growth.

Opponents of the concept argued that many students with specific learning disabilities would be right back where they started from. They would fail to receive the special treatment they required to deal with their learning interferences. they argued further that regular classroom teachers would not receive the training they required to deal with the sudden influx of students with learning disabilities in their classrooms. Refer to Figure 6.1 for additional information. Use the reproducible as needed, but especially for informational meetings on the subject of special education placement.

6.1 – INCLUSION

Definition of Inclusion:

The Learning Disability Association of America describes inclusion as "... full inclusion, full integration, unified system, inclusive education as 'terms used to describe a popular policy/practice in which all students with disabilities, regardless of the nature or severity of the disability and need for related services, receive their total education within the regular education classroom in their home school.' ... LDA ... believes that many students with learning disabilities benefit from being served in the regular education classroom, but that the regular education classroom is not the appropriate placement for a number of students with learning disabilities who may need alternative instructional environments, teaching strategies, and/or materials that cannot or will not be provided within the context of a regular classroom placement. LDA does not believe that the least restrictive environment and the regular education classroom are synonymous."

LDA's Concerns about the use of full inclusion:

1. It is a violation of the law.

2. Introduced and promoted without involvement of regular educators who will implement this initiative.

3. There has not been systematic in-servicing and training of regular educators to help them teach students with special needs.

4. Regular educators, resistance to provide modifications and accommodations.

5. Increased academic standards and rigid standardized competency testing, often without accommodations, threatens the success of these students.

6. Parents are uninformed.

7. Funding issues may result in diminished services.

8. Each student with learning disabilities has unique needs, and inclusion will not allow for an individualized program tailored to meet the needs of the student.

9. Placement will need to be made on an individual basis.

10. Will eliminate the continuum of alternative placements.

11. Placement of ALL children with disabilities in a regular education classroom violates IDEA as does placement of ALL children in separate classrooms.

La, Nelle S. Gallagher, Inclusion, Reform, Restructuring and Practice, *LDA/Newsbrief, May/June 1994, pg. 19*

Interestingly, their opposition to REI paralleled the growing discomfort many educators felt for trends like school reform and restructuring. Opponents of both REI and school reform argued that even a rudimentary understanding of system theory suggested that such significant changes in schools would require much more than good intentions. "Restructuring" school curricula, administrative decision making, and the instructional methodologies needed not only for students with learning disabilities but for all students would require comprehensive change strategies—something historically foreign to many, maybe most, of the nation's schools.

To consider inclusion within its proper perspective, then, we must first consider a few important facts. A few years after the introduction of REI, a full 35 percent of the nation's five to six million students with learning disabilities were placed in regular education classrooms. For the first time, more students with learning disabilities were placed in regular classrooms than in resource centers or separate special education classes. Unfortunately, those "included" in freshman classes were discovered to be 10 percent more likely to fail one or more courses than peers who were included only half time.

Opponents of full inclusion argue that these students were placed in settings that caused their original problems. For example, studies found that only one in five regular teachers had the training needed to teach students with specific learning disabilities, and less than half the special needs students placed in regular classrooms were watched over by special education teachers. Such problems are compounded by the fact that students with learning disabilities are consistently the largest group of disabled students in this country.

MAKING THE MOST OF INCLUSION

The benefits of including students with learning disabilities in regular classrooms, however, are still valid. They benefit from involvement with their peers and need a sense of normalcy in their lives. Students with learning disabilities, however, also require an appropriate education and, by law, must receive educational placement on an individual basis after the development of the IEP. "Full inclusion," by definition, violates the law and is contrary to the needs of most students with learning disabilities.

Partial inclusion, however, is still desirable and can benefit the emotional, social, and educational growth of students—if they receive an *appropriate* education. Aye, there's the rub, you say. We agree. If students with learning disabilities are to receive an appropriate education in regular, mainstreamed classes, several accommodations must be made for them. Perhaps the most important is that they receive instruction that is consistent with their learning styles and that recognizes and accommodates their learning interferences.

For this to happen, mainstreamed teachers must receive the kinds of professional growth experiences that promote their understanding of the needs of students with learning disabilities. The child who is unable to discriminate auditorily is subjected to daily frustration and inevitable failure in a classroom where lecture is the dominant methodology. The child who is handicapped by poor visual memory requires auditory and kinesthetic experiences to master course content.

The ultimate goal of any educational experience for students with learning disabilities is to help them integrate the necessary compensatory skills to become independent learners. For this to happen, classroom teachers must understand the variable characteristics of students with learning disabilities in order to teach them without sacrificing or "watering down" course content.

Figure 6.2 categorizes the problems of students with learning disabilities. In essence, these are the behaviors that interfere with student learning and that mainstreamed teachers must accommodate if students who are "included" in their classrooms are to be successful. This is no easy task. For example, while the student with poor study skills is struggling to change from one task to another, the student with poor interpersonal skills will be racing ahead of the teacher without rhyme or reason.

Expecting regular classroom teachers to not only understand but accommodate these different and often contradictory behaviors in special needs students is asking a lot. Administrators who simply hand teachers the reproducible in Figure 6.2 to read and eventually to master are not doing their jobs. Similarly, administrators who distribute the material in conjunction with a large-group in-service program that explores each of these behaviors may still not be doing their jobs.

EFFECTIVE MAINSTREAMING INCLUDES PROFESSIONAL GROWTH

Teachers are life-long learners. Like all professionals, they must keep abreast of changes in their field. Teachers achieve excellence by degrees, by regularly improving their professional skills. To achieve such growth, they need help. School administrators must provide this help by assessing the needs of teachers, then satisfying those needs by providing comprehensive professional growth experiences for the entire staff.

Answers to the questions in Figure 6.3 help administrators assess the level of faculty understanding of teaching students with learning disabilities. Use the reproducible with administrators and department heads to develop assessment instruments or to promote discussions during department meetings. When the most pressing needs have been identified, provide professional growth experiences that satisfy them.

The development of effective professional growth programs warrants special mention. Teachers must explore a range of topics and eventually integrate new knowledge into their instructional repertoires. Such knowledge results, first, from in-service training experiences that introduce and explore innovative instructional techniques. This introductory experience should be followed by supervisory activities that enable teachers to practice the techniques in a risk-free atmosphere in order to master them.

Finally, evaluation activities must determine that teachers are successfully using the techniques. To the degree that they are not using them successfully, in-service and supervisory activities must be reintroduced to provide additional information and practice. The process of in-service training, supervision, and evaluation, therefore, is self-renewing and should result in improved knowledge of instruction for all teachers, especially those who will be working with students with learning disabilities.

6.2 – THE CHARACTERISTICS OF LEARNING DISABILITIES

Following are characteristic problems of students with learning disabilities. No student will have all of these problems. In essence, these are the behaviors that mainstream teachers must accommodate in their classrooms.

Study Skills

Inability to change from one task to another
No system for organizing notes and other materials
Difficulty scheduling time to complete short- and long-term assignments
Difficulty completing tests and class assignments without additional time
Difficulty following directions, particularly written directions

Interpersonal Skills

Impulsivity
Difficulty delaying resolution to a problem
Disorientation in time — misses class and appointments
Poor self-esteem

Reading

Difficulty reading new words, particularly when sound/symbol relationships are inconsistent
Slow reading rate — takes longer to read a test and other in-class assignments
Poor comprehension and retention of material read
Difficulty interpreting charts, graphs, scientific symbols
Difficulty with complex syntax on objective tests

Writing

Problems in organization and sequencing of ideas
Poor sentence structure
Incorrect grammar
Frequent and inconsistent spelling errors
Difficulty taking notes
Poor letter formation, capitalization, spacing, and punctuation
Inadequate strategies for monitoring written work

Oral Language

Difficulty concentrating in lectures
Poor vocabulary, difficulty with word retrieval
Problems with grammar

Math

Difficulty with basic math operations
Difficulty with aligning problems, number reversals, confusion of symbols
Poor strategies for monitoring errors
Difficulty with reasoning
Difficulty reading and comprehending word problems
Difficulty with concepts of time and money

Adelman, Pamela, and Debbie Olufs (1986). Assisting College Students With Learning Disabilities: A Tutor's Manual. *Association of Handicapped Student Service Programs in Postsecondary Education, P.O. Box 21192, Columbus, OH 43221 (Currently called AHEAD). Reprinted with permission.*

196

6.3 – Assessing Faculty Needs

- What is their underlying knowledge of learning disabilities or attention deficit disorder?
- Do they understand the documentation used to determine the existence of a learning disability/ADHD?
- Can they identify signals of undiagnosed LD or ADHD?
- Do they know what are appropriate accommodations for students with LD or ADHD?
- Do they know who is responsible for providing teachers with the assistance in adequately providing appropriate accommodations?
- Do they know the legal requirements for accommodating students?
- Do they know what resources are available to assist them with working with students with LD or ADHD?
- Do they know how to inform students that accommodations are available with appropriate documentation?
- Do they know who is available to assist them in understanding how certain accommodations help specific students learn?
- Do they understand how teachers maintain integrity of their course material and still provide accommodations in curriculum modifications?
- Have the teachers developed teaching techniques or strategies to use with students with learning disabilities or ADHD?
- What information would be helpful to teachers in working with students with special needs?
- How does the teacher deal effectively with students requesting special accommodations or curriculum modifications?
- How do the faculty evaluate students' work if they are unable to meet the tasks of the class because of the learning disability?
- How can faculty differentiate between learning disabilities and lack of motivation, limited learners, or underachievers?
- How sensitive are the faculty to students with learning disabilities or ADHD?
- How comfortable are faculty about discussing the learning disability with the student?
- Does the faculty member feel required to overcompensate for the disability?
- Is the faculty member comfortable allowing the student to tape record the lecture or to provide the student with the lecture outline?
- Does the teacher know how to use a multimodality approach to instruction?
- Is the teacher familiar with the resources available for the student?
- Does the teacher need assistance in developing innovative ways to help students receive and transmit information?
- What is the procedure for working out conflicts between teachers and students when a request meets with resistance?
- Is the faculty member properly prepared to teach to students with special needs?

Just a glance at the list of responsibilities in Figures 6.4, 6.5, 6.6, and 6.7 suggests the depth of understanding mainstreamed teachers require to accommodate students with learning disabilities in their classrooms. These suggestions are also appropriate for all students, and serve as excellent resource and reference materials for all classroom teachers. Special education departments and all department heads should have copies to share with teachers as questions arise or whenever teachers seek advice regarding their work with students with learning disabilities.

Each figure also represents the focus for in-service training activities, follow-up supervisory processes, and subsequent evaluative sessions. The reproducibles contain valuable information for teachers, but they are insufficient without additional explanation and a range of risk-free opportunities to practice. One-shot deals, whether they involve handouts like the ones in Figures 6.4 through 6.7 or large-group in-services, fail to promote the kind of professional growth in teachers that good, nonjudgmental supervision provides.

The following process should be considered when promoting the professional growth of all teachers, especially those who have the added responsibility of working with special needs students:

◆ Conduct a comprehensive needs assessment to determine areas in which teachers require additional information and practice in order to work effectively with special needs students.

◆ Provide one or more in-service training programs to present and explore the needed information. Such in-service programming need not involve only large-group presentations. Small-group sessions, reading materials, videotapes, visits to other schools or to other teachers within their own schools, and other forms of in-servicing can also provide the information teachers need to expand their knowledge of instruction.

◆ Involve the staff in a process that enables them to practice the information that was provided during in-service sessions. Such practice can be conducted with department heads or with other teachers—in groups or in tandems. Whatever the format, the practice must be scheduled regularly and involve relatively nonjudgmental feedback that provides a mirror of the teacher's performance with the new information.

◆ Administrators or others in the building can then evaluate the teachers' successful use of the new information. Such evaluation is effective or, for that matter, fair only after the teachers have had sufficient time to practice the techniques or teaching strategies. They may require as much as one or two years to master the concepts.

◆ Finally, the administration can review the evaluations of teacher performance and conduct further needs assessments to determine the success of the original in-service training or to identify areas of additional need. If the original in-servicing was unsuccessful or when complementary needs have been identified, new in-servicing can be developed to give the teachers the information they need to promote their continued professional growth.

6.4—SUGGESTIONS FOR INSTRUCTING STUDENTS WITH LEARNING DISABILITIES

Following are some suggestions for teaching students with learning disabilities. We will be discussing these items in in-service training sessions and in supervisory activities throughout the year. If you have questions, please contact your department chair.

- Begin each class with a review of material covered previously.
- Repeat or rephrase instructions or directions.
- Use multiple formats of instruction, emphasizing as many student modalities as possible.
- Preview material that will be covered at the start of each class.
- Explain assignments or new concepts verbally and in writing.
- Keep directions simple; use numbered lists of directions.
- Rephrase complex directions as needed.
- Stick to the topic being taught.
- Summarize what is covered prior to adding new information.
- Clearly explain transitions from one set of information to another.
- Teach difficult concepts in small segments.
- Allow enough time for questions and answers.
- Encourage students to ask questions.
- Provide sufficient time for students to copy from transparencies or board.
- Use handouts that highlight important information.
- When using the chalkboard, do not talk with back to students.
- Speak clearly and at a reasonable pace.
- Write key words or new terms on the chalkboard or a transparency.
- Illustrate abstract concepts with concrete examples.
- Use visuals to explain abstract information.
- Emphasize major points using body language or voice inflection.
- Face the students while talking.
- Beware of using clichés or jargon when talking.
- Check for understanding frequently.
- Use eye contact prior to calling on a student.
- Avoid asking questions when student appears unfocused.
- Ask questions when student appears on task.
- Engage students in as much cooperative group work as possible.
- When possible, tandem students and encourage them to help each other.
- Offer opportunities for hands-on activities.
- Use positive reinforcers.
- Give distinct clues to emphasize important information.
- Phrase evaluative comments in a positive way.
- Do not water down the requirements of the course.

6.5 – Suggestions for Organizing Classrooms With Students With Learning Disabilities

Students with learning disabilities have organizational needs that must be met if they are to succeed in regular classrooms. Please keep the following suggestions in mind when planning instruction for them.

- Provide a detailed course syllabus.

- Provide a list of required reading prior to the beginning of class.

- Provide a monthly assignment sheet with due dates.

- Identify what is expected of the student.

- Give strategies on taking notes for the class.

- Identify students in class who can take notes and have them assist you whenever possible.

- Encourage use of computers.

- Permit the use of calculators, if appropriate.

- Help students manage time effectively.

- Encourage students to use calendars.

- Provide suggestions for learning material and for studying for tests.

- Be sure all handouts are readable.

- Make all directions short and simple.

- Give assignments in advance.

- Notify students of course changes.

- Provide alternative ways to earn extra credit.

- Offer review sessions.

- Provide tips and strategies on how to memorize or learn material.

- Provide breaks during extended classroom time.

- Handle problems effectively with a controlled, calm voice.

6.6 — SUGGESTIONS FOR RELATING TO STUDENTS WITH LEARNING DISABILITIES

Following are some suggestions for relating to students with learning disabilities. That such students have special needs goes without saying. Teachers must keep several points in mind when instructing them and when seeking to establish relationships with them.

- Request appropriate documentation for identified accommodations.
- Talk to the student to provide support and encouragement.
- Ask students for suggestions of effective ways to accommodate them.
- Consult with tutors or LD specialists to get suggestions.
- Identify for students what is expected of them.
- Beware of using clichés or jargon when talking with them.
- Be open to suggestions of what may be helpful to the student.
- Be structured and predictable.
- Learn ways to teach to different learning styles.
- Be supportive.
- Use positive reinforcers.
- Be educated about learning disabilities.
- Be sensitive to students who have difficulty reading in front of others.
- Be aware of nonverbal and verbal signs of anxiety.
- Be aware of the characteristics of attention deficit disorder.
- Be aware that new tasks or concepts can cause anxiety.
- Never label a student.
- Never discuss the disability with others without the student's permission.
- Be sensitive and patient.
- Focus on the student's areas of strength.
- Encourage self-esteem.
- Help student to value independence.
- Do not overcompensate. Students with learning disabilities can be amazingly resilient. If expectations are clear and their needs have been accommodated, they can achieve as well as — sometimes better than — any student in school.

6.7—Suggestions for Evaluating Students With Learning Disabilities

Following are a few suggestion when evaluating students with learning disabilities. Consider these items when checking for understanding during class, for quizzing, or for testing at the end of a unit or semester.

- Consult with tutors or LD specialists for suggestions.
- Identify what is expected of the student.
- Repeat or rephrase instructions or directions.
- Allow students extra time to complete tests and quizzes.
- Provide study questions for exams.
- Provide examples of format and content of upcoming tests.
- Permit the use of calculators, if appropriate.
- Provide suggestions for studying for tests.
- Construct tests that require recognition rather than recall.
- Provide a word list for fill-in-the-blank sections.
- Keep options to 4 in multiple-choice exams.
- Make sure that tests have only one right answer.
- Be sure all tests and handouts are readable.
- Make all directions short and simple.
- Underline, capitalize, bold, or color-code key words on quizzes and tests.
- Give several quizzes and tests over longer units and assignments.
- Be open to suggestions of what may be helpful to the student.
- Provide alternative ways to earn extra credit.
- Offer review sessions.
- Provide tips and strategies on how to learn material.
- Do not penalize for spelling errors if deficit is in this area.
- Phrase evaluative comments in a positive way.
- Emphasize skill building, not competition.

The process, therefore, is cyclical. It begins with in-service training and concludes with an evaluation and needs assessment format that identifies more reasons for in-service training. Only with such a self-renewing process can schools expect teachers to refine their skills in order to integrate research and new knowledge on effective teaching and to accommodate the unique needs of students with learning disabilities.

TAKING ANOTHER LOOK AT SELF-ADVOCACY

Self-advocacy for students with learning disabilities is so important, it warrants another look. In Section 5 we discussed the "what" and the "why" of student self-advocacy. Now, consider answers to the question, "How do I self-advocate?" Figure 6.8 provides a detailed list of concrete suggestions for students and their parents. The reproducible is appropriate for IEP meetings, MDCs, annual reviews, and sessions for reviewing psychoeducational evaluations and for making placement decisions.

The suggestions are as appropriate for parents as they are for students. If parents understand the specifics of student self-advocacy, they will know when and how to encourage their children and when to avoid involving themselves in situations requiring the child's intervention. Like the suggestions for teachers, these items require exploration and practice. Students can receive both in meetings with their counselors, case managers, and other special education personnel.

Such meetings should be relatively frequent and should focus on individual items rather than the entire reproducible. If students are to "Be comfortable talking to instructors", it takes practice and a working knowledge of ways to approach and talk to teachers. The same is true of items such as "Plan ahead," "Develop good time management skills," "Set realistic goals and priorities," and "Let instructors know if accommodations are not being provided."

These items require the student's understanding of everything from positive confrontation techniques to goal setting, time management, and planning activities. Such understandings don't come easily, particularly to students who already struggle with self-confidence and learning issues. They need help to learn and practice the techniques and to use the goal-setting and planning strategies in practical situations.

In addition, items like "Do not miss classes" and "Take notes while reading assignments" may appear self-explanatory, but they require explanations that clarify the rationale behind them and that serve to promote the student's good intentions. So, like their teachers, students with learning disabilities must be encouraged to explore and practice certain behaviors in order to use them comfortably in situations that require them.

6.8 — THE STUDENTS' ROLE IN RECEIVING ACCOMMODATIONS — HOW TO SELF-ADVOCATE

- Have current documentation on file.
- Be able to articulate the learning disability.
- Be willing to assist instructors with solutions to problems.
- Continue to develop compensatory skills to bypass the area of weakness.
- Be comfortable talking to instructors.
- Have accommodation needs identified.
- Be sure to have a complete understanding of all the necessary recommendations for instructors.
- Meet with each instructor at the beginning of each course.
- Let instructors know what can and cannot be done.
- Request alternate assignments or assessments when appropriate.
- Register for Recordings For The Blind in time to receive the materials.
- Request a note-taker, if appropriate, in the beginning of a course.
- Take notes while reading assignments.
- Request permission to tape-record lectures.
- Do not miss classes.
- Do not arrive late to classes.
- Request a course syllabus at the beginning of each course.
- Verify assignments when they are given.
- Keep an assignment book and use it daily.
- Estimate how long each assignment will take to complete.
- Use only one calendar with assignments, appointments, and plans.
- Identify priorities.
- Have a separate notebook for each course.
- Plan ahead.
- Sit in the front row of classes if possible.
- Write down any questions you have.
- Develop good time management skills.
- Never miss completing an assignment.
- Ask for help as soon as it is necessary.
- Locate tutors early in the semester for future reference.
- Consider taking a minimum load of courses.
- Allow ample time for studying.
- Find a quiet place to study.
- Set realistic goals and priorities.
- Let instructors know if accommodations are not being provided.
- Join support groups.
- Do not use the disability as an excuse.

CLASSROOM TEACHERS IN SPECIAL EDUCATION SETTINGS

"Comfort" is a key word when adapting new behaviors. Although the involvement of regular classroom teachers in special education really doesn't involve new behaviors, it does impose a whole new set of expectations that discomforts many teachers. Special education jargon—with its occasional dip into psychology, sociology, and medicine—unnerves many teachers. Perhaps even more unnerving are the new roles that classroom teachers are expected to perform and the many added responsibilities they discover when they begin to teach students with learning disabilities. Traditional methodologies and modes of interaction must be redesigned to accommodate students who learn and relate differently from other students.

Teachers must also learn to share their observations in meetings with school psychologists, social workers, counselors, and special education personnel. This is no easy task, given the fact that the school's curriculum and traditional instruction are regarded as part of the problem during the diagnostic process. Schools labor long and hard to maintain the sequence, continuity, and integration of the curriculum, only to learn that the transitions they establish between elements of the curriculum are confusing to certain students.

Similarly, teachers who develop stimulating techniques and materials to enhance lecture as a method of direct instruction discover that some of their techniques actually inhibit student learning. These are shocking discoveries to some teachers, especially the traditionalists among us. Some of them enter such meetings actually expecting to defend themselves rather than to offer insights into the diagnosis or the treatment plan.

Pupil Personnel specialists must be sensitive to the needs of classroom teachers during such meetings. Classroom teachers are breaking new ground when they discuss curriculum and instruction within a special education perspective. They must be encouraged to share their special insights into student learning and behavior as complements to the diagnostic and treatment processes. They are integral members of the diagnostic and treatment team and must not be regarded as outsiders who are permitted momentary access to special education's inner circle.

The role of classroom teachers is greatly enhanced when they understand the purposes of the several meetings they attend as well as when they understand the role they are expected to perform. Figure 6.9 provides a reproducible to share with teachers prior to their involvement in meetings with special education personnel. It can also be included in teacher handbooks or distributed during in-service training sessions for the entire staff.

Accommodation and the Classroom Teacher

The reproducible in Figure 6.10 is also appropriate for distribution during in-service training sessions or for sharing with individual teachers when accommodation is discussed. The form discusses the legal issues involved in accommodation and allays teacher concerns as well as provides an easy way to address the issue with students who may need such help. Teachers would be encouraged to discuss the reproducible in department meetings or with special education personnel.

6.9 — RESPONSIBILITIES OF CLASSROOM TEACHERS

IEP, MDC, Annual Reviews

Classroom teachers are essential professionals in the diagnostic and treatment process for students. The teachers have daily contact with the students, and are able to provide insight into academic, emotional, and environmental behavior. This information is extremely important in the diagnostic evaluation of the student and later in determining the recommendations and treatment plans and reevaluation.

Individual Educational Plan

Student _____

Counselor _____

Case Manager _____

Teacher _____

    Subject _____ Period _____

Teacher _____

    Subject _____ Period _____

Teacher _____

    Subject _____ Period _____

Date _____

Purpose of the Meeting _____
_____

Classroom teacher's role prior to the IEP meeting _____
_____
_____

Classroom teacher's role during the IEP meeting _____
_____
_____

Classroom teacher's role after the IEP meeting _____
_____
_____

Other individuals invited to the meeting _____
_____
_____

Signature of individual in charge _____

Multidisciplinary Conference

Student _____

Counselor _____

Case Manager _____

Teacher _____

    Subject _____ Period _____

Teacher _____

    Subject _____ Period _____

Teacher _____

    Subject _____ Period _____

Date _____

Purpose of the Meeting _____
_____

Classroom teacher's role prior to the MDC meeting _____
_____
_____

Classroom teacher's role during the MDC meeting _____
_____
_____

Classroom teacher's role after the MDC meeting _____
_____
_____

Other individuals invited to the meeting _____
_____
_____

Signature of individual in charge _____

Annual Review

Student _____

Counselor _____

Case Manager _____

Teacher _____

    Subject _____ Period _____

Teacher _____

    Subject _____ Period _____

Teacher _____

    Subject _____ Period _____

Date _____

Purpose of the Meeting _____

_____

Classroom teacher's role prior to the Annual Review _____

_____

_____

Classroom teacher's role during the Annual Review _____

_____

_____

Classroom teacher's role after the Annual Review _____

_____

_____

Other individuals invited to the meeting _____

_____

_____

Signature of individual in charge _____

6.10 – HOW CAN I GET STUDENTS WITH LEARNING DISABILITIES TO TALK TO ME?

Faculty who are concerned about their legal responsibilities to students with learning disabilities (LD) frequently wonder how to get these students to ask for appropriate accommodations such as use of a tape recorder in lectures or testing modifications. Many faculty would be willing to discuss and provide accommodations, but they do not find out until too late because students do not come forward and identify their needs.

Often faculty ask for a list of students with learning disabilities at the beginning of each semester so that the instructor could approach the student if the student did not initiate contact. Although this willingness and concern is commendable, it is neither legal nor necessarily in a student's best interest for such a list to be circulated.

Legally, students have the right *not* to be identified as disabled if they so choose. Accommodations are not required unless students self-identify. Moreover, it is critical that students with learning disabilities develop the independence and self-advocacy that will help them outside the classroom and beyond college. Students with learning disabilities *need* to learn how to explain their disability, describe their strengths and weaknesses, and negotiate appropriate accommodations. Their need for accommodation will always exist, so the skills required to obtain such accommodations should also be developed on a "permanent" basis.

For all these reasons, it is appropriate for students to take the responsibility of identifying themselves and their need for accommodation to you, rather than vice versa. There is, however, something that can be done to help students in this process. It is very difficult to have to identify yourself, time after time, as being "different" — and more so for the student whose disability is invisible. Students will feel more comfortable about identifying themselves if they are approaching someone whom they believe to be receptive to the discussion. You might try including a sentence like this in every course syllabus you put together:

"If there is any student in this class who has special needs because of learning disabilities or other kinds of disabilities, please feel free to come and discuss this with me."

This approach demonstrates to students that you are someone who is sensitive to and concerned about meeting the needs of *all* students you teach. Such an invitation to discuss individual needs can go a long way toward encouraging the student with a learning disability to approach the instructor early.

Adapted from materials available from AHSSPPE-now called AHEAD — Trio Training, 1988.

CONSIDERING THE FUNDAMENTAL ISSUES OF ACCOMMODATION

Teachers must also explore other issues involved in accommodation. Certainly, they need not be experts about the legal issues affecting special education, but they should understand the fundamentals that relate to their classroom responsibilities. Figure 6.11 provides a concise explanation of when accommodations should or should not be provided. It also defines what constitutes reasonable accommodations.

Forms like this one should be included in teacher handbooks and be available for distribution to teachers during in-service training sessions or upon individual request. Accommodation is an educationally and legally sensitive issue and warrants discussion and broad treatment in all schools. Figure 6.12 helps provide such treatment by outlining several possible ways for teachers to accommodate students in mainstreamed classes.

The list is classified according to the nature of the student's disability and suggests specific accommodations. It is self-explanatory and can serve as a resource—and a periodic reminder—for most classroom teachers. It, too, should be distributed during in-service training sessions for the staff or given to teachers on an individual basis.

Accommodation requires both student self-advocacy and teacher approval. Figure 6.13 can be used by special education personnel, the students' parents, and/or the students themselves to inform teachers of the need for accommodation. The form should be initiated by students requesting meetings with teachers to discuss needed accommodations.

Once the teacher and the student have identified one or more accommodations, the teacher can use the form in Figure 6.14 to document the agreement. The teacher should forward the completed form to the special education department for filing and, as determined by special education, for mailing to the student and his or her parents. Copies of the agreement should also be given to the teacher and his or her immediate supervisor for additional documentation.

Sharing the form with supervisors alerts them to a very important consideration. Classroom teachers who go the extra mile to accommodate the unique and sometimes complicated needs of students with learning disabilities deserve recognition for extending themselves beyond the generally accepted limits of their jobs. Teachers "accommodate" students in a variety of ways. Many go well beyond simply permitting them to use calculators in class or to have extended time on tests.

Many teachers also spend considerable time studying learning disabilities. They take courses or read books and articles in order to understand and provide the adjustments students with learning disabilities require to be successful in regular classrooms. Such adjustments are not made easily. Many of the adjustments outlined in Figures 6.4 through 6.7 require not only commitment, but flexibility. Teachers who accomplish this deserve recognition.

6.11 – SHOULD ACCOMMODATIONS BE PROVIDED?

Does the student have a diagnosed learning disability?

"Specific learning disability" means a disorder in one of more of the basic psychological processes involved in understanding or in using language, spoken or written, which may manifest itself in an imperfect ability to listen, think, speak, read, write, spell, or do mathematical calculations. The term includes such conditions as perceptual handicaps, brain injury, minimal brain dysfunction, dyslexia, and developmental aphasia. The term does not include children who have learning problems which are primarily the result of visual, hearing, or emotional disturbance, or of environmental, cultural, or economic disadvantage. (USOE, 1977, P. 65083) Mercer, Cecil D.; Jordon, LuAnn; Allsopp, David H.; Mercer, Ann R., "Learning Disabilities Definitions and Criteria Used By State Education Departments," *Learning Disability Quarterly*, Volume 19, Fall 1996, p. 218.

- If the answer is yes, the student must provide current (within three years unless otherwise requested) documentation.

  Is the documentation appropriate?

  1. It must be provided from a licensed clinician who is qualified to make the diagnosis.

  2. The documentation must clearly identify a learning disability

  3. The documentation must provide psychoeducational testing that measures the student's aptitude, achievement, and processing information.

- If the documentation is appropriate then the student must prove that he/she meets the prerequisites to participate in the program/course.

Does the student meet the prerequisites?

1. Does the student have the necessary, required prerequisites to meet the academic and technical requirements of the course? (#504 regulations)

2. Will the requested accommodations allow the student to fulfill the requirements of the course?

3. Will providing these accommodations not pose a threat to the personal or public safety of others?

- If the answer is yes then it must be determined if the accommodations being requested are "reasonable."

What are reasonable accommodations?

- Reasonable accommodations are ones that provide academic adjustments to ensure that the student receives an equal chance to participate. Accommodations that would place an undue burden or hardship on the provider or require a fundamental alteration to the course, is not considered to be "reasonable."

    1. Is the requested accommodation based on information from the student's documentation?

    2. Do the accommodations requested meet the student's individual needs?

    3. Do the accommodations allow the student to be in the most integrated environment?

    4. Do the accommodations allow for no alterations to the course that are essential components of the course?

    5. Do the accommodations guarantee no personal or public threat to others?

    6. Will the provider not be under undue financial or administrative burden by providing the requested accommodations?

    7. Are the accommodations being requested of a nonpersonal nature?

- If the answers are yes then accommodations must be provided. There should be no additional charges for these accommodations.

Information gathered from Scott, S. (1994), "Determining Reasonable Academic Adjustments for College Students With Learning Disabilities." Journal of Learning Disabilities, 27 (7), pp. 403-412. and The Student Disability Resource Center at Harvard University.

6.12 – Tips for Accommodating

Written or Receptive Language Deficits

- Use a word processor
- Use spellchecker
- Use a grammar check
- Use of a Franklin Speller, dictionary
- Allow oral responses
- Allow rewrites
- Do not mark off for spelling errors
- Do not use complex sentences
- Use of a note taker
- Use of a scribe
- Tape record lectures
- Outline of each lecture
- Tutorial assistance
- Reading skills classes
- Study groups
- Proofreader
- Review previous assignment prior to introducing new material
- Summarize at the end of each class
- Put key words or terms on the chalkboard or transparencies
- Use handouts
- Use visual aids
- Extra time for assignments and exams
- Kurzweil Reader

Deficits in Mathematics

- Use of calculator
- Use of lined paper or graph paper
- Handouts done in large, bold print
- Underline key words
- Test retakes
- Partial credit for answers
- Repetition
- Check for understanding
- Extra assignments that help student to learn new concepts
- Present material in organized and structured fashion
- Buddy system

6.12 continued

- Extended time
- Tutoring

Auditory Deficits

- Note taker
- Tape recorder
- Lecture notes
- Outline of each chapter
- Extra time
- Memorization strategies
- Computers
- Speak slowly and clearly
- Repeat often
- Review notes

Visual Perception Deficits

- Large-screen computer
- Extended time for exams
- Taped texts
- Note taker
- Tape lectures
- Provide color-coded handouts
- Test questions read aloud

Attention Deficit Disorder

- Distraction-free environment for tests
- Seat in front of classroom
- Note taker
- Cues to get the student refocused
- Structure
- Buddy system
- Peer tutor
- Frequent breaks
- Organization techniques
- Study skills assistance
- Monitoring
- Check for understanding

6.13—REQUEST FOR ACCOMMODATIONS

To _____
Name of instructor

We are informing you that _____
Student name

is registered to take your course _____
Name of course

for the semester beginning _____
Date of beginning of course

This student will request to meet with you to discuss his/her particular situation. The student's identity should remain unknown to anyone else in your class. The student may request the use of a note taker or permission to tape-record your lectures. It may be useful to help the student identify another student who could take notes. It may also be helpful to provide the student with a seat in the front of the classroom.

The student is eligible for the following accommodations:

_____ Extended testing time

_____ Distraction-free environment for tests/quizzes

_____ Reader

_____ Oral tests

_____ Computer/spellchecker

_____ Calculator

_____ Scribe

_____ Alternative testing

_____ No accommodations necessary

_____ Other

If you would like to be responsible for providing these accommodations, please make arrangements with the student. However, if you are unable to provide these arrangements, please let the student know that other arrangements will have to be made. Appropriate accommodations must be ensured. In order to avoid concerns of test security, lost tests and testing times, it is important that arrangements be made well in advance of the testing day.

For your reference we have included a copy of the Rehabilitation Act of 1973, Section 504 and The Americans With Disabilities Act (ADA), 1990.

If you have any questions please contact the Director of Support Services.

6.14–ACCOMMODATIONS TO BE PROVIDED

During _____ _____ in _____
         Semester   Year   Course

with _____
                                   Faculty name

_____
                                   Student name

will be provided with accommodations for:

_____ Exams

_____ Tests

_____ Papers

_____ Class presentations

_____ Projects

The accommodations requested are:

_____ Quiet place to take exam

_____ Reader

_____ Tape recorder

_____ Scribe

_____ Computer

_____ Calculator

_____ Proctor

_____ Extended time _____ Amount of time requested

_____ Alternative testing

_____ Meetings with instructor

_____ Note taker

_____ Books of tape

_____ Reader

_____ Tutoring

_____ Writing assistance

_____ Monitoring

_____ Proofreading

_____   _____
       Student signature   Date

_____   _____
       Faculty signature   Date

BEYOND ACCOMMODATION

Let's put accommodation and inclusion in perspective. As important as both are to students who struggle with learning disabilities, they can be harmful if teachers misinterpret them. Students with learning disabilities must be "included" in courses that intellectually challenge them, and they must be "accommodated" so that disabilities are not allowed to interfere with the expression of their native abilities.

Inclusion requires placement in regular classes—not easy classes. And accommodation requires nothing more than an equal chance to participate in those classes. Students with learning disabilities don't want fewer challenges; they want opportunities to meet those challenges and to realize the same levels of success and self-satisfaction that other students realize. The school that "includes" them in easier courses or "accommodates" them by spoon-feeding does them a disservice.

Share the reproducible in Figure 6.15 with regular classroom teachers and provide them with the in-service training they need to teach these skills effectively. The high school student with learning disabilities who plans to attend college requires these skills to compete successfully at that level. Special education personnel and regular classroom teachers must do all they can to provide them.

TAKING A FINAL LOOK AT THE REGULAR CLASSROOM

Regular classroom teachers who teach one or more students with learning disabilities assume a significant responsibility. They understand or soon learn that education's creation of the homogeneous classroom is about as likely as Diogenes' discovery of a completely honest man. Though each is desirable, neither seems possible in the real world. Our differences as human beings, even when they involve marginal dishonesty, make life interesting.

Saying that students with learning disabilities can make life interesting for the regular classroom teacher is like saying that teenagers make life interesting for their parents. Both statements are laughable. Making life "interesting" only hints at what challenges students with learning disabilities provide for regular classroom teachers and what teenagers provoke in their homes.

The teacher who undertakes such a responsibility deserves our applause and all the help we can provide. Regular classroom teachers may find themselves in a world that causes problems for students with learning disabilities. A few may even cause some of the problems. Most, however, are elements in the solution. Their knowledge of instruction and curriculum and their commitment to young people are invaluable adjuncts to the work of counselors and special education personnel.

We ask them, then, not only to teach organizational and time-management skills, to promote motivation and self-esteem, and to encourage creativity and self-discipline in students with learning disabilities but to assess each student's academic and behavioral progress. It does involve extra work for them, and we should guard against punishing proper performance, but the information they provide complements the work of special education and influences the subsequent development of IEPs, transition plans, and placement decisions.

6.15 – Recommendations for Teachers in Preparing Students With Learning Disabilities for College

If teachers are to assist students in preparing for the demands of a college curriculum, they must help students attain the knowledge in a curriculum that is consistent with their abilities. It is not helpful to water down the curriculum or to merely keep students functioning at the minimal level of their ability. The following recommendations may be useful in guiding teachers who are involved in helping students with learning disabilities prepare for the transition to college.

- Do not keep students enrolled in remedial courses, but rather encourage them to take some risks and challenge themselves to higher level, mainstream courses that will prepare them for college-level work. Be sure that students are enrolled in college preparatory core courses in mathematics, English, social studies, laboratory science, and foreign language, if possible.

- Prepare the students for the demands of college-level work by assigning work that is challenging and promotes independent thinking, critical analysis, research, essay writing, and comprehensive reading.

- Work with students to help them learn how to read new materials and comprehend what they are reading.

- Work with students to help them understand various forms of charts and graphs to be better prepared to tackle science reasoning, statistics, mathematical concepts, and other technical materials.

- Work with students to develop study skills that are necessary to learn college-level material. These skills should include test-taking strategies, organizational skills, time-management skills, note-taking skills, outlining, reading skills, writing skills, and stress management.

- Work with students on ways to structure their time and to prepare for multiple assignments and exams at one time.

- Have students spend time reading more challenging reading assignments and identifying new vocabulary words to prepare for the demands of college-level reading.

- Assign writing assignments across the curriculum.

- Spend time working with students on the concepts of lecture-taught courses, including identifying key words and phrases, and staying focused.

- Require the students to become proficient on using a computer.

- Develop research skills by using the library.

- Have the students learn to use a cassette recorder with a digital numbering system for note-taking assistance.

- Practice taking multiple formats of tests to familiarize students with essay, short answer, multiple choice, fill-in-the-blanks.

- Work with students on oral presentations

- Use multisensory approaches to work, for example, videocassette, read out loud

- Utilize student's mastery of lower level skills as the stepping stone to facilitating the acquisition and use of higher level knowledge.

218

Share the form in Figure 6.16 with the classroom teachers responsible for one or more students with learning disabilities. Their cumulative responses will influence special education's reevaluation of placement decisions, IEP goals, transitional activities, and general treatment plans. Such a form should be completed at least yearly—perhaps at the conclusion of each semester.

LET'S WRAP IT UP

Mike has taught educational leadership to graduate students for more than twenty years and has spent a major part of each semester convincing his classes that the school's most important activity takes place in its classrooms. Administrators, especially aspiring administrators, enjoy the notion that the school's critical decisions are made in the principal's office. Administrators who believe such nonsense obscure classroom instruction within the fog of their own self-importance. Some never do see clearly enough to focus on the preeminence of classroom instruction.

Those administrators do significant damage to untold numbers of students. Anyone in the school who forgets that the classroom is the focus of the school's most important activity does students and teachers—as well as the community—a disservice. For this reason, special education departments must work collaboratively with classroom teachers, particularly those who teach students with learning disabilities, to share the information and materials they all require to do their jobs well.

One of inclusion's biggest problems is the lack of support regular classroom teachers receive when they work with students with learning disabilities. Such support must come in the form of materials to help them in the classroom, activities to enhance their professional growth, and the continuing message that their work and their opinions are not only valued but essential if the school is to help students successfully compensate for their learning disabilities.

The materials and the processes outlined in this section represent only the first step in providing teachers such support. Anything classroom teachers learn about students with learning disabilities is appropriate for other students as well. Nothing in Figures 6.4 through 6.7 relates only to students with learning disabilities. Emphasis on checking for understanding, providing time for questions and answers, and focusing on student modalities improves the learning experiences of all students.

The more closely we work with classroom teachers, therefore, the more likely we are to improve our relationships with them, benefit from their expert opinions during meetings, and enhance the learning of all students. To help promote such a working relationship, distribute the reproducible in Figure 6.17 to inform teachers of the availability of support personnel throughout the building. You might even include it in your school's teacher handbook.

We must also recognize that a good working relationship is more relationship than work. It is like a dependable automobile. It will get us where we want to go, comfortably and reliably, if we don't drive it too hard. Classroom teachers spend considerable time planning and delivering instruction. Meetings in the special education department and information requests take valuable time from them. Such impositions on their time should be requested sparingly.

If the requests are appropriate, however, and if classroom teachers feel confident that their time and opinions are valued by counselors and the special education department, their investment and insights establish a synergy within the school that results in direct benefit to all students. As important, they will receive the support they need to make inclusion the valuable experience it is designed to be for students with learning disabilities.

6.16 – CLASSROOM TEACHER'S EVALUATION

Student Name _____   Teacher _____

Course _____   Date _____

Study Habits:

Lacks good habits	Adequate habits	Reasonably good habits	Self-starter	Excellent habits
/_____ /	_____ /	_____ /	_____ /	_____ /

Organizational Skills:

Totally disorganized	Adequate organization	Reasonably good skills	Good skills	Excellent skills
/_____ /	_____ /	_____ /	_____ /	_____ /

Time-Management Skills:

No concept of time	Adequate skills	Reasonably good skills	Good skills	Excellent skills
/_____ /	_____ /	_____ /	_____ /	_____ /

Self-advocacy:

Unable to Advocate	Adequate advocacy	Reasonably good skills	Good advocacy	Excellent advocacy
/_____ /	_____ /	_____ /	_____ /	_____ /

Articulation:

Difficulty with adequate articulating ability	Reasonably good skills	Good articulation	Excellent skills
/_____ /	_____ /	_____ /	_____ /

Motivation:

Lacks motivation	Adequately motivated	Reasonably well motivated	Good motivation	Excellent motivation
/_____ /	_____ /	_____ /	_____ /	_____ /

Self-esteem:

Low self-esteem	Adequate self-esteem	Reasonable self-esteem	Good self-esteem	Excellent self-esteem
/_____ /	_____ /	_____ /	_____ /	_____ /

Attention:

| Low attention span | Adequate attention span | Reasonably good attention | Good attention | Excellent attention |

/_____ / _____ / _____ / _____ / _____ /

Coping Skills:

| Limited coping skills | Adequate coping skills | Reasonably good coping skills | Good skills | Excellent skills |

/_____ / _____ / _____ / _____ / _____ /

Realistic:

| Unrealistic | Adequate reality | Appropriate reality | Realistic | Extremely realistic |

/_____ / _____ / _____ / _____ / _____ /

Creativity:

| Lacks creativity | Adequate creativity | Reasonably creative | Creative | Extremely creative |

/_____ / _____ / _____ / _____ / _____ /

Academic Potential:

| Underachiever | Success in some areas | Potential for growth | Strong potential | Excellent potential |

/_____ / _____ / _____ / _____ / _____ /

Interest in Learning:

| No interest | Mildly interested | Interest in some areas | Strong interest | Extreme interest |

/_____ / _____ / _____ / _____ / _____ /

Maturity:

| Immature | Age appropriate | Above average | Very mature | Extremely mature |

/_____ / _____ / _____ / _____ / _____ /

Socialization:

Difficulty relating	Age appropriate	Reasonable interaction	Good interaction	Excellent
/_____ /	_____ /	_____ /	_____ /	_____ /

Discipline:

Very little discipline	Fairly disciplined	Reasonable discipline	Well disciplined	Excellent discipline
/_____ /	_____ /	_____ /	_____ /	_____ /

Sense of Humor:

Minimum humor	Some humor	Reasonable humor	Good humor	Terrific humor
/_____ /	_____ /	_____ /	_____ /	_____ /

6.17 — Sample List of Support Personnel for Classroom Teachers

Following is a list of support personnel within the building who are available to help classroom teachers, especially those who work with students with learning disabilities. Call upon them as needed to answer questions or to receive the help you may need to accommodate the special needs of some of your students.

Position	Name	Phone Extension
Special Education Chair	Claire Jones	2356
#504 Coordinator	Paul Lynn	2357
Testing Coordinator	Linda Reason	2366
Counselor(s)	Robert Moore	2490
	Beth Krance	2559
	Edward Sales	2233
	Marty Kuhn	2211
Social Worker(s)	Molly Mott	1004
	James Reagan	4421
	Alysa Thomas	9560
Psychologist(s)	Lydia Blume	1750
	Ken Beane	8884
Psychiatrist	Dr. Jeanne Carr	1000
Substance Abuse Director	Jeff Branny	4300
Speech Therapist	Wendy Pearl	4444
Reading Specialist(s)	Miriam Sands	1044
	Kay Severny	9999
	Penny Frank	6565
Case Manager(s)	Stephanie Grodon	1990
	Carol Blue	0035
	Allison Linsey	9963
	Connor Rudy	2345
Tutor(s)	Sherry Goldstone	5252
	Lynne Lusky	1509
	Gail Florman	6667
Behavioral Specialist	Cathy Dritt	5080
Learning Specialist	Alice Whitty	1010
Writing Specialist	Jeff Green	0025
Screening Committee	Patrick Moon	0773
	Susan George	0774
	John Sweeney	0775
Dean(s)	Scott Kane	9898
	Ellen Gray	9897
Educational Tester(s)	Pam Thomas	0104
	Paul Brody	1042
Alternative Classroom	Kevin Moore	2222
Learning Resource Center	Judy Dimple	4448
English Chair	Susan Hopery	8888
Math Chair	Marvin Dunne	7777
Social Studies Chair	John Haynes	6666
Science Chair	Vinny Laket	5555
Foreign Language Chair	Elaine Wise	4437

223

TRANSITION PLANNING— THINKING ABOUT COLLEGE

First, a quick story . . .

Rather than share a story to introduce this section, we'd like to share a letter. It was written by Imy Wax—at the time of the writing, the mother of a sophomore in college:

"My daughter has just completed her sophomore year in college. Just to be able to say 'enrolled in college' out loud, overwhelms me. I have so many deep emotional feelings. It's true that most parents feel a pang when they know it's time to separate. It's true, too, that most parents have mixed emotions as they see their children take this major step toward the future. But, for me, this was also a time of reflection, of looking back over the long years of watching, waiting, hoping, and trying to encourage changes....I remember the stab of pain I felt when those who gave me the diagnosis that my daughter was severely learning disabled followed...with a negative prognosis. All those professionals who would not believe that an academic future would be possible for my child should sit up and take notice that my daughter and the other students with learning disabilities...are making all kinds of tracks.

"...All I recall are the many times when professionals believed that we should not have expectations for our child, so they subtly, or not so subtly, tried to kill the wish—and the dream. I knew from my professional training that when dreams are killed for parents, the spirit and the desire to provide the stimulating environment that will make the difference go with it. Parents need to believe that nurture can compensate for what nature has failed to provide. They need to recognize that in the long run their efforts can provide a child with 'that special edge.'

"Believing and hoping are options each one of us needs when faced with crises. As parents, we decide whether to buy into the negative message or challenge it and go on. Lack of hope paralyzes the will, paralyzes the brain, and paralyzes the movement. If we as parents give in to despair, then we cannot create. If we cannot have a vision, we cannot move forward. As parents, we must believe that what we provide for our child will make a difference in the long run. The message I wish to share is that though the future is unknown, everything is possible.

"At the age of two, my daughter was given a bleak prognosis. We were told that there was concern for her ever being successful in a traditional school system. I struggled with this news but kept the glass 'half full.' Now my daughter has fulfilled my dreams and wishes for her. She embarked on her own, taking with her all the experiences and survival strategies that she learned. Have we taught her enough? Will she use good judgment? These are typical thoughts. . . . I am grateful that she took what we provided; I am grateful for the special help she willingly received, and I am bursting with pride for the remarkable human being she has become, far surpassing the expectations of those who could not 'believe.'

"The future is hers. The dreams and wishes now belong to her. Good luck, my baby."

"THE LITTLE ENGINE THAT *CAN*"

Were parents of children with learning disabilities to express their feelings, many would tell similar stories. Such stories are inspirational and reflect the undeniable power of courage and commitment. Unfortunately, a lot of these parents are struggling against a torrent of opinion that rejects the notion that belief in oneself can overcome even the severest obstacles. People who hold such opinions have accepted life's apparent realities; many are even quite well adjusted.

They embrace the story of the little engine as an endearing message, but they really don't believe it. It sounds good to them, but they reason that life just doesn't work that way. Too many of them have reconciled themselves to a comfortable but restricted concept of reality. And it works for them. Many of them are quite happy. Their beliefs, however, are only part of the message to be shared with children with learning disabilities.

Certainly, children with disabilities must learn to acknowledge this wind of prevailing opinion, but, like so many kites, they must also use it to elevate themselves higher and higher in their own minds and in the minds of others. Certainly, we must all learn to accept our limitations. To a large extent, we agree with the old saying, "The smaller the head, the bigger the dream."

We have also learned, however, that a blanket acceptance of our weaknesses also smothers our strengths. When we struggle, we grow. To a very real extent—and this may be a perspective that is inconsistent with the feelings of a lot of people—children with learning disabilities are fortunate. Mother Nature has introduced adversity into their lives, an opportunity to display their courage and to develop the character and realize the sense of self-satisfaction that comes only from overcoming obstacles.

Courage for a good many youngsters is letting go of the safety bar on a roller coaster. For children with learning disabilities, it's letting go of the safety found in anonymity. By letting go, such students risk being labeled and being misunderstood by others. But they learn the value of good advice: "To grow, let go." They discover a process that may not involve the momentary thrill of a roller coaster but that rewards risk takers with lasting personal satisfaction. This section was introduced by a mother who sensed this opportunity and helped her child realize its benefits.

COLLEGE AS AN OPPORTUNITY

Figure 7.1 illustrates the problems as well as the solutions that enter the lives of students with learning disabilities, particularly those who identify college as a goal. Recent statistics indicate that as many as 50 percent of all students with learning disabilities may be planning on college at some time in the future. In fact, students with learning disabilities represent one of the fastest growing populations in postsecondary education.

The diagram in Figure 7.1 illustrates the complexity of the situation for them, as well as for everyone who is associated with them. The top part of the diagram illustrates the range of disabilities, the bottom part the levels and kinds of interventions required to compensate for the damage the disabilities may have done.

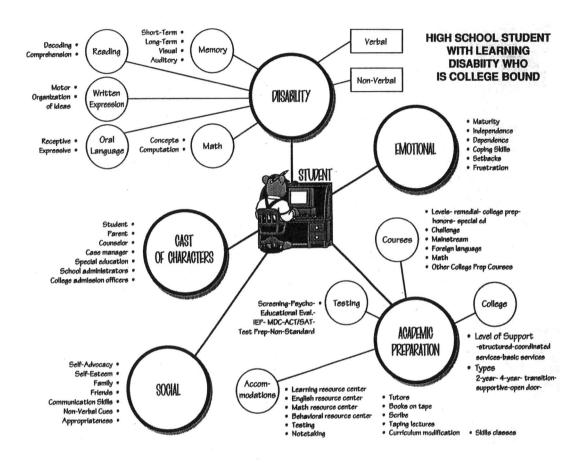

If the "Cast of Characters" provides the emotional, social, and academic assistance the student requires, he or she can anticipate success in college. If this assistance is not provided, success is less likely. This is not to say that success is impossible. Even without such assistance, some students possess such a relentless will to achieve that they develop their own compensatory strategies. It's simply a whole lot easier for them when professionals and parents help pave the way.

Use this reproducible to explain the process in large-group meetings with parents and students, or to share with them individually. It is also appropriate during meetings with teachers and other professionals to underscore the need for collaboration among the persons involved in the diagnostic and treatment processes for students.

PROVIDING TRANSITION PLANNING

Students with learning disabilities require planning that enables them to transition from their current educational setting to another involving either work or more education. Figure 7.2 explains both the process and the products of such planning. As indicated on the bottom of the figure, the process is mandated by law, should be accommodated during IEP meetings, and is cyclical throughout the student's high school career.

To conduct the additional transitional planning meeting recommended on the bottom of the form, use Figure 7.3. This Transitional Planning Guide identifies and discusses a wide range of possible services to ease the transition from high school to college for students with learning disabilities. The form suggests everything from a vocational evaluation and career counseling to job placement assistance, academic training, and social skills instructions. It even addresses guardianship, case management support, and transportation assistance.

As such, this additional Transitional Planning Meeting promotes a discussion of everything the student will need to function successfully in college or the community. Severely handicapped students require a broad range of services and, often, the involvement of someone to assure that these services are provided. Even those students who are planning on college require more than academic training to meet the unexpected social and emotional demands of a university campus.

The Transitional Planning Meeting, therefore, may be one of the most important meetings the student and his or her parents will attend during the last couple years of high school. For students who may still be struggling with self-esteem issues and/or the apprehension of the increased social and educational demands of college, such a meeting can provide the preparation they need to enjoy rather than fear the challenges of college. Certainly, such a meeting will reduce the uncertainty about the future by anticipating any needs that are likely to arise.

DEVELOPING A HIGH SCHOOL PLAN FOR TRANSITIONING TO COLLEGE

Former British Prime Minister Benjamin Disraeli once said, "What we anticipate seldom occurs; what we least expect generally happens." The key for high school personnel, parents, and students, therefore, is to hope that we capture as many contingencies as possible within the framework of our planning. Figure 7.4 provides such planning during high school and makes the Transitional Planning Meeting that much easier during the junior and senior years.

The information in the figure is especially good because it discusses the foundations that must be established during the early years in high school to make the transition to college that much easier. Foundations are not developed easily; fortunately, they are the most enduring. The foundations established during the freshman year must endure if the recommended activities during the junior and senior years are to be successful.

Consider just a few examples of the skills that constitute the foundation. Students with learning disabilities must "Develop compensatory skills," "Work on study skills," "Develop self-advocacy skills," and "Develop an individualized learning style." It is unrealistic to expect any child to do this within one year. Most of these skills take years to develop and refine; but they must constitute the focus of the student's early high school experiences if college is ever to become a realistic future goal.

7.2—THE TRANSITION PLANNING PROCESS

Illinois Transition Project (1990)
Southern Illinois University, Carbondale, IL 62901

1

Assist student in determining preferences and interests related to postsecondary life:
- interviews with student and family
- formal and informal assessments
- structured observations in work, community, and home settings

2

Product: Develop an individualized postschool vision in the form of an outcome statement describing desired career, postsecondary education, and community living situation.

3

Conduct transition planning meeting:
- includes the student and an interdisciplinary team
- may utilize Transition Planning Guide; Personal Futures Plan; or informal planning processes

4

Provide written notice of annual review to:
- the student and parents
- all other agencies targeted as providing annual needed services

5

Conduct IEP meeting/annual review:
- includes the student, parent, school personnel, and outside agencies
- annual transition goal and annual needed services determined based on postschool vision (outcome-oriented postsecondary goal statement)

6

Product: Written Statement of:
- long-term goal
- annual needed services based on long-term goal

These steps are mandated by law. Transition services must be addressed at the IEP meetings for students receiving special education services ages $14^{1}/_{2}$ and over. An additional, separate annual transition planning meeting is a recommended best practice. This process is cyclical and ongoing over several years.

7.3 – TRANSITION PLANNING GUIDE (TPG)

Services that may be needed in the next year to attain desired Postschool Outcomes:

____ *Vocational Evaluation:* Refers to a wide variety of activities that result in the collection of assessment information regarding a person's work and work-related behaviors in integrated community employment situations.

____ *Career Counseling/Guidance:* Refers to specific discussions with a student regarding his/her career goals and related guidance regarding curriculum choices associated with identified goals.

____ *Career/Vocational Education Classes:* Refers primarily to classes sponsored by vocational education that provide career awareness and/or specific vocational abilities.

____ *Community Work Experiences:* Refers primarily to high school vocational placements in integrated work settings. These work experiences are typically paid and may be unsubsidized or subsidized by another source (e.g., rehabilitation).

____ *Job Placement Assistance:* Refers to activities that result in the hiring of students in employment situations that are expected to continue beyond high school.

____ *Post-Employment Support:* Refers primarily to assistance provided following placement to enable a person to maintain employment. These supports might include transportation assistance, job coaching.

____ *Academic Training:* Refers primarily to secondary curriculum experiences that are designed to prepare a person for postsecondary community college or university programs.

____ *Domestic Skills Instruction:* Refers to curriculum activities for individuals in need of instruction to participate more actively in the home setting. Self-care skills, meal preparation, and household chores are examples of domestic curriculum objectives.

____ *Community Skills Training:* Refers to curriculum activities for individuals in need of instruction to facilitate their participation in the local community. Grocery shopping, mobility, and use of community services are examples of community skills curriculum objectives.

____ *Social Skills Instructions:* Refers to curriculum activities designed for individuals in need of social-interpersonal instruction. Exchanging greetings, handling criticism, and making requests for assistance are examples of social-interpersonal objectives.

____ *Self-Advocacy Training:* Refers to curriculum activities designed to assist individuals to express their opinions, advocate for their legal rights, act assertively, and make personal decisions.

____ *Recreation/Leisure Instruction:* Refers to activities for individuals in need of instruction to facilitate participation in personally preferred recreation leisure options. Hobbies, sports, and movies are examples of recreation/leisure objectives. These objectives are relevant for both secondary and postsecondary situations.

____ *Postsecondary Educational Support:* Refers to support services that may be required after a person leaves high school to facilitate his/her performance in community college, technical school, or other adult education program. Specialized student services resources and/or special classes are examples of services in this category.

_____ *Residential Services/Support:* Refers to the need for involvement in a supervised residential option and for need for specific support services including income support to enable a person to live more independently.

_____ *Social Support:* Refers to the establishment of social support networks. This may involve the identification of an individual or group of individuals that are available to assist the process in participating in social activities. In some communities formal social programs exist, while in other communities this is handled more informally.

_____ *Family Support:* Refers to unique family supports, including monetary or programmatic resources that enables individuals to remain with their families. These family supports may be needed during high school, but may assume a higher priority beyond high school.

_____ *Income Support:* Refers to programs such as SSL, AADI, food stamps, or Medicaid. These programs should be considered in relation to their support of the individual's desired lifestyle.

_____ *Transportation Assistance:* Transportation refers to a person's need for assistance to travel in the community. Refers to personal attendant care/special transit beyond what is available through public transportation. The specific transition services needed by an individual for community travel should be described.

_____ *Medical Needed Therapies:* Medical services refer to the individual's need for specialized medical assistance on a frequent basis (daily or weekly). Specific descriptions of these services should be included.

_____ *Assistive Tech/Adaptive Devices:* Refers to a variety of unique arrangements that enable an individual to participate more fully in community life. These include augmentative communication devices, mobility aids, feeding adaptations, rehabilitation engineering.

_____ *Case Management/Advocacy:* Refers to the need of certain individuals for ongoing assistance in assessing and using multiple community services. Typically these will be selected in the transition year.

_____ *Guardianship/Advocacy:* Refers to persons in need of assistance in assuring that his/her legal rights are being protected. Although these services may be needed during high school, typically these will be selected in the transition year.

_____ *Affordable Housing:* Refers to housing where costs are no more than 30 percent of the gross monthly income so that persons with disabilities can afford to stay where they choose to live.

_____ *Other:* Refers to services not included in this section.

_____ *No Support Needed:* Use this category when Transition goal documentation shows no assistance is needed.

7.4 – FOUR-YEAR HIGH SCHOOL PLAN
FOR TRANSITIONING TO COLLEGE

Freshman Year

- Develop an academic plan for high school
- Identify strengths and weaknesses
- Utilize services and accommodations
- Develop compensatory skills
- Work with Special Education to develop an individualized learning style
- Work with special education/counselor to develop an Individualized Educational Plan (IEP)
- Work on study skills
- Get involved in extracurricular activities
- Learn to articulate learning disability
- Develop self-advocacy skills
- Attend IEP/MDC Conferences

Sophomore Year

- Meet with counselor
- Review course selections
- Take as many mainstream courses as possible
- Continue to work on study skills
- Understand what services/accommodations are necessary for success
- Continue to utilize appropriate services/accommodations
- Begin to explore colleges
- Determine what level of services is appropriate in college
- Take the PLAN if offered
- Attend IEP/MDC conferences
- Explore the world of work
- Identify potential career and academic choices

Junior Year

- Meet with counselor
- Review course selections
- Enroll in mainstream courses if possible
- Register for ACT/SAT (nonstandardized if appropriate)

- Review understanding of learning disability with special education
- Be able to articulate learning disability
- Practice interviewing techniques
- Identify criteria for college choices
- Prioritize criteria for college choices
- Visit colleges
- Talk to Director of Support Services on college campuses
- Submit special applications to college programs requiring early applications
- Attend IEP/MDC Conference
- Narrow potential career choices
- Narrow academic areas of emphasis
- Identify colleges that offer the areas of emphasis

Senior Year

- Meet with counselor
- Review course selections
- Be sure psychoeducational evaluations are current
- Release documentation to colleges of choice
- Submit applications to colleges of choice
- Request recommendations from faculty
- Retake ACT/SAT if necessary
- Review strengths/weaknesses with Special Education
- Verify that colleges offer necessary accommodations/services
- Accept college of choice by May 1
- Arrange for final transcript to be sent to college

Students with learning disabilities must have a realistic appraisal of their strengths and weaknesses if, during their junior year, they are to narrow their fields of study and identify one or more colleges that can further their vocational and educational interests. Similarly, they must know how to self-advocate if, at some time in the future, they hope to interview successfully with officers of admission and/or the Director of Support Services on one or more college campuses.

The skills and activities recommended during the junior and senior years are relatively easy compared with those recommended during the earlier years. That's why the focus on the freshman and sophomore years is so important. It is not the time to start threatening youngsters with the "C" word (college), but it is the time to emphasize the development of the skills that will make the expectation of college that much less threatening in the future.

Share Figure 7.4 with parents as soon as possible—especially if they have indicated college as a future goal for their children. Even when such a goal seems hopelessly unrealistic, it should be the focus of continuing discussion with parents to determine if alternatives to college are possible. The number of college-bound students in some communities is so large that college, for many parents, seems to be the only option for their children. Sometimes just the awareness that alternatives exist is enough to refocus the goals of unrealistic parents.

Figure 7.4 should be shared with even the most unrealistic parents. The information it contains provides a measuring stick to assess the child's progress toward personal and educational self-sufficiency. Parents may discover during the sophomore year, for example, that mainstream courses are too difficult for him or that his vocational interests require something other than a college education. These are important moments of discovery for parents, and they provide the substance for discussions with school professionals that lead to realistic future goals for students.

That's why it's wise to share Figure 7.4 with counselors and selected mainstreamed teachers as well. Many of them have ongoing contact with parents and students and can help them accomplish many of the activities. They also can help to reestablish goals if present circumstances seem to suggest the need for a different direction. Because each of the activities listed in the reproducible is so important, we recommend that special education personnel meet with counselors and teachers prior to their use of the form to discuss its several uses.

IMPORTANT REASONS FOR TRANSITION PLANNING

Meetings with counselors, teachers, and parents are also a good time to emphasize the important differences between high school and college for students with learning disabilities. The information in Figure 7.5 can be shared whenever the time seems right, preferably near the end of the student's junior year or early in the senior year. Just a glance at the form indicates the fundamental differences between high school and college regarding such specifics as teaching methods, the monitoring of student progress, the availability of support systems—even the right to due process.

7.5 – Difference Between High School and College For Students With Learning Disabilities

High School	College
• Right by law to go to school	No given right
• Many tests & quizzes	Fewer tests & quizzes
• Extra-credit work allowed	Not much extra-credit work
• Allowed to retake or redo work	Rarely allowed to retake or redo
• Teachers discuss test material	Rarely discuss test material
• Instruction modes are varied	Instruction is usually lecture
• Teachers reach out to students	Students must seek assistance
• Assignments are structured	Assignments are less structured
• Receive credit for motivation	Grades based on a few tests
• Teachers trained to teach	Professors not trained to teach
• Student progress is monitored	Students monitor own progress
• Class attendance is mandatory	Attendance often not a factor
• Family and faculty available	Support system is often limited
• Courses last 18 weeks	Some courses last 14 weeks
• Class sizes are often small	Class sizes are often large
• Schools must test and identify LD	No obligation to test or identify
• Must evaluate if suspect LD	No obligation to evaluate
• Must develop IEP and monitor	Student develops own plan
• Must alter courses	Not required to alter courses
• Must provide waivers or substitutions	No right to fundamental changes
• Right to due process hearing	May file a grievance; it is not a right

That parents and students understand these differences is critical if they are to make realistic decisions about which college to attend and what adjustments to expect. Distribute the form to counselors and teachers, so they can emphasize the differences during meetings with parents and students. The teachers of senior courses can even use a modification of the form with all students to prepare them for the transition to college.

Many of the items on the form must be discussed at some length to emphasize the implications of such things as large class sizes, limited extra credit, lecture as the primary methodology, and fewer tests and quizzes. To most students, a circumstance involving fewer tests and quizzes is as undesirable as a reduction in parental controls. What parents and school officials are likely to perceive as a potential problem, most students will welcome as new-found freedom.

Unfortunately, Will Rogers probably was correct when he said, "[Freedom] doesn't work as well in practice as it does in speeches." He knew that new-found freedoms provoke as much self-indulgence as self-discipline. The student who understands the differences listed in Figure 7.5 and has the self-discipline to attend class regularly, to meet periodically with professors, to self-monitor, and to anticipate fewer tests and quizzes by devoting more time to them is likely to enjoy a successful college experience.

HELPING STUDENTS ASK THE RIGHT QUESTIONS

Students must ask several important questions in order to find the college that offers the educational and social opportunities that meet their special needs.

Questions They Should Ask of Themselves

College is not an end in itself. It is a process that leads to the realization of educational and career goals. To establish such goals, students must understand not only their vocational and social expectations of college but their feelings about leaving home and fighting their academic battles without the immediate support of family and friends. The assessment instrument provided in Figure 7.6 promotes an exploration of their feelings as well as their expectations of success.

It should be administered in the student's sophomore year to explore post high school experiences, again in the junior year to reassess needs and to use during the Transitional Planning Meeting. Students should answer the questions honestly and be expected to attend follow-up meetings with the counselor and/or case manager to discuss especially sensitive issues.

7.6—STUDENT READINESS ASSESSMENT

READINESS ASSESSMENT FOR SOPHOMORES AND JUNIORS IN SPECIAL ED

Student _____

Counselor _____

Case Manager _____

Date _____

1. As I begin this process of planning for "life after high school" I feel: (Check as many as apply)

   ____ Excited   ____ In charge
   ____ Uneasy   ____ Confident
   ____ Scared   ____ Ready to go
   ____ Worried   ____ Other: Please specify

2. The quality of my academic record so far will:

   ____ Let me have many choices that are very acceptable to me
   ____ Mean that I have to plan carefully to ensure that I have choices

3. My strengths are _____

   _____

   _____

4 My weaknesses are _____

   _____

   _____

5. The reason I am receiving Special Ed services is _____

   _____

6. I have already participated in the following as it relates to post high school planning: (Check as many as apply)

   ____ A meeting(s) with my parents, college counselor, and Case Manager
   ____ Conference with my counselor

____ Conference with Career Consultant and Case Manager

____ Met with career representatives

____ Met with college representatives

____ Did a Career Search

____ Did a College Search

____ Talked things over with my parents

7. I need help with: (Check as many as apply)

____ Getting started

____ Understanding what I'm supposed to do next

____ Knowing how to use resources

____ Understanding class rank and test scores and college options

____ Planning my junior or senior year course work

____ Signing up for ACT, SAT

____ Knowing my interests

____ Planning ahead

____ Financial Aid

____ Understanding where my parents fit in

____ Other: Please specify

Developed for Deerfield High School by Marybeth Kravets

The Parent Readiness Assessment in Figure 7.7 asks similar questions of parents to determine the extent of their agreement with their children's observations and feelings. Significant perceptual discrepancies between the student and his or her parents should alert the counselor and case manager to the need for further exploration of the issue(s) affecting the family. In addition, the form invites parents to find help understanding their child's involvement with special education and additional alternatives for the future.

Both readiness assessment instruments are designed to open the door to further communication among students, parents, and school personnel and to reduce the stress that accompanies decisions to attend college. It's well known among psychologists that stress provokes in most people a return to previously learned behaviors. The job of special educators, social workers, and counselors, therefore, is to help reduce the stress in students with learning disabilities so that they and their parents can function at current, improved levels.

The more information we provide and the broader the opportunities to discuss such information, the better prepared students and their parents will be to make a successful transition from high school to college. Some of the information is designed to help students and their families find even more information—in essence to be self-sufficient when high school personnel are no longer available to answer questions.

Questions They Should Ask of the Colleges

The student's likelihood of success is further assured, therefore, if he or she asks the right questions of—and about—schools when conducting a college search. Some of the questions should be asked of college personnel, some of the student himself or herself. Some of the questions are general, the kinds that all students ask when considering the appropriateness of a particular school. Others involve specific issues regarding learning disabilities and the services provided by the college.

Many of these questions are difficult to answer and require not just introspection but lengthy discussion with parents, special educators, and counselors, as well as university officials. The reproducible in Figure 7.8, therefore, should be shared with students and their parents during meetings when college selection and admission are the primary topics of discussion. Elements within it should be explained and explored during such meetings, and follow-up meetings should be scheduled if additional discussion seems warranted.

ANTICIPATING QUESTIONS
THE COLLEGES MIGHT ASK

College officials will ask some very pointed questions, too. Such questions should be anticipated and explored before the student and his or her parents visit schools for interviews or informational meetings. The questions in Figure 7.9 are representative of the kind that might be asked by college officials. They are tough questions and presuppose of the student considerable self-knowledge and planning within the past several years.

7.7 — Readiness Assessment for Sophomores and Juniors in Special Ed

PARENT FORM

Student _____

Parent _____

Counselor _____

Case Manager _____

Date _____

1. As your student begins this process of planning for "life after high school" you feel: (Check as many as apply)

    ____ Excited

    ____ Uneasy

    ____ Scared

    ____ Ready to go

    ____ Worried

    ____ In charge

    ____ Confident

2. The quality of your student's academic record so far will:

    ____ Allow for many choices that are very acceptable to you and your student

    ____ Mean that the student has to plan carefully to ensure several choices

3. Your student's strengths are _____

    _____

4. Your student's weaknesses are _____

    _____

5. The reason your student is receiving Special Ed services _____

    _____

6. Your student has already participated in the following as it relates to post high school planning: (Check as many as apply)

    ____ A meeting, or meetings, with parents, college counselor, and Case Manager

    ____ Individual conference with student's counselor

    ____ Conference with Career Consultant and Case Manager

    ____ Talked things over with you

    ____ Met with career representatives

    ____ Met with college representatives

    ____ Career Search

    ____ College Search

7. You feel your student needs help with: (Check as many as apply)

    ____ Getting started

    ____ Understanding what should be done next

    ____ Knowing how to use the College and Career Resource Center

    ____ Understanding class rank and test scores and college options

    ____ Planning for junior or senior year course work

    ____ Signing up for ACT, SAT

    ____ Knowing about individual interests

    ____ Planning ahead

    ____ Financial Aid

    ____ Understanding where you fit in

    ____ Other: Please specify:

8. You, as a parent, would like some help with:

    ____ Understanding why your student is receiving Special Ed services

    ____ Understanding options available for your student after high school

    ____ Understanding your student's strengths/weaknesses

    ____ Understanding the time frame for postsecondary planning

9. My concern (as it relates to your student's life after high school) is _____

_____

10. My student has already made specific decisions about post high school plans. The plans are _____

_____

11. Please feel free to make any other comments that you think will help your student's counselor/case manager.

7.8—QUESTIONS STUDENTS MAY ASK ABOUT COLLEGES

General questions

- How close to home do I want to be?
- What is the size of the student body that is right for me?
- Where is the college located (urban, suburban, rural)?
- What does the campus look like?
- What are the food arrangements? How many meals are required?
- What are the security measures taken on the campus?
- Is transportation nearby?
- What degrees are offered?
- What are the general entrance requirements?
- What are the graduation requirements to exit the college?
- How is the general maintenance of the college?
- What is the makeup of the student body?
- What percentage of students live on campus?
- How many students leave the campus on weekends?
- What is the typical number of students in each class?
- Is the college "need blind" financially in the admission process?
- How large is the Greek system?
- What are the extracurricular activities?
- What are the rules about cars on campus?
- Who advises students and how are they selected?
- How successful is the job placement center?
- What is the full cost for attending?
- What is involved in freshman orientation?
- How difficult is it to register for courses?
- Are there job opportunities on or near campus?
- Is the health center staffed by a physician?
- What types of athletic opportunities are available?
- What clubs and organizations are available?

Specific questions regarding learning disabilities

- What is the philosophy of the college toward learning disabilities?

- Who is the contact person on campus for students with learning disabilities?
- What documentation is required to receive services?
- Who are the staff working with students with learning disabilities and what are their qualifications?
- Does the college offer basic services or a more structured program?
- What is the admission procedure for students with learning disabilities? Is a special application required? Special testing? Interview? Does it differ from general admissions?
- What are the admission requirements? Is there any flexibility?
- Who is responsible for admission decisions for students with learning disabilities?
- Should the LD documentation be sent to the admission office or the director of support services?
- Does the admission office ask for recommendation or input from the LD service provider?
- Are there fees for services?
- Does the college offer remedial or developmental courses?
- Does the college offer skills courses?
- What is the process for requesting course substitutions or waivers?
- What services and accommodations are available?
- What classroom modifications are available?
- Are support groups offered?
- What percentage of the classes are taught by professors?
- How are professors notified of a student's learning disability?
- How many students with learning disabilities are enrolled on campus?
- Who provides services for students with attention deficit disorder (ADHD)?
- What is the graduation success rate for students with learning disabilities?
- What tutorial services are available?
- Are services available after freshman year?
- Can students with appropriate documentation use calculators or computers in exams?
- How are professors trained to teach to students with learning disabilities?
- Is there a learning resource center? What services are provided?

7.9 – QUESTIONS COLLEGES MAY ASK STUDENTS WITH LEARNING DISABILITIES

- When was the learning disability diagnosed?

- What accommodations are being utilized in high school?

- What accommodations are needed in college?

- Can the student articulate the learning disability?

- Does the student know strengths and weaknesses?

- What does the student want to study? Is this choice appropriate?

- What courses has the student taken in high school? What percent of the courses were mainstream, college prep courses?

- Does the student accept the learning disability?

- Can the student be a self-advocate?

- What are the student's goals? Are they realistic?

- Does the student understand the difference between services provided in high school and in college?

Share the reproducible with students and parents early in the college search process. If the student is still struggling with self-advocacy, the development of educational and career goals, and an acceptance—maybe even an understanding—of his or her learning disability, much more must be done before the actual college search process begins.

The decision to go to college provokes an important self-assessment: Are my career and educational goals realistic? Have I prepared for them? Are they consistent with my strengths? Do I have a clear understanding of my disability? Can I articulate it to others and advocate for whatever accommodations I require? The answers to such questions are critical and represent issues of more immediate importance than college decisions. That the college search process provokes such questions is good. Questions like these must remain foremost in the minds of students and parents during the entire process.

PREPARING FOR THE COLLEGE INTERVIEW

Answers to these questions are essential if students hope to impress college officials during interviews. Someone once said that conversation is the least reliable form of communication—second only to newspapers. Interviewers, therefore, must ask good questions and consider the quality of a person's answers if such conversation is to result in reliable information and a confident decision regarding the student's admissibility.

It follows that if students are to make favorable impressions, they must answer questions confidently and intelligently. The process outlined in Figure 7.10 prepares students to make such answers. It promotes an exploration of their high school experience, consideration of the kinds of questions they may want to ask college personnel, and an understanding of the guidelines for a successful interview.

Interviewing is as stressful as anything students will ever do—particularly for those seeking an identity and struggling with a problem they scarcely understand. Questions asked of them during interviews can probe sensitive areas, reopen wounds, and underscore the frailty of their egos and the limitations of their self-knowledge. The more help they receive prior to the actual interview, the more comfortable they will be throughout the process to favorably represent themselves to college officials.

To help students gather the specific information they require to make such impressions, Figure 7.11 should be given to students and their parents well before the first interview, probably sometime early in the senior year. The form forces students and their parents to revisit past experiences in order to anticipate future needs. It provokes a good deal of discussion over the dinner table and encourages students and/or their parents to schedule meetings with one or more school officials to discuss the relative success of intervention strategies, current progress, and future needs.

7.10 — PREPARING FOR AN INTERVIEW

Useful information for students to have about their high school experience

1. Explanation of the learning disability.

2. Ability to describe the way in which their learning disability affected them (listening, writing, spelling, speaking, taking notes, etc.).

3. What assistance was received in high school (note taking, tutoring, proofreading, extended testing time, etc.)? Which were helpful and why?

4. History of learning disability: when was it first diagnosed and did the student receive extra help in elementary or junior high school?

5. Ability to describe any service or help from sources outside the school setting (tutors, speech therapists, etc.).

6. Be able to describe the current high school (including: competitiveness, percent of students continuing on to college, student body, community life).

7. Which high school courses were easier for the student?

8. Which high school courses were more difficult for the student?

9. Which were the student's favorite courses, and why?

10. Which were the student's least favorite courses, and why?

11. In what areas does the student want to improve?

12. Is it easier for the student to remember information given during class discussion or lecture, or what the student reads from a textbook?

13. How well can the student do on a written assignment?

14. Is correct spelling difficult for the student? If so, is the student able to use computer spell check?

15. Comment on abilities in the following areas: attention, memory, time management.

16. What is the level of skill and/or strategy in test-taking? In note-taking?

17. What is the student's interest in studying?

18. What are the student's long-term goals?

Questions students and families may want to ask of the interviewer to better understand the admissions criteria and services at the college

1. What are the admission requirements for the college and are these requirements flexible for students with documented learning disabilities?

2. What are the procedures and timelines for applying for admission to the college, and to be eligible to receive services?

3. What accommodations are available on campus? How do students access these services?

4. Are there additional charges for services?

5. Are there special courses designed for students with learning disabilities or remedial or developmental courses available? Will college credit be granted for these courses?

6. Is there someone who will help the students obtain the necessary services and accommodations?

7. Who is responsible for considering petitions for modifying course requirements or waivers?

8. Is there a counselor available who is knowledgeable about learning disabilities?

9. Are there organized support groups for students with learning disabilities?

10. Are there courses available to help students with time management, study skills, organizational skills, note taking, and test-taking strategies?

Guidelines for a successful interview

1. Develop a list of questions that probably are not covered in the college catalogue.

2. Be able to talk about what you want in a college support program.

3. Make a short list of information about yourself that may not appear in your application.

4. Practice interviewing so that you are comfortable with the situation, and are able to answer questions clearly and honestly.

5. Be able to describe your strengths and weaknesses and how you compensate. Are these strategies for compensation successful or unsuccessful? Be honest.

6. Be able to answer some questions that may not involve your application or disability, such as how you spend your summer, or a book you read lately.

7. At the conclusion of the interview, ask the interviewer for a business card so that you have a reference of whom you met with and can also send a thank-you note.

8. Be able to write some notes to yourself afterwards about the visit, listing the important information you may have received. (You may even ask if you could tape-record the interview so that you could verify the information you have given the interviewer.)

7.11 – College Interview Preparation Form

Name _____ Date _____

Address _____ Phone _____

Description of learning disability _____

When diagnosed _____

Special help received:

___ Tutoring   ___ LD Resource   ___ Remedial Reading   ___ Study Skills   ___ Other

Which were helpful and why? _____

Current high school _____

Describe this school _____

GPA _____   SAT _____   ACT _____

Comment on your abilities in the following areas and describe:

Memory _____

Attention _____

Time Management _____

Time Orientation _____

Describe strategies you have used to compensate for your learning disability _____
_____

Why were these strategies successful/unsuccessful for you? _____
_____

When was your last diagnostic testing? _____

What is taking these kinds of tests like for you? _____
_____

Describe your skills in the following areas. If your learning disability interferes in any of these areas, describe strategies you have used to compensate:

    Reading _____

    Writing _____

    Spelling _____

    Math _____

    Test taking _____

    Note taking _____

What is your favorite subject? Least favorite? _____

How would your favorite teacher describe you? _____

7.11 continued

How would your least favorite teacher describe you? _____

What do you see as your own personal strengths? _____

What are your weaknesses? _____

What kinds of activities are you involved in? _____

What do you hope to get out of college? _____

What do you want in an LD college program? _____

Which of the following services will be appropriate for you?

_____ Untimed tests _____ Distraction-free environment for tests

_____ Taped texts _____ LD specialist

_____ Skills courses in time management/test taking/organization/note taking

_____ Tutors _____ Note takers _____ Counseling _____ Reduced course load

_____ Study skills _____ Support group

What are your career interests? _____

_____

_____

_____

_____

_____

_____

_____

_____

_____

Just Before the Interview

Students should do the "homework assignment" provided in Figure 7.12 several days before the actual interview. If they have worked with the forms provided earlier in this section, they should have no trouble with this assignment. They already will have given considerable thought to most of the questions. In addition, they should be encouraged to include many of the answers in a small notebook they plan to bring to the interview. For example, the three questions they want to ask during the interview should be written down in the notebook. Such a notebook serves at least two purposes. It can be used to jot down relevant information provided by the interviewer or to record reminders of "things to do" after the interview. It also can be used as a "cheat sheet" for students to refer to periodically to assure they cover everything they had planned for the meeting and to remind them of the answers they prepared for anticipated questions.

Be sure to emphasize with students that the résumé suggested in Figure 7.12 need not be detailed. It should be restricted to one page and should contain only relevant information. Have them use the model in Figure 7.13 when they develop their own resource. As a friend once said, "Presentation is half the sell job," so tell them to keep it simple but to develop a pleasing format. Tell them to bring several copies to the interview. The interviewer will want one for his or her records and probably will want to share one or two with the office of admissions.

SELECTING THE BEST SCHOOLS

First of all, "best" is a relative term. Many students express interest in certain schools because friends plan to apply, the football team is nationally ranked, parties abound on campus, it has a deserved—or an undeserved—reputation for academics or "fun," or it's currently the "in" school. As evidenced in Figure 7.14, the reason(s) for selecting a particular school extend well beyond the relative difficulty of admissions standards or the last time it won the Rose Bowl. All students should be expected to research the information requested in Figure 7.14, if only to discover the several variables involved in their ultimate decision.

For example, the number of part-time students in a school—one of the items on the form—may be irrelevant to most high school seniors, but once they become serious about a school and discover that it's a "suitcase college," they might start looking elsewhere. The same is true of the distance of the school from the largest town or city. Some students prefer schools that are comfortably isolated from the rest of the world; others need the experiences that only a metropolitan area can provide.

Without an awareness of such characteristics, students are unable to use them to make intelligent decisions about "best" colleges. Most important, they must research information about academic requirements: when majors must be declared, who teaches the courses, the student-to-faculty ratio, and the specific requirements of the preferred course of study. Does the school provide study abroad or co-op study programs?

7.12—HOMEWORK ASSIGNMENT TO PREPARE FOR AN INTERVIEW

1. Think about yourself:
   Values
   Goals
   Specifics about life experiences

2. List three strengths:
   One academic
   One nonacademic
   One elective
   Provide samples of each; write them out.

3. Record one weakness—must be presented in a positive way:
   Acknowledge weakness with signs of improvement (e.g., procrastination—in freshman and sophomore year I tended to procrastinate a great deal and handed in many assignments late. However, I am improving.)

4. List three questions you want answered during interview:
   One academic
   One nonacademic
   One elective

   Cannot be *too* general nor *too* specific; questions must be ones you truly want answered and *must* relate to your interests.

5. Prepare a *one* page résumé; use *only* those aspects of school and life you want to share:
   Test scores
   Honors
   Activities
   Work experiences
   Interests

Don't include *anything* that is not true and that you don't want to talk about.

7.13 — SAMPLE RÉSUMÉ

Buster Fraser
1119 Wagner Road
Deerbrook, Illinois 60033

Education:	Senior at Deerbrook High School
Graduation date:	June 6, 19__
Class rank:	122/422
Test scores:	ACT 26
	SAT 1190
Honors:	Regular Honor Roll each semester in high school
	French Honor Society
	Principal's Award 19__
	Regional Swimming Champion 19__, 19__
Activities:	Literary magazine editor
	French tutor
	Varsity swim team
	Community helper
Work Experience:	Assistant Manager of Little Tot Swim House
	Camp counselor
Interests:	Reading French literature
	Gardening
	Guitar
	Stock market
Strengths:	Foreign languages
Weaknesses:	Mathematics
Activities to be pursued on the college campus:	Literary journal
	Intramural swimming
	Jazz band
	Admissions tour guide

7.14 – EXPLORING COLLEGES

Name of college _____

Address _____

Telephone: (_ _ _)_ _ _-_ _ _ _   e-mail _____

Director of Admissions _____

Director of Financial Aid _____

Director of Support Services _____

Telephone: (_ _ _) _ _ _-_ _ _ _

Calendar _____   Application deadline _____

Cost: Tuition in-state _____   out-of-state _____

    Room and board _____   Fees _____   Books _____

Admission policies: Class rank _____   GPA _____   ACT _____

    SAT:I _____   SAT:II _____   _____   _____

    Courses required _____

    _____

    _____

    Essay _____   Recommendations _____   Interview _____

    Early Decision _____   Binding _____   Deadline date _____

Freshman profile: Applied _____   Accepted _____

    Mid 50% ACT score _____   Mid 50% SAT:I score _____

Student body:

    Number of full-time undergraduates _____

        Males _____   Females _____

    Part-time students _____

    Graduate students _____

    Diversity _____

    Religious makeup _____

    Percent in-state _____   Out-of-state _____

Location: Urban _____   Rural _____   Suburban _____

Number of acres _____   Number of buildings _____

Population of nearest city/town _____

Distance from closest large town/city _____

Transportation to college: air _____   train _____   bus _____   car _____

7.14 continued

Distance from home town _____
Travel time to campus _____

Degrees in undergraduate school _____

_____

Degrees in graduate school _____

Major(s) of interest _____

    Depth of course offerings _____

    Entrance requirements _____

    When major must be declared _____

    Majority of courses taught by: Professors ____ TA's ____

    Student/faculty ratio: _____ PhD's: _____

    Distribution requirements for graduation _____

    Course requirements in major _____

    _____

Clubs/organizations of interest _____

_____

Housing options _____

Fraternity/sorority percentages _____

Athletic conference _____

    Intercollegiate sports for men _____

    _____

    Intercollegiate sports for women _____

    _____

    Intramural sports _____

    _____

    Athletic facilities _____

    _____

Special Programs:

    Study abroad _____ Co-op Work/Study _____

    Internships _____ Honors Program _____

    Credit by exam (AP,CLEP) _____ Career Center _____

    Job placement _____ Independent study _____

Support Services for students with learning disabilities:

Learning Center _____ Tutoring ___ Computer lab _____

LD Specialist(s) _____ Support groups _____

Note takers _____ Scribes _____ Proctors _____

Testing accommodations _____ Books on tape _____

Distraction-free environment for testing _____

Priority registration _____ Advisors _____

Skills classes _____

Financial Aid: Forms required: FAFSA _____ Profile _____

College form _____ Other _____

Percent of students receiving aid ___

Need blind _____ Need aware _____

Aid based on need _____ merit _____

Deadline date _____ Loans _____

Scholarships _____

Is job placement high? Is there a learning center for students with learning disabilities? Are LD specialists available? What about access to tutors or books on tape? Is a distraction-free environment available for testing? How big is the school? How large are the classes? Am I going to get lost in the shuffle? These are all important questions and can be answered only after the student researches the characteristics of several schools. Figure 7.14 will be helpful not only to record the information but to use later when comparing one school with another.

Visiting College Campuses

The rational approach to college selection is important, but it has its limitations. One of the biggest factors in deciding on a college is how the student feels about it during and after the visit. Realistically, the student's emotional reaction to the campus and its student body is one of the determining factors in the final decision. Parents and school personnel must work hard to encourage students to trust these emotional reactions—but within the framework of the rationality that preceded the college visit.

In essence, emphasize the process outlined in this section to identify a list of colleges that meet the student's and the parent's needs and expectations of a college program. Having identified this prioritized list of colleges, use Figure 7.15 to arrange a visit to several or all of them. Then have the student use Figure 7.16 to summarize the highlights of the visit. The student will have to give a lot of thought to a few of the items and will be ready to discuss them with his or her parents or someone at school.

Special Education personnel must share each of these forms—for that matter, all the forms that have been mentioned in this section—with counselors, students, and parents at appropriate times throughout the school year to promote the kind of planning that results in good college choices. They must also encourage the students to discuss with parents or counselors the information they have gathered and the feelings they have experienced.

The discussions provoked by these forms probably do more good than the forms themselves. Such discussions are possible, however, only after the student has gained enough information about schools to evaluate them intelligently. During these discussions, parents and school personnel should encourage the student to share his or her feelings about each campus. *All else being equal*, the student's *feelings* will determine which school he or she is likely to want to attend.

Figures 7.17 and 7.18 will help the student and his or her family make the final decision. Figure 7.19 provides a comprehensive review of the important criteria involved in the final selection. Students might be encouraged to read it prior to discussing their feelings and making a final decision. Once they have made this decision, the search and selection processes are complete.

This is not to say that decisions can't be reevaluated and changed. New information can provoke a new decision at any time prior to the student's enrollment at a particular college. The point is, if students use the materials in this section, the processes they establish will result in a decision that is realistic and satisfying. The decision is realistic if it promises to accommodate the student's special needs and unique interests. It is satisfying if the student feels comfortable with his or her preliminary experiences on the campus and anticipates academic and social success.

7.15 — THE COLLEGE VISIT

- Identify colleges that meet priority criteria.
- Plan to visit while college is in session.
- Call admissions office for appointment at least three weeks in advance:
  - time and date of visit
  - who will be visiting
  - interview or just general visit and tour
  - a request for meal on campus
  - a request for overnight accommodation if available
  - a request to visit a class
  - a request to meet with professor or department chair
  - a request to audition if necessary
- Arrange meeting/interview with director of support services.
- Call ahead if arrival on campus will be delayed.
- Read about college *prior* to visit.
- Make a list of questions to ask.
- Be prepared to share pertinent information.
- Arrange to meet with currently enrolled students.
- Do not visit too many colleges in one day.
- Take pictures while on campus.
- Sample food on campus.
- Visit residence halls.
- Tour facilities.
- Observe for deferred maintenance.
- Walk around the surrounding area of campus.
- Take notes.
- Write thank-you notes.

7.16 — Campus Visit and Interview

Name of College _____

_____

Interview date/time/location _____

_____

Name of interviewer _____

Impression left after interview _____

_____

Tour guide's name _____

Impression left after tour _____

_____

Names of faculty or support staff met _____

_____

Classes attended _____

Overnight visit scheduled _____

Name of student host _____

Name of dormitory _____

General impression from visit _____

_____

Questions to follow up on _____

_____

_____

_____

7.17 – COLLEGE COMPARISON WORKSHEET

Comparative criteria   *College A* ____   *College B* ____   *College C* ____

Total Undergraduate Enrollment:

Cost/Tuition/Room and Board:

Amount of financial aid dollars available:

Course admission requirements:

Mid 50% range of ACT/SAT scores:

Mid 50% range of class rank:

Mid 50% range of GPA:

Majors of interest:

% living in university housing:

% of commuters:

% who graduate in 4 years / 5 years:

% going on to higher degree:

Faculty-student ratio:

% of fraternities / sororities:

Religious diversity on campus:

% who stay on campus on weekends:

Campus security available:

Campus crime statistics:

Foreign language required to graduate:

Thoughts / observations:

7.18—LD College Comparison Worksheet

Criteria	College A	College B	College C
General Information			
1. Size of student body			
2. Location			
3. Degree of difficulty for admissions			
4. Cost for college			
5. Fee for program			

Your criteria for program

1.
2.
3.
4.
5.
6.
7.
8.

Your thoughts

1. Pros—Positive
2. Negatives
3. Parents' thoughts

Order of preference

Chance for admission

Developed for Deerfield High School by Marybeth Kravets

7.19 – College Selection Criteria

Learning Disability Services or Programs

There are six levels of service available to students with learning disabilities for their postsecondary educational experiences and it is important to identify the appropriate option that will lead to ultimate success:

Level I: Postgraduate year in high school. Some students would benefit from a fifth year of high school and the chance to build better academic foundations. There are various high schools in the country that offer specific fifth year experiences for students with special learning needs, and many of these high schools offer a residential experience.

Level II: Transition Programs. Some students are not ready to tackle college level work, but are ready for an experience in residential living. These programs are usually not for college credit, but do provide an opportunity for students to strengthen academic skills and abilities to survive in the working world.

Level III: Highly Structured Programs. These college programs provide full-fledged learning disability services. Students must submit psychoeducational evaluations, have interviews, and usually submit special applications. The admission decision is usually made by the Director of the Support Program or jointly between the Director of the Program and the Director of Admissions. Once admitted, students develop an Individual Educational Plan similar to the one used in high school, and usually sign a contract regarding attendance and investment in the program. Usually these programs have an additional fee for services.

Level IV: Coordinated Services. These services differ from Highly Structured Programs in that the services are not compulsory. Students may submit a special application, and the Director of Support Services could be involved with the admission decision. However, no contract is signed and students voluntarily request the services.

Level V: Services. Most colleges will provide services that comply with Section #504 of the Rehabilitation Act of 1973. Sometimes the services are directed by someone who is knowledgeable about learning disabilities. Services do not begin until the student is enrolled and on campus, and the degree of services available vary from college to college. The Director of these Support Services is not involved in the admission process and the degree of services is usually minimal.

Level VI. Supportive Institutions: These are colleges that do not have specific services or programs, but the small size of the student body and the involvement of faculty provide plenty of nurture and assistance.

Academic Programs

One of the first priorities should be the availability of majors that interest the student. It is not sufficient for a major just to be offered; students must evaluate the strength of the offerings and the department (number of courses and depth, number of faculty, and placement of graduates, etc.).

Many students, however, are undecided about a college major. If this is the situation, students should consider what studies they would like to continue in college and what new avenues they would like to explore. Also, it is helpful to know if students will be able to get involved in courses not in their major. For example, can students get involved in the drama department if they are not majoring in drama?

Type of Institution

Is a coeducational college absolutely important or will the student consider a single-sex institution? Does the student have a preference between a public and a private institution? Cost, size, diversity of students, course offerings, administrative control, and admissions criteria are factors that vary between public and private colleges.

Size of the Institution

Students will find colleges with 250 students and those with 50,000. While the quality of a college is not determined by size, enjoyment may be. Here are some factors which may be affected positively or negatively by the size of the institution:

> Extensiveness of course and program offerings
> Diversity of student body and faculty
> Faculty/student ratio
> Class size, especially in introductory courses
> Use of graduate teaching assistants
> Academic and social contact with students and faculty
> Availability and accessibility of facilities
> Involvement in leadership and extracurricular activities
> Dependence on fraternities and sororities for social activities
> Degree of personal discipline, independence, and aggressiveness required of a student
> Competition for support services

Location

Where would students like to be geographically? Do they want an urban or rural setting, and in what part of the country? Students may significantly add to their educational experience by attending college in another part of the country, yet there may be reasons why it is important for students to be near home. Students and parents should discuss this topic early in the process to allow for time to be spent exploring possible options instead of impossible dreams.

Size of the Community

Students should consider the community and area around a college. Is it important to be near a city or would it be preferable to be in a smaller college town? Is public transportation convenient? What is the area bordering the college? What is the relationship between the college and the community?

Facilities

Campus facilities—their availability and their condition—should also be of concern. Outstanding facilities in a particular area may reflect the strength of the program and the college's commitment to it. These are also practical considerations: An astronomy major will want an observatory; music majors will want adequate practice rooms; if students want to live in a single-sex or substance-free dorm, the college should have these options; athletic facilities, bookstores, student unions, libraries, and dining options are important.

Competitiveness

The competitiveness of a college is important in the college selection process. It will help students make realistic college applications, and will lead to a challenging yet comfortable academic environment. The question is not only can the student be admitted, but can the student be academically successful? Easy entrance does not always mean easy to stay in! Most college guides categorize colleges as to their competitiveness, but students must ask questions to really determine the degree of competitiveness. What is the ACT/SAT score, GPA and class rank of the middle 50 percent of incoming freshmen? How many students enter with AP credits? What is the average GPA of the returning sophomores?

Costs

This factor will be a significant consideration for students and parents. The comprehensive fee (tuition, room and board) for a year may be as high as $25,000. This figure does not include entertainment, transportation, clothing, fees, books, spending money, and sorority/fraternity costs.

In determining the cost criteria, decide on a range within which a student and family can operate. Scholarships and financial aid are available to students with demonstrated need, and many colleges offer scholarships based on no-need. Although students should not exclude an institution solely on the basis of cost, it is important to be cognizant of the fact that *not* all colleges are need blind. *Need blind* means admitting a student not based on financial need. Some colleges are "need conscious" and financial need may be a factor in admission. Students should consider colleges that may be a cut below their first-choice college, as many colleges offer full, no-need, scholarships to students who may not be in the top 10 percent or with ACT of 30+ or SAT of 1300+. These colleges could offer an equally challenging educational experience and offer scholarship money.

Religious Orientation

Is the college affiliated with any religious group? How much emphasis is placed on the religious conviction? Are services or chapel required? Is there a Hillel or Neuman Club or other club of interest to the student? Where are the nearest churches or synagogues?

Fraternities and Sororities

How important is the Greek system on campus? Is it very competitive to join a fraternity or sorority? What are the general costs of belonging? Do students live in fraternity or sorority houses? Is the student interested in these social groups?

Special Interests

Be sure to include in the list of college requirements everything the college should have to be considered as ideal: Fraternities, sororities, athletics, music, drama, TV/radio stations, ROTC and others. Whatever is important should be put on the list.

Having defined the criteria and researched the colleges, students are now in a position to make an informed decision on which colleges will receive their applications. Students must remember that they need to "own" this process and not leave the decision making to others. Students should also remember that parents are an important part of the "team" and should be part of the decision-making process.

The student and his or her parents can then put the process to rest. If the selection criteria have been reviewed carefully, the student's admissibility is guaranteed and his or her success is relatively assured. On that basis, students should avoid the status charade that characterizes the college application process for so many students across the country. Many seek acceptance to as many as ten to fifteen schools, thinking that their status in high school is enhanced with each additional school that accepts them.

What they fail to realize is that, once a family seeks admission to ten to fifteen different schools, high school personnel and many students begin to assume that they haven't done their homework. Many even begin to question the family's understanding of the purposes of a college education. Let's put it this way. The search for status is to the search for knowledge what cosmetics are to intelligence! Putting on more makeup does nothing to increase intelligence. As a matter of fact, an excess of the former makes us wonder about the existence of the latter!

High school personnel must be careful, therefore, to encourage students and their parents to search for the right schools, visit as many as possible, then select the ones that satisfy the needs and expectations of the student. Submission of the applications, and the student's eventual acceptance should complete the process, with the student enrolling in the college that best meets his or her needs.

PERSONAL ESSAYS AND RECOMMENDATIONS

The application process may require a personal essay from the student and/or a set of counselor and teacher recommendations. The essay may require answers to questions such as: "What is the defining moment in your life?" "What distinguishes you from every other student in this building?" These are challenging questions for all students, but they can be downright threatening to students with learning disabilities.

Many 17-year-old high school students, especially those with learning disabilities, are only recently able to grasp the subtle abstractions lurking behind every nuance of the school's curriculum. Most are avoiding the inevitable struggle to "define your future," and their parents are revisiting "work" or the "C" word every time they sit down to dinner.

Then someone asks them questions like these and provokes a numbing search for a level of enlightenment barely achieved by Buddha. Most 17-year-olds enjoy introspection almost as much as alarm clocks, homework on weekends, and Dad's lectures. They fear such suspiciously deep psychological waters. Their apprehension is complicated by their learning disabilities and the uncertainty that awaits them in college.

It's important to recognize, however, that the admissions process is characterized by close scrutiny of student transcripts, letters of recommendation, and personal essays. One admissions officer indicated to us that "…the recommendations and essay put the meat on the bones of the application." In essence, well-constructed and interestingly written personal essays, and recommendations from counselors and teachers bring students to life. This is especially important for students with learning disabilities. Their educational histories—even their life stories—are not only revealing and interesting but often inspirational.

They involve stories that must be shared with admissions officers to enhance the admissibility of certain students. Consider the dean who indicated to us that he and his admissions counselors accept students *for the university faculty.* He and his colleagues seek to populate the university with intellectually curious, creative students who can complement the faculty's love of learning. Many students with learning disabilities are the very kinds of students this school and others like it are seeking.

Share Figure 7.20, therefore, with all students who will be expected to include personal essays with their applications for admission. The form provides valuable information for students by suggesting topics as well as organizational tips that impress college admissions officers. In addition, recommend that students be as creative as possible when writing essays.

A purely expository approach to the topic may provide important information, but it may not sustain the reader's attention. Information and readability are both necessary in a good personal essay. Share Figures 7.21 and 7.22 as illustrations of good essays. You might also recommend that students request help from their English teachers when writing essays. The additional help might make the difference between acceptance to and rejection by a highly selective school.

The closest any of us ever comes to individual perfection is when we write a personal essay or fill out a college or job application! But that's OK. In fact, a whole lot of "horn tooting" is perfectly appropriate for personal essays. If we don't blow that horn, few others will do it for us. So encourage teachers, parents, and others to provide all the help students require when they write a personal essay. The time is well-spent.

LOOKING AT "MOVE-IN" DAY

Someone once said, "Don't agonize. Organize." It's a piece of advice that pretty well wraps up the thrust of this entire section. Having organized the college search and selection processes, students and parents must organize the actual move to college. Many students with learning disabilities will have a hard time finding their classes, their advisor's office, and the Office of Financial Aid in the administration building, let alone exploring the library's maze of computerized card catalogues, research sections, and periodicals files.

The adjustment to college becomes additionally difficult when the student moves into the dormitory and, although he has his toothbrush and notepads, suddenly discovers he needs a screwdriver, batteries, a bottle opener, a laundry bag, even a sewing kit and an extra pillow. Many of these needs are unanticipated, so share Figure 7.23 with students and their parents just after they've been admitted to college. They may not need all the items listed on the form, but it serves as an excellent reference guide when the student and his or her parents are preparing for the move.

7.20—Tips on Writing Personal Statement or Essay

Importance of Essays

- Make the facts in folder come alive
- Insight into depth of student
- Illustrate writing style
- Fill in gaps
- Provide a better understanding of obstacles navigated

Describe yourself

- Disclose and describe learning disability
- When diagnosed; impact on academics; strengths/weaknesses
- Describe services being utilized; compensatory skills developed; services to be utilized in college
- Describe accomplishments
- How experiences have shaped who you are
- Emphasize what has been learned from the experience

Describe an interest:

- Activities or involvement beyond high school
- An important person in your life
- Research accomplished
- Job
- Poetry/artwork

Reasons for selecting college:

- What will be your major
- What you hope to accomplish on campus
- What is offered in curriculum that is important to you

Tips:

- Gather data about yourself: activities; shortcomings; most valued personality traits; learning disability
- Write a draft
- Do not be vague
- Use specific examples
- Be clear and concise
- Avoid simplistic answers and reasons
- Be error free
- Be organized
- Use comfortable language
- Proofread
- Keep audience in mind
- Don't try to rush—allow enough time to write
- Neat and readable—use of computer is fine

7.21 – Sample Personal Statement

As you review my transcript I would like to provide you with some information that could be helpful in making an admission decision. Throughout elementary, junior high, and high school I was extremely successful in English and social studies courses, but from my transcript you can see that mathematics has always been difficult for me. As a junior in high school, I was tested for learning disabilities and the results indicated that I do indeed have a specific disability in the area of mathematics and computation. However, I have not deserted the math curriculum, but rather continued to take additional courses as a senior. I am receiving some accommodations of extended testing time and the use of a calculator. These accommodations are helpful and my current grade in Algebra II is a B-.

I would like to request that you review my transcript, keeping in mind that the disability was not identified until late in my high school career, and the earlier grades have been averaged into my grade point average and class rank. My current rank of 34 percent would be much higher if I removed the three years of math and the physics and chemistry courses, which also involved mathematical concepts. During those courses, I was not being accommodated. Without those courses, my class rank would rise to the 67 percent.

I thank you for your consideration of this issue. I sincerely feel that had I been accommodated earlier in my high school career my grades would have been better. I am very excited about studying at "X" University and pursuing a degree in Journalism, a major that is highly regarded at your college. I have included copies of articles I have written that have been published in various journals. I am hopeful that this information will have a positive impact on my admission decision.

7.22 – Sample Essay

"Nine Little Words Changed My Life"

As a little child, I thought it was funny that I simply could not get the dance steps in the right order. The other girls in my class would giggle as I continued to twirl while all the others were bowing. Little did I know that they were laughing at me and not with me. As I entered fifth grade, my parents could not understand why I was unable to remember to do specific chores, keep my room in order, purchase a number of items at the grocery store, or complete specific homework assignments. I was continually being "grounded," punished, kept after school, and repeatedly being given additional assignments when I couldn't even finish what was originally assigned.

I had developed a wonderful sense of humor and a great "gift of gab" that kept a number of peers and teachers on my side, but I was continually frustrated by my lack of success in school and at home. By junior high school I had begun to shut down. I refused to do homework, had constant stomachaches just before the school bus arrived, and spent an enormous amount of time in the nurse's office or with the counselor or social worker. Then suddenly, Thomas Edison's light bulb went off in someone's head and I was referred for diagnostic testing. I was thrilled. Finally, someone may be able to figure out why I always felt confusion in my brain as materials were being presented. I would just be focusing on the first point of information and the teacher would be ten concepts ahead.

The results were "manna from heaven." Nine little words said it all: "Persisting problems following/comprehending oral class presentation hampers achievement." Additionally, it was determined that I have attention deficit disorder, which results in impulsivity and distractibility, impeding success. It was determined at the multidisciplinary conference that I should be given resource assistance five days weekly to help me develop compensatory skills to assist with disorganization, focus, note-taking strategies, and time management. Additionally, I was offered extended testing time, direction clarification, and a note taker for lecture classes.

I decided to learn to use a tape recorder with a numbering system that allowed me to tape the lecture and refer to a number of the recorder that referred to a place in the lecture where I missed the words. This accommodation has allowed me to be independent and rely on my own resources for lecture notes. The extended time for tests and some class assignments has provided me with the appropriate accommodation to level the playing field and allow me to be successful on my tests and with my class assignments. I have also learned to use a planning calendar and to date have not missed an assignment.

I still have a wonderful sense of humor and gift of gab, but more important, my self-esteem has flourished. Before, I would laugh on the outside and cry on the inside; before, I would comply on the outside to punishment but scream on the inside for the unfairness; before, I would shut down and now I ask for tips, strategies, suggestions, and am the best self-advocator. I am comfortable approaching teachers and suggesting ways to help me learn the material; I am comfortable explaining my learning disabilities and attention deficit disorder; I am comfortable articulating the specifics of the disabilities. I am currently the president of the Coping Support Group and I am a mentor to others who are learning to deal with their diagnosis.

I often think about the unfairness that I have been saddled with this disability, but I also think about how much I have gained from learning to deal with frustration, stress, and setbacks. There is no way that I will be held back or held down. I am willing to take longer, work harder, say "no" to peers who want to party and play when I have work to be completed, and have the confidence that I can do anything if I have the motivation.

As you review my transcript and test scores, you will note a tremendous upward trend based on BA and AC—Before Accommodations and After Accommodations. My grades are all A's and B's; my ACT went from a 16 to a 24 composite; and my class rank has steadily improved. I keep reminding myself that class rank compares me with everyone in my class and that field is definitely not leveled. It is comparable to running a track race, but I have to run the race with one leg tied behind my back. Please consider my progress, my motivation, my true abilities as documented in my psychoeducational evaluation, and the comments from my teachers. If you really want to see progress, I invite you to visit my bedroom and see my neatly organized closet and drawers, all of my study books organized by curriculum, and the giant calendar on my wall with all of my assignments. Nine little words changed my life.

7.23 — What to Have on Hand for "Move-in" Day

- Necessary papers: financial aid forms, registration materials, personal identification, copy of medical insurance card, social security card
- Flashlight
- Different sizes of batteries
- Masking tape
- Scissors
- Solid kneaded adhesive to hang posters
- Sticky putty
- Small hammer
- Hooks
- Screwdriver
- Nails
- Thumbtacks
- Picture wire
- Extension cords/cheater plugs
- Extra light bulbs for study light
- Bottle and can opener
- Erasable memo board for door
- Bulletin board
- Grow bar (fits in closet to make two hanging shelves)
- Shoe rack
- Cardboard boxes for under bed
- Small cardboard dresser/bookshelves
- Trunk (to transport blankets, sheets, towels, etc., and then to be used as coffee table or refrigerator stand or seating, etc.)
- Clip-on lamp
- Desk lamp
- Pencil holder
- Pencil sharpener
- Study pillow
- Canvas backrest for beach or lawn
- Lap desk
- Chair (director's chair is easy to pack, comfortable and handy)
- Beach towels
- Extra pillow

- Sleeping bag
- Whistle (can be put on chain—good safety measure)
- Hangers (regular, skirt, slack, etc.)
- Wastebasket
- Bathroom rug or throw rug
- Snack foods
- Popcorn popper
- Large plastic bowl with lid
- Plastic plates, cups, mugs, silverware
- Heating coil
- Hot pot
- Knife
- Notepaper
- Laundry basket
- Laundry bag
- Iron
- Sewing kit
- Pitcher with lid
- Foil, baggies
- Bike and lock
- Lock box with small combination lock
- Shelf liner
- Drawer liner
- Cleaning supplies (rags, air spray, cleaners, etc.)
- Stereo/headphones/speakers/speaker wire
- Records
- Tape deck, tapes, disk player, VCR (if lucky enough to own these)
- TV
- Clock radio
- Another alarm clock (if you have trouble waking up)
- Gym bag
- Pail with handle (holds bathroom items)
- Boxes or jars for change or pins
- Telephone, address book

- Answering machine

- Fan

- Posters, pictures

- School supplies (less expensive from home)

- First-aid kit that includes favorite headache, sinus, and cold tablets.

- Enough stationery and stamps to carry you through the first few weeks of news or home-sickness and quarters for first loads of laundry.

- Pictures of family, pets, and friends and high school yearbook to personalize room and help new friends get to know you

- Camera to record memories and a scrapbook to keep them in

- Backpack, umbrella, duck shoes, boots and raincoat/poncho

- Sports equipment

- Computer, printer, disks

- Computer paper

- Reference books—dictionary, thesaurus, almanac, book of quotes, term paper guide, grammar book

- Plastic milk-style crates for storage

- Soap container

- Toothbrush container/cup

- Two sets of linens for bed, plus mattress pad

- Laundry lesson before leaving for school (so that white shirts don't turn pink.)

In addition:

  – Open a checking account on campus

  – Get ATM card

  – Have a physical, dental, eye exam

  – Arrange for phone installation in dorm

  – It's time to pack!

LET'S WRAP IT UP

This has been a long section, probably because the decision to attend college and the resulting move can be so confusing and potentially threatening to students and their parents. The materials in this section should ease their anxiety and promote good decision making. The more students and their parents understand the selection and application processes, the more comfortable they are with their respective roles.

For example, students who understand the organization and purposes of college entrance tests, though perhaps still anxious about them, are energized to register and prepare for them. Figure 7.24, therefore, should be shared with students at appropriate times in the junior year to inform them of the particulars of these tests and to reduce their fears by showing them how to register for nonstandardized testing.

Similarly, Figure 7.25 discusses the different admissions policies for students with learning disabilities. It, too, should be shared with juniors, probably near the end of the year, to explain college admissions processes and their impact on students with learning disabilities. Students and their parents want to understand the opportunities as well as the obstacles they will face during the college application process. The better they understand them, the better they will be able to plan for them.

Finally, Figure 7.26 answers the question, "When is college appropriate?" This is a tough question for any high school student, but it's a real puzzler for students with learning disabilities—maybe more so for their parents. Students who have struggled with the formative years of their schooling inevitably question not only their ability but their desire to attend college. Their parents want only the best for them, but they, too, wonder about the appropriateness of college for their children.

Figure 7.26 lists the very skills that have caused the biggest problems for these students and could discourage them if handled insensitively by school personnel and parents. A discussion of the items is essential, however, if students are to understand the demands of college, perfect their compensatory skills in high school, become effective self-advocates, and enter college with the same kind of drive and determination that made them successful in high school.

If a high school student is still struggling with a pronounced disability—the ability to use verbal symbols and concepts, for example—his or her junior and senior years are the time to master the strategies that will lessen the impact of the disability not only in college but during the remaining years of high school. As indicated so often in this book, the student, his or her parents, and school personnel must not allow a learning disability to remain "hidden." It must be discussed openly, and it constantly must be explored in relation to current activities and future goals.

Successful students, like great athletes, may come dangerously close to defeat—but they don't realize it. They are too focused on their goals. They are too busy overcoming their limitations and gaining self-confidence to even consider the possibility of failure. And if they do fail, they learn from the experience and, with our help, use it as a stepping stone to future success. Will Rogers once said, "Even if you're on the right track, you'll get run over if you just sit there."

Our job as special educators, counselors, teachers, and parents is to assure that our students don't just sit thre. The closer we work with them to understand and to overcome their limitations, the more college will become not only a reality but the pathway to additional success for them.

7.24 – COLLEGE ENTRANCE AND PLACEMENT TESTS

What you need to know about Admissions Tests:

The Scholastic Assessment Test: (SAT:I): Reasoning Tests of the College Board have two sections, verbal reasoning and mathematical reasoning. The verbal section emphasizes reading and the math portion emphasizes the ability to apply mathematical concepts and interpret data. Calculators are permitted for the math section and students produce and "grid-in" their own answers on ten questions. It is important to know that there is a guessing penalty for the SAT except for the ten questions in the math section requiring students to grid their own answers. In all other sections each wrong answer results in points deducted. Therefore, if students cannot make a solid educated choice on a question, they are better off leaving it blank. Scores range from 200-800 on each section with 500 as the average on both the verbal and math.

The SAT:II: Subject Tests of the College Board, required by many highly selective colleges, measure a wide variety of skills and areas of knowledge. Students may select from eighteen specific subjects in the areas of: writing, literature, foreign language, history, mathematics, science, and English as a second language. Generally students are required to take three tests and the writing test (with essay) is one of the tests recommended or requested. Students must check each college catalogue to determine the Subject Test requirements. Each test is one hour, and students take one to three Subject Tests on the same days as the administration of the SAT:I. Be very observant as to which Subject Tests are being offered and on which dates, as all Tests are not offered each time the SAT:I is offered. Scores on Subject Tests range from 200-800.

The American College Test (ACT) has four tests: English, Mathematics, Reading and Science Reasoning. Students receive twelve scaled scores on the ACT assessment including four test scores (range of scores 1-36), seven sub scores (range of scores 1-18), and a composite score (range of scores 1-36). There is no additional penalty for a wrong answer. Therefore, if time begins to run out, take ACTion and fill in the dots as quickly as possible. Some colleges will accept the ACT in place of SAT: I and II Subject Tests.

Standardized or non-standardized tests:

Standardized tests are those tests taken under normal testing conditions on national testing dates. Nonstandardized tests are tests taken with modifications such as: extended time, quiet room, reader, cassette player, large print, or scribe.

To be eligible for nonstandardized tests students must:

- have a disability that requires testing accommodations
- have documentation on file at school (IEP, 504 Plan, or evaluation by a qualified professional stating diagnosis and need for accommodation)
- be receiving accommodations in school or submit an evaluation by a qualified professional explaining reasons for accommodations

How to register for Nonstandardized tests:

- complete the regular application form
- complete a special application form
- have documentation that verifies the request
- submit special application and documentation to the testing centers
- permission for modifications is granted by ACT/SAT

7.25 – Admission Policies for Students With Learning Disabilities

Helpful Hints

- Review admission criteria: course requirements, grade point average, tests required, and minimum scores
- Identify LD services and/or programs
- Research availability of specific majors
- Be aware of course substitution policies
- Review graduation requirements from the college

Open Admissions

These colleges admit students on a rolling or continuous basis. Very often these colleges are community colleges and two-year colleges, although there are many four-year colleges that offer open enrollment. As soon as all credentials (application, transcript, test scores, other supporting data) have been received, the application is processed and a decision is usually made within six weeks. Students with documented learning disabilities are admitted automatically in the same manner as students with no disability as long as they have a high school diploma or its equivalent.

Vocational Technical Schools

These schools offer programs in various occupations. Students are trained to enter specific fields such as construction, health services, childcare, and office occupations, and the training time can vary from two weeks to two years. Students with learning disabilities are admitted in the same way as students with no disability and most of these schools have an open enrollment policy. The main criterion is the student's desire to learn a particular occupation.

Technical Institutions

These schools are usually two-year programs and are considered more challenging than the skilled trades but less demanding than the professional level. Admission can be competitive and many of the programs will have specific entrance requirements. Students with learning disabilities will need to explore these requirements and determine if they have the necessary skills required to successfully complete the program.

Trade Schools

These schools offer training in a specific trade within an occupational group. Students should have a specific interest in the trade such as truck driving or diesel mechanics. Admission is typically open enrollment.

Traditional Admission

These colleges usually have stated admission criteria utilizing class rank or grade point averages, test scores, and course requirements. Very often the criteria will be based on a sliding scale, which means that low test scores can be offset by better grades or vice versa. There may be some flexibility with a student with a documented learning disability. These colleges will either admit on a rolling basis (decisions are sent as soon as all of the information has been reviewed) or at a specific time during the admission cycle.

7.25 continued

Admission at Selective Colleges

These colleges usually admit students who have been successful in high school and have taken a challenging curriculum of college preparatory courses. These colleges will review all of the information and expect the students to have been successful in their high school courses as well as college admission tests. Although these colleges admit many students who have not taken Advanced Placement or Honors classes, these types of courses are always helpful in an admission decision. Students with learning disabilities are encouraged to self-disclose if there are deficit areas on the transcript that need explaining. Many colleges will take this information into account in making an admission decision.

Admission at Highly Selective Colleges

These colleges usually require the submission of ACT/SAT scores; Advanced Placement or Honors courses in high school courses; high class ranks and/or grade point averages; essays; recommendations; and involvement in school and community activities. Students with learning disabilities who have not taken advanced courses, do not have superior class ranks and grade point averages, and do not have high test scores, will probably have difficulty being admitted to these colleges.

Admissions at Colleges With Structured Programs

These colleges typically have a special admission process for students with learning disabilities. Usually there is a separate application for the program as well as the submission of the general college application. Students usually provide their most recent psychoeducational evaluation and any other documentation relating to the learning disability. Very often they do not place much emphasis on the ACT/SAT. The application and documentation are reviewed by the program director either independently or in conjunction with the Office of Admission and a decision is made that may utilize different criteria from those of the general applicant.

Admission at Colleges with Comprehensive Services

These colleges could be selective or less selective; however, they provide more flexibility in admission for students with documented learning disabilities. Students typically have GPAs and test scores that are near the stated criteria, but the college is willing to look at the testing, teacher comments, student personal statement, and upward trend in high school courses and grades in making an admission decision. Often the Director of Support Services is part of the Admission team.

Early Admission

This program admits students at the end of the junior year of high school. Such a program is usually reserved for truly exceptional students of proven maturity. This plan should not be confused with Early Decision or Early Action. Students with learning disabilities would do better by staying in high school for the full four years and taking as many college preparatory courses as possible.

Early Decision

Students who have done their research thoroughly, and have definitely decided on a first-choice college, may want to consider an Early Decision application. Many of the colleges whose regular reply date is April 15 offer an Early Decision (ED) plan. Students apply by November and usually receive a decision by December 15. (Some colleges offer multiple ED plans at different times during the cycle). Students not accepted ED are often reconsidered for admission during

276

the regular decision time. Students must be certain of their college choice, because colleges offering ED require withdrawal of any other applications filed if the student is accepted. Students considering Early Decision must read the college catalogue carefully to assure that they complete all the necessary tests (ACT/SAT:I or SAT:II) by the stated deadlines. Students with learning disabilities must be confident that their needs will be met at the college prior to committing to an early decision option.

Early Action

Some colleges offer an Early Action plan. The timetable is the same as for Early Decision (apply by November and receive notification by December), but the student is not required to withdraw other applications if accepted, and has until May 1 to accept or decline the offer. There are some variations on Early Decision and Early Action at different colleges. Read the literature and small print *very carefully*. Students with learning disabilities would not put themselves in jeopardy with this type of a plan, because there is no obligation to accept the offer of admission until the May 1 reply date.

Deferred Admission

Students delay enrollment for a semester or a year to earn money, travel, or pursue special educational programs. Many colleges will allow this, but it is necessary to consult with the college regarding the specifics.

Other Admissions Considerations

After reviewing school records, recommendations, testing, and motivation, the college admissions committee's first concern is whether the students can handle their academic program with success and reasonable comfort.

In the more highly competitive college, where academically qualified candidates outnumber the spaces available, the next question is which of the academically qualified applicants are admitted. A number of other admissions factors then become important:

1. *Special talents.* It is helpful to submit a tape of a musical or a debate, slides of artwork, a sample of creative writing, or evidence of exceptional athletic ability or other evidence of being special.
2. *Alumni connections.*
3. *Geographical mix.*
4. *Exceptional academic talent.*
5. *Extracurricular involvement.* In general, colleges are impressed by students who have made a significant commitment to one or two areas rather than one with superficial involvement in many areas.
6. *Diversity of backgrounds and cultures.*

A formula, based on school records and testing, is used as the basis for admission by some colleges. Usually, these are state institutions where numbers prohibit individual consideration of each applicant.

Many colleges have special admissions, probationary admissions, conditional admissions, and summer admissions. Students should consult with the admissions office or the support services office.

7.26 – Is College the Appropriate Option?

To be successful in college students should have the following:

1. *Motivation* is the key to success in college. Students with motivation have the ability to work longer and harder.

2. Good *study habits, test taking skills* and the necessary knowledge to use the resources and references on campus.

3. Strengths in *oral and written communication.*

4. Ability to *stay focused* on assignments and the *organizational skills* to keep up with the required work.

5. Ability to be a *self-advocate* and request help when needed; disclose the learning disability to the professors before classes begin; identify the modifications and accommodations that are necessary; and provide the professor with an understanding of the particular learning disability and how it impacts academics.

6. *Emotional stability.*

7. Ability to *live independently* from the family: manage checking account, be responsible for good and healthy eating habits, do own laundry, manage time, etc.

8. Ability to *interact socially* with peers.

9. Willingness to *work on assignments* and projects until they are completed.

10. *Acceptance* of the fact that college could take longer than four to five years.

11. *Computer skills.*

12. Willingness to *utilize the resources* and services provided.

13. *Realistic goals* that are consistent with strengths.

14. Ability to *deal with stress, frustration, setbacks.*

15. A good *sense of humor.*

TRANSITION PLANNING— FOCUS ON CAREERS

First, a quick story...

Moe was a high school sophomore with an undiagnosed learning disability and a grade point average with more goose eggs than Canada. To make matters worse, his learning problems were magnified by a mistrust of authority, an inability or a refusal to follow rules, and an unfocused anger that alienated him from friends, faculty—even family. His counselor suspected parental abuse, even referred him once to the Department of Children and Family Services, but the case worker could find nothing to substantiate the counselor's suspicions.

Moe was well down the road to dropping out of high school before his counselor finally overtook him. One of the few people Moe would talk to, his counselor helped him to look down the road a little further and decide if his likely destination seemed worthwhile. Predictably, more meetings revealed Moe's poor self-concept, generalized anger, and a learning problem that neither of them understood.

At that time, special education wasn't even on the drawing board in most schools, so Moe's counselor spent a great deal of time meeting with his teachers to encourage them to go above and beyond the call of duty—no easy task with a student who was likely to fight them every step of the way. Teachers and counselors don't require sophisticated diagnostic guidelines, however, to realize that something's wrong with a student's learning. Once Moe's teachers realized that a learning interference was frustrating, angering, and even immobilizing him, they worked more closely with him.

No one at that time was able to specify Moe's disability, but all his teachers eventually realized that something was wrong and that he needed help. His counselor realized that Moe would never be a high achiever in school but that they might hang on to him in school if they could find a niche somewhere in the community. Maybe a job would provide the "hook" they needed to keep Moe in school, earn a diploma, and develop the self-confidence he needed to redirect his life.

It worked. The local student hangout needed a cook, a part-timer to handle side orders. Moe's counselor called Tony, the owner, and Moe got the job. In a matter of weeks, Moe was handling much of the ordering and substituting for Tony when business or family matters took him out of the restaurant. Moe's transformation startled his teachers—even his counselor— but it was unnoticed by Tony, who didn't know Moe prior to his joining the restaurant. Tony said often that Moe was the best thing to happen to him since he opened the restaurant.

And Moe's grades improved—hardly a threat to the valedictorian and barely out of the bottom quartile of his class—but he walked across the stage on graduation day like the leading man coming out for an encore. He also kept his job with Tony for several more years. Eventually, he moved on and lost contact with his counselor and classmates.

Several years later, his counselor saw him on Christmas morning in a nearby cafe having breakfast with his family. He and his wife had three children; he was living in a nearby suburb, and managing a restaurant in downtown Chicago.

SATISFACTION OF WORK

Henry Ward Beecher once said, "In the ordinary business of life, industry can do anything which genius can do, and very many things which it cannot." Genius is a gift, often undeserved, but work and the rewards it provides are always earned. Fortunately, there is much more to life than term papers and IQ tests. Students who stumble over academic hurdles often find smoother running in the world of work, where they are more in control of their life's causes and effects.

Work, no matter when it occurs in life, can instill responsibility and be a source of great satisfaction and fulfillment. The child who regularly empties the garbage, the teenager who earns much of his college expenses, and the woman who sells stocks and bonds all benefit from the challenges and the sense of accomplishment experienced only through work. It can work occasional magic for students like Moe, and it represents a lifetime of similar experiences for millions of Americans.

For all high school students, work is sometimes a journey and, except for a few very privileged youngsters, always a destination. Few high school students find careers in part-time work after school and on weekends. Invariably, high school is a time to assess abilities and interests and to explore the world of work to find career opportunities to satisfy them. A daunting responsibility for all students, it is particularly difficult for students with learning disabilities.

It is difficult for their parents, too. They find themselves walking a fine line. Most of them realize how important it is to "keep the dream alive," to excite their children about the limitless opportunities that await them, but they also seek to protect them from the failure that results from the inability to accept their limitations. Parents often need help walking this line, especially as their children approach graduation from high school and begin planning for careers immediately or after college.

CAREERS AND TRANSITION PLANNING

Transition planning is primary for all high school students but especially for students with learning disabilities. We have already discussed transition planning as it relates to college. Figure 8.1, "Taking Action," explores the process as it relates to careers. It discusses a few of the student's responsibilities in junior high school, then identifies the more specific responsibilities for career and vocational exploration in high school.

Such responsibilities as "reassessing interests and capabilities," "identifying gaps of knowledge," "identifying skills that need to be addressed," and "identifying postsecondary institutions" are significant tasks and require the ongoing involvement of parents as well as school personnel. If these kinds of tasks are performed poorly, the success of future decisions is seriously jeopardized.

8.1 – Taking Action

All students will eventually leave school and transition to college, trade school, work, military, or other options. This transition process is part of the IEP in high school and must include a statement of the services needed by the student by the time the student is 16. The following information is from the National Information Center for Children and Youth with Disabilities (Nichcy).

In Junior High School: Start Transition Planning

- Become involved in career exploration activities.
- Visit with a school counselor to talk about interests and capabilities.
- Participate in vocational assessment activities.
- Use information about interests and capabilities to make preliminary decisions about possible careers—academic vs. vocational, or a combination.
- Make use of books, career fairs, and people in the community to find out more about careers of interest.

In High School: Define Career/Vocational Goals

- Work with school staff, family, and people and agencies in the community to define and refine transition plan. Make sure that the IEP includes transition plans.
- Identify and take high school courses that are required for entry into college, trade schools, or careers of interest.
- Identify and take vocational programs offered in high school, if a vocational career is of interest.
- Become involved in early work experiences, such as job tryouts, summer jobs, volunteering, or part-time work.
- Reassess interests and capabilities, based on real world or school experiences. Is the career field still of interest? If not, redefine goals.
- Participate in ongoing vocational assessment and identify gaps of knowledge or skills that need to be addressed. Address these gaps.

If you have decided to pursue postsecondary education and training prior to employment, consider these suggestions:

- Identify postsecondary institutions (colleges, vocational programs in the community, trade schools, etc.) that offer training in career of interest. Write or call for catalogues, financial aid information, and applications. Visit the institution.
- Identify what accommodations would be helpful to address your special needs. Find out if the educational institution makes, or can make, these accommodations.
- Identify and take any special tests (PSAT, SAT, ACT) necessary for entry into postsecondary institutions of interest.

- In your last year of secondary school, contact Vocational Rehabilitation (VR) to determine eligibility for services or benefits.

After High School: Obtain Your Goals

- If eligible for VR services, work with a VR counselor to identify and pursue additional training or to secure employment in your field of interest.

- If eligible for Social Security Administration (SSA), find out how work incentives apply to you.

- If not eligible for VR services, contact other agencies that can be of help: state employment office, social services offices, mental health departments, disability-specific organizations. What services can these agencies offer you?

- Also find out about special projects in your vicinity (Projects with Industry, Project READY, supported employment demonstration models, etc.). Determine your eligibility to participate in these training or employment programs.

- Continue to work your plan. Follow through on decisions to attend postsecondary institutions or obtain employment.

National Information Center for Children and Youth with Disabilities (NICHCY), Transition Summary, Number 7, September 1991, p. 22.

In essence, every student who expects success in the workplace—or in college, then the workplace—requires some basic skills:

♦ Students must be able to read and understand the kind of information that characterizes the nature of their jobs.

♦ They must be able to communicate in writing—letters, memos, reports, even flowcharts and diagrams.

♦ They must be active listeners, able to interpret both verbal and nonverbal cues.

♦ They must be able to use basic math.

♦ They must speak clearly and intelligently.

These skills must be complemented by the ability to:

♦ Identify problems, create or select appropriate solutions, and monitor plans of action.

♦ Develop goals and make decisions about ways to realize them.

♦ Acquire new knowledge and use sound reasoning techniques independently.

The inability of students with learning disabilities to do some of these things creates doubt and frustration, both for them and their parents. Their parents, however, must not allow their own frustrations to interfere with their ability to help their children either develop these skills or master strategies to compensate for them. In addition, parents must promote a sense of responsibility and honesty in their children and fortify their self-esteem and self-discipline. These, too, are qualities of effective workers.

Such qualities make for success not only in the workplace but in the home, school, and community. Students who realize this are well on their way to personal and vocational happiness. They also are able to work closely with parents, friends, and school personnel to assess their own strengths and weaknesses and to get help with the exploration and the ultimate selection of a desirable job. Then, they need help with the application process, even with the particulars of developing a résumé and a cover letter, choosing the right clothes, and using effective interviewing techniques.

Regarding the assessment of strengths and weaknesses and the exploration of potential jobs, the questions in Figure 8.2 help teachers, counselors, and parents establish a sense of direction for students. The questions evaluate the student's knowledge of potential careers, the nature of the academic preparation they have received, their ability to self-advocate.

If students struggle with answers to these questions, they might need to spend time working on one or more of the activities in Figure 8.3. The process used to introduce these activities or to ask the questions in Figure 8.2 must be nonthreatening and relaxed. It must involve a dialogue that explores the student's knowledge of each of these areas and encourages him or her to gain a sense of competence in gathering such information and answering such questions.

8.2 — TRANSITION PLANNING — THINKING ABOUT CAREERS

Student _____

Date _____

1. What type of work are you interested in pursuing? _____
   _____

2. Do you think you would like to be in a job that is stressful and competitive?
   _____

3. Do you think you would like to be in a job that is low keyed and relaxing?
   _____

4. What career do you see yourself pursuing? _____

5. What courses have you taken that will help you prepare for this career? _____
   _____

6. What part-time or summer jobs have you held that have provided experience for your
   career choice? _____

7. What kind of post-high school education is necessary to pursue this career?
   _____

8. Do you feel that you have the necessary skills and abilities to be successful in this career?
   _____

9. What kind of assistance do you need from your high school in pursuing your career plans?
   _____

10. Is there anything you should have done in high school to better prepare yourself for your
    future career? _____

11. What special talents do you have that are important for your future career?
    _____

12. If you plan to go directly from high school into a job, how will you begin your job search?
    _____

13. What types of accommodations will you need on the job? _____
    _____

14. What are your rights under Federal law regarding accommodations? _____
    _____

15. Are you capable of being your own self-advocate? _____
    _____

8.3—How to Identify Future Career Interests

It is important that you spend time exploring and understanding your interests and aptitudes in order to zero in on particular careers that will meet your interests, skills, and dreams. The following is a list of suggestions to help you proceed as you begin this exploration.

1. Identify the courses in school that you have enjoyed and why these have been enjoyable.

2. Identify your skills, values and interests by taking an interest inventory assessment such as the Kuder or Strong-Campbell.

3. Focus on developing skills in time management, organization, and stress management.

4. Talk with other students, friends, faculty, family, and professionals to find out about their career searches, careers, occupations.

5. Be sure to experience working with many different types of people to open your eyes to the diverse populations in our country.

6. Develop computer skills and learn word processing and spreadsheet programs.

7. Develop a list of activities, honors, interests, work experiences, and educational history that can be continually updated.

8. Develop good self-advocacy skills.

9. Work on skills that will help you manage yourself, such as loyalty, friendship, maturity, honesty, motivation, enthusiasm, flexibility, independence, dependability, confidence, and conscientiousness.

10. Work on skills that are important for all situations such as critical thinking, communicating, decision making, oral and written work, problem solving, interacting, teaming, accepting, listening, working cooperatively, scheduling, managing time, neatness, and accuracy.

11. Develop short- and long-term goals.

12. Meet with individuals in your area of interest.

13. Develop friendships with teachers, peers, current employers, and supervisors.

14. Maintain an updated résumé.

15. Request recommendations for your file.

16. Volunteer.

17. Increase your knowledge of various job settings.

18. Continue to gain new skills and education in fields of interest.

19. Read journals and books related to areas of interest.

20. Get involved in internships.

21. Go on informational interviews.

22. Attend career seminars or career fairs.

23. Write for information and research job listings in your area of interest.

24. Use the Internet to research.

25. Use electronic job and résumé banks.

26. Research in all parts of the country.

27. Network and identify organizations that can be helpful.

28. Develop cover letters for various jobs.

29. Conduct some mock interviews and tape them.

30. Read the local and national newspapers.

31. Submit résumés and cover letters.

32. Have a back-up plan.

33. Prepare a living expense budget.

34. Have an idea of the entry-level pay for the career.

35. Be patient.

Above all, students must understand that, by federal law, their disabilities may not be permitted to interfere with their right to a particular job. They must also understand, however, that they must be qualified in all other respects to perform the job successfully. That's what this section is all about—to encourage students to enhance their qualifications for particular jobs, then to understand the processes to find and to apply for them.

UNDERSTANDING THE SEARCH AND APPLICATION PROCESSES

The first step in the application process probably is the development of a résumé. Figure 8.4 lists and discusses the characteristics of a well-developed résumé. Share it with all students who are seeking employment after graduation from high school. It might even be shared with college-bound students for their future use. Be sure that they notice that the information in the résumé makes no reference to their learning disabilities. Such specific information is essentially irrelevant to application processes and ultimate employment.

Figure 8.5 provides a sample résumé and should accompany Figure 8.4. Students are much more comfortable developing their own résumés when they have models to study. In addition, the sample can provide answers to questions they may have when counselors and teachers are unavailable to them. When they have completed their résumés, they should share them with their parents and school personnel for critiquing prior to finalization.

Following the development of the résumé, the job search and application processes begin. Figure 8.6 outlines these processes from "Identifying the jobs you would like to pursue" to the steps following the actual job interview. It is a comprehensive outline of the job search process and should involve dialogue among students, parents, and school personnel. The reproducible simply outlines the steps in the search process. It must be complemented by a discussion that leads the student through the process and explains each step along the way.

THE INTERVIEWING PROCESS

The Rehabilitation Act of 1973 (RA), specifically Section 504, stipulates that "No otherwise qualified handicapped individual in the United States . . . shall, solely by reason of...handicap, be excluded from the participation in, be denied the benefits of, or be subjected to discrimination under any program or activity receiving Federal financial assistance." The Americans With Disabilities Act (ADA) further restricts employers from discriminating based on disability or handicap.

It should be mentioned to students and parents that the ADA has broader application than the RA. The RA applies to employers who receive Federal financial assistance. The ADA applies to private as well as public employers as long as they employ fifteen or more people. Parents and students must understand their rights as specified within these two statutes in order to understand what employers may or may not do not only during interviews but afterward during employment.

8.4–Developing a Résumé

Job Objective: A brief overview of the job the student is looking for and why a particular job being advertised sounds interesting.

- Describe the experience you will bring to the job.
- Describe the experience you hope to gain from the job.
- Describe skills you have that are important for this job.
- Describe previous experiences that may have prepared you for this job.

Education: This section will include information about the schools you have attended, the dates you attended, the addresses of the schools and phone numbers. You should put the latest grade and school (or college) first and go in descending order to your earliest year in school. This is the place to add any important information about honors, special reports or projects, special courses, or particular courses taken that might be important for the job.

- List the latest grade you are in with courses in progress.
- List your course grades in each of the subjects currently being taken if these grades are good.
- List any diplomas you have already received.

Work Experience: This is the section to list all previous jobs, work-study programs, or volunteer work. The most recent job should be listed first and then list past jobs with the last entry being the first job ever held. This information should include the name of the company, address, phone number, and dates of employment.

- Identify each job held and your responsibilities.
- List these jobs in descending order with the most recent job first.

Special Talents: This is a space for you to highlight important attributes and talents about yourself that you would like the employer to know. This is the one place on the application where you are able to give yourself some depth and breadth and describe abilities that might not show up anyplace else in your application or résumé.

- Identify the skills or talents and briefly describe them.
- Begin with the most important talent or skill.
- Include talents such as a photographic memory or a good voice.
- Highlight your people skills and communication skills.

Hobbies and Extracurricular Activities: This is the place to identify the things you like to do with your free time. This will provide the employer with an idea of what interests you outside of the work week.

- Include athletic interests, volunteer experiences, clubs and organizations.
- Describe the things you do with your down time such as read, listen to music, garden, build model airplanes, cook, train animals.
- Be brief.

Hours of Employment: This section should include your availability with dates you can begin and how many hours you will be able to work. If you are willing to work either part time or full time you should include this information.

- Let the employer know how flexible you are.

8.5 — Sample Résumé

Martin Bethany
202 Deerpath
Lakeside, IL 60600
847-202-1222

JOB OBJECTIVE: I am looking for a job as a teacher aide. I am currently enrolled in my second year of Child Development in high school, and I enjoy being with children and teaching them new things. My future plans are to gain experience working with children and to ultimately pursue a degree in Early Childhood Education. This job opportunity would provide invaluable experience for me and also provide supervision and guidance from a master teacher.

EDUCATION:

1994-1998   Deerpath High School
303 Deerpath
Lakeside, IL 60600
847-202-3120

Current courses for senior year include:
– Senior English
– Advanced Child Development
– Adolescent Psychology
– Nutrition
– Sociology
– Physics Survey
– Weight Lifting

WORK
EXPERIENCE:

1996-present   Kiddie Day Care
part-time   (address and phone number)
3:30-6:30
Mon.-Thurs.

Position: Assistant Teacher

Responsibilities: Responsible for after-school activities including art projects, reading, game time, and cleanup

1990-present   *Position:* Babysitter for neighbors
weekends   *Responsibilities:* In charge of three children ages 2-6 including meal time and bedtime

8.5 continued

SPECIAL TALENTS:

Artist: Awarded first place in Arts in Lakeside Competition 1995-present
Circus Master: Master of Ceremony for yearly Lakeside Circus
Thespian: Appeared in several community plays

EXTRACURRICULAR
ACTIVITIES:

Wood carving: make wood-carved vent covers
Oil painting; paint extra large murals and portraits
Reading; specifically poetry and plays
Volunteerism; volunteer weekly for church youth group; also spend
one Saturday a month at a Children's Soup Kitchen

HOURS OF
EMPLOYMENT:

Availability: August 1
Hours: Available to work any shift and request full time

REFERENCES: Upon request

8.6—FINDING AND SECURING THE RIGHT JOB

It is important to have a well-organized strategy for researching and finding a job. All aspects of the job search need to be reviewed including rejection. A good support system is very important to provide encouragement, direction, strategies, leads, and focus. The following list will provide some suggestions in helping to make the job search more manageable.

1. Highlight the various parts of the job search in priority order.

2. Determine how you will handle the disclosure of the learning disability, e.g., disclose or not disclose.

3. Identify strengths and what jobs would complement these strengths.

4. Identify the jobs that you would like to pursue.

5. Determine why you are interested in these jobs and write your thoughts down on paper.

6. Write your résumé and have it proofed and then printed.

7. Begin networking; talk to your family and friends.

8. Practice interviewing; develop questions you will ask and identify questions you may be asked.

9. Go on some informational interviews; these are interviews where you can gain some insight into the job you may be researching, but generally will not be where you would apply for a job.

10. Go to the library and research possible job opportunities using newspapers, journals, and magazines.

11. Once you identify various job opportunities, do some research on the company. Try to get some information on the company mission, the products or services being offered, any recent information that may have been printed about the company.

12. Request an application from the company and information about the interviewing process.

13. Duplicate a copy of the application; fill out the duplicated copy first and review it for mistakes or questions you may not understand. Carefully complete the actual application and have someone proof it before mailing it back to the company. Be sure to include a copy of your résumé.

14. If you do not hear from the company within a reasonable amount of time (2-3 weeks), call to verify that your materials have arrived and inquire as to when you may hear from them. Keep a record of everything you send out, date, to whom it was sent, and time and date of any conversations and with whom you speak. It might also be helpful to jot down the key points in any conversations you have.

15. Once you are called for an interview, begin preparing for the appointment:

    • Be sure you know your route to the appointment.

    • Know the name(s) of person you will be meeting and title.

    • Have copies of your résumé and samples of work if appropriate.

    • Select your interviewing outfit and make sure you are comfortable and that it is clean and ironed.

- Be sure that you have had a recent haircut, that your nails are polished or clean, shoes are polished, and that you have the right accessories selected to wear or take with you.

- Determine beforehand how you will deal with your learning disability. There are definitely times when it would be better to reserve this information for later in the process or even after being hired.

- Be sure you have thought about why this is a good job for you and how you will highlight these reasons.

16. On the day of the interview:

   - Arrive early.

   - Be sure you have all your information with you.

   - Know your social security number.

   - Make immediate eye contact with whoever greets you in the office and offer your hand and your name.

   - Be sure to give a firm handshake and repeat the person's name as you say your greeting so that you have a better chance of remembering the name.

   - Remember this is a two-way conversation; have questions to ask as well as be prepared to answer questions.

   - Be prepared for more than one person in the interview and be comfortable addressing the different people as you answer their questions.

   - Do not say negative things about past jobs or past employers, as this will leave the interviewer with concerns about what you might say about them some day.

   - Try to avoid any nervous habits you might have, like biting your fingernails or twirling your hair.

   - Always thank the interviewer for seeing you and provide information on how you can be reached.

   - If you are asked to read something and need more time, ask for the time or ask if you can read it at your leisure and get back to them with your thoughts.

   - If you are asked to take any type of on-site test, you may need to disclose your disability and ask for accommodations, if it impacts your ability to take the test.

   - Be upbeat and positive and motivated.

17. After the interview:

   - Jot down your impressions of the interview after leaving so that you have this to refer to at a later date.

   - Write a thank-you letter, and if you want the job be sure to include your interest.

   - Follow up with a phone call if you do not hear from the company.

   - Continue to look for additional job opportunities as you await a decision on this particular job.

What this means for employers is that they must be careful about the kinds of questions they may ask during the interviewing and selection processes. Figure 8.7 lists specific questions that employers may and may not ask. Share this reproducible with students to acquaint them with the information they should or should not share with employers. Also share Figure 8.8 to direct them to the appropriate federal office in the event they are discriminated against during the interviewing or hiring processes.

CONSIDERING ACCOMMODATIONS ON THE JOB

If accommodations are not required during appropriate preemployment testing situations, employees need not inform employers about the need for accommodations until such accommodations are needed. Within the provisions of the law, employees must establish that they are "otherwise qualified with or without reasonable accommodations for the job, promotion, or employment benefit being sought."

"Otherwise qualified" means simply that the employee can perform the essential functions of the job with or without reasonable accommodations. An accommodation is reasonable when it does not create undue hardship for the employer. If, for example, the accommodation were to change the nature of the task to be performed, it would create an "undue hardship" on the employer. Accommodations that do not create undue hardships for employers and that enable employees to perform their jobs more effectively must be provided.

Figure 8.9 provides examples of the kinds of accommodations that are sometimes provided in the workplace. Share this reproducible with students and parents to acquaint them with specific examples. Encourage them to review the form to identify the kinds of skills they must develop in order to benefit from one or more of these accommodations. They might also keep the form for future reference.

LET'S WRAP IT UP

Someone once said, "Most people like hard work, particularly when they're paying for it." And as a close friend used to say, "That may be funny, but it ain't no joke." Most employers want to hire perfect employees—people who understand the job, are competent, go about their tasks enthusiastically, and never complain. But perfection can be found only in commercials and occasionally in the advice we give others. Our advice to employers, therefore, is to hire the best people you can find and then do what you can to help them perform their jobs competently.

We offer similar advice to students with learning disabilities. Be the best you can be, and when your disability gets in the way, advocate on your own behalf to seek the kinds of accommodations you require to resume being the best you can be, whether in school or in the workplace. Parents, counselors, and teachers must help students work toward such growth by giving them the information and support they require to realize such success.

8.7 – QUESTIONS INTERVIEWERS MAY AND MAY NOT ASK

It is important that you know the laws about what an interviewer is allowed to ask and what questions are against the law. You must be comfortable with your rights and be able to inform an interviewer that the questions being asked may not be appropriate.

Questions interviewers may ask:

1. Your name, address, and telephone number.
2. The job that you are interested in.
3. Your skills for this particular job.
4. Your educational background.
5. Any licenses you might have.
6. Your work experience.
7. Your hobbies and extracurricular activities.
8. Your special talents.
9. How you heard about this job.
10. If you disclose the learning disability, the interviewer may inquire if you will need specific accommodations for this job, but these questions should be kept at a minimum.
11. Do you like to read and write?
12. Are you computer literate?
13. Will you be able to comply with the work schedule of the company?
14. Do you enjoy working with people or do you prefer to work on projects on your own?
15. Do you like to be in an office where a lot of activity is taking place?
16. Do you prefer to manage your own calendar or have someone else manage your appointments?
17. Do you enjoy the competitive environment?

Questions interviewers may not ask:

1. Do you take any prescription drugs?
2. Do you have a disability?
3. Have you ever been treated for drug or alcohol addiction?
4. Are there accommodations that you will need on the job? (See question 10 above.)
5. Do you have difficulty with reading, math, or memory skills?
6. Do you need to be in a quiet place to do your work?
7. Have you ever been tested for a learning disability?
8. Have you ever taken Ritalin?
9. Did you take the ACT/SAT in a nonstandardized form?
10. Did you receive special education services in high school?

8.8 – SAMPLE GRIEVANCE/COMPLAINT PROCESS AT WORK

Equal Employment Opportunity

1. "Very Best" company provides equal employment opportunities to all employees and applicants for employment without regard to marital status, race, color, religion, sex, national origin, age, or handicap. This policy applies to all terms and conditions of employment, including, but not limited to, counseling, hiring, placement, promotion, termination, layoff, recall, transfer, leaves of absence, compensation and training.

2. "Very Best" prohibits any form of unlawful harassment.

3. Improper interference with the ability of the employees to perform their expected job responsibilities is not tolerated.

4. "Very Best" maintains an equal employment opportunity policy for all applicants and employees. All qualified persons are given consideration and all employees are afforded the opportunity for advancement according to their individual abilities.

5. No opportunity for promotion, transfer, or any other benefit of employment will be diminished through discriminatory practices.

6. It is illegal and against company policies for any employee to create an intimidating, hostile, or offensive working environment by participating in racial, ethnic, religious, sex, handicap, or age harassment against any other employee or person.

Employee Resolution/Complaint Procedure Within the Workplace

1. Managers are responsible for providing discrimination-free environments.

2. Employees are responsible for respecting the rights of their co-workers.

3. Employees who experience job-related harassment or believe they have been treated in a discriminatory manner, must report the incident in writing to the Director of Human Resources.

4. The report will be investigated within two working days after it is received.

5. The investigation will be conducted by individuals not involved in the alleged harassment or discrimination.

6. Everyone involved is guaranteed complete confidentiality.

7. The Director of Human Resources will determine the validity of the report based on the evidence provided.

8. Any substantiated report will result in appropriate corrective action being taken.

9. If the report is not substantiated, the matter will be closed.

10. The employee who lodged the complaint will be advised of the results of the investigation.

11. Retaliation against any employee for filing a bona fide complaint or assisting in a complaint investigation is forbidden.

12. If it is proved that an employee is identified as providing false information regarding the past complaint, the employee may be referred to counseling for filing a false complaint or giving false information.

*Employee Resolution/Complaint Procedure Outside the Workplace**

1. The Americans With Disabilities Act provides equal opportunities for individuals with disabilities and forbids discrimination against these individuals.

2. If an employee feels that discrimination took place in the workplace and that the company did not handle the complaint fairly, the employee may file a complaint with the Equal Employment Opportunity Commission (EEOC).

3. Charges must be filed within 180 days of the discriminatory act or within 300 days in states with enforcement agencies that have been approved.

4. The EEOC may take 180 days to investigate the complaint after it has been filed.

5. The EEOC may conclude after the investigation that the complaint is unfounded or that a lawsuit should be initiated against the company or provide the employee with a letter giving the "right to sue" the company.

6. The employee has 90 days to file a lawsuit.

7. The EEOC has a referral agreement with the Office of Civil Rights which provides that the attorney general may investigate complaints, pursue compliance reviews, and initiate a lawsuit.

*Promoting Postsecondary Education for Students with Learning Disabilities, *Loring C. Brinckerhoff, Stan F. Shaw, Joan M. McGuire, 1993, Pro-Ed, Austin ,Texas, pp.48-49.*

8.9 – Ways to Provide Accommodations on the Job

Each individual has different strengths and weaknesses and accommodations that will need to be individualized. The Dale Brown article suggests several ways to provide accommodations.

Problem: An employee has difficulty reading instructions.

Suggested solutions:
- Assign a co-worker to read.
- Put written communications on voice mail.
- Have supervisors give instructions orally.
- Highlight the important information.

Problem: An employee consistently turns in reports with misspelled words and grammar errors.

Suggested solutions:
- Put spellcheck on the computer.
- Provide secretarial services.

Problem: The employee frequently makes errors in following directions.

Suggested solutions:
- Give instructions slowly and clearly in a quiet place.
- Write the instructions.
- Have the employee take notes on the instructions and have these reviewed for accuracy.
- Have employee repeat instructions to supervisor.

Problem: The employee frequently forgets procedures.

Suggested solutions:
- Put up pictures to reinforce procedures.
- Have employee use mnemonic devices and acronyms.
- Have employee draw diagrams or flowcharts.

Problem: The employee transposes numbers in math calculations.

Suggested solutions:
- Have employee say the numbers out loud and touch numbers on the calculator to be sure they are correct.
- Use a talking calculator.

Problem: Employee has difficulty with time management and deadlines.

Suggested solutions:
- Teach the employee how to use daily calendar with alert function to remind him or her of particular appointments.
- Have employee use a signal watch.
- Have employee prioritize tasks and improve management skills.

Problem: Employee has difficulty working in an open space with distractions.

Suggestion solutions:
- Provide a quiet place to work.
- Allow work to be taken home.
- Permit the use of other quiet offices or library.

LDA/Newsbrief, *May/June 1993, Dale S. Brown, Adult Issues Committee, p. 7.*

Parents and school personnel must also share their knowledge of learning disabilities with others in the community to assure that employers understand the characteristics of students with disabilities. We know, for example, that students with learning disabilities tend to be brighter than normal, more creative, and more sensitive to the needs of others. They may require accommodations at times, but they more than compensate for such trifling inconveniences with high energy levels, creative insights, supportive organizational relationships, and a powerful desire to succeed.

Once potential employers understand this, they will be far more likely to hire students with learning disabilities, and certainly to accommodate their needs once on the job. Special education personnel and counselors are encouraged, therefore, to meet with community and fraternal organizations to share their knowledge of learning disabilities in order to impress on the business world the benefits of hiring students who are so disabled.

Let us close this section with one last quote. "Let me tell you the secret that has led me to my goal. My strength lies solely in my tenacity." The source of the quote is French chemist Louis Pasteur, a man who succeeded as much in his field as anyone in history. In his youth, he learned the value of hard work and, through his life and accomplishments, convinced the world that his tenacity benefited others as well as himself. He, too, suffered a learning disability.

LEARNING DISABILITIES AND THE LAW

First, a quick story...

Phyllis had problems almost from the moment she started school. Happy and well adjusted as a preschooler, she started kindergarten with the usual trepidation but soon developed a relationship with her teacher, made friends, and enjoyed most of the daily activities. First grade provoked a problem or two. It became evident to her teacher, even to a few classmates, that Phyllis struggled with numbers and letters. Her mother noticed the same thing at home.

As the years passed, Phyllis enjoyed school less and less. She talked to classmates a little too often, disregarded assignments, and got into fights on the playground. Her father reacted by grounding her and taking away her allowance, her mother by meeting with teachers to try to revive Phyllis's love of school. Nothing worked. When her mother requested testing to determine the specifics of her problem, teachers insisted that Phyllis was a slow learner. When she became angry at the school's intransigence, the counselor and school principal attributed Phyllis's behavioral problems to poor parenting.

Held back twice during her first seven years of school, Phyllis finally received tutoring in a special program for limited learners. She really liked one of the tutors, a local mother with some special education background. The teacher did more to improve her self-esteem than her understanding of fractions, but her grades improved, and the teacher insisted to the school that she be tested for a learning disability.

Testing in eighth grade revealed a possible learning disability. Nothing was conclusive because Phyllis's intelligence test results were slightly below average, but the school documented a discrepancy between Phyllis's verbal IQ and her achievement in reading and English. One of the testers indicated that Phyllis had problems with expressive language and that writing would be difficult for her throughout school. The committee failed to recommend special education placement, but they did suggest increased involvement in the tutoring program.

Phyllis graduated from elementary school, still ineligible for special education services, entered high school as a 16-year-old freshman, and immediately began failing English and social studies. Her high school counselor called Phyllis's mother to discuss Phyllis's report card and to request more information about her educational background. The counselor also suggested a meeting in order to discuss Phyllis's special program in junior high school and to develop a "plan of attack" for the remainder of the semester.

After months of phone calls to her former school and a discussion with her elementary school tutor, Phyllis's counselor referred her for a screening. The screening committee reviewed the available information, met with Phyllis's mother, secured permission to request the testing information from elementary school, and finally recommended a diagnostic evaluation with the school psychologist.

Phyllis's problems with expressive language were rediscovered by the school psychologist, and she was declared eligible for special education. During the final meeting to declare her eligible and to secure parent permission for placement, Phyllis's mother was informed of her legal rights, was given a few handouts, and responded to the committee by simply shaking her head. When asked if something was wrong, she responded simply: "Where were you guys seven years ago when we really needed you?"

INFORMING PARENTS

How many parents find themselves in similar situations? Even if the child is receiving services, how many are aware of their rights when they find their children "included" in regular education classes? For that matter, how many teachers are aware of their rights when they suddenly discover students with learning disabilities on their class lists? Some teachers may find as many as five to ten students with learning disabilities in each of their classrooms at the beginning of the year.

How many of them realize that they have a right to participate in the IEP process to assure that they receive the proper training or assistance, to make adjustments in the curriculum, and to provide the special instruction such students require? Conversely, how many receive administrative support in the form of free time or substitute teachers to accommodate the time demands of the many IEP meetings they will be expected to attend?

How many parents and teachers realize that schools are in violation of the law if an IEP, which includes reference to placement in mainstreamed classes, fails to provide reasonable benefit to the student? Certainly, parents and teachers recognize that the services provided students may vary from year to year, depending on the child's emotional, social, and educational progress. They also deserve to know, however, that the only reasonable—and legal—reason for a change in services must relate to the child's needs, not to adjusted school policies.

UNDERSTANDING SPECIFIC RIGHTS

Eligibility or ineligibility for special education or inclusion in regular education classes must result from the diagnostic and IEP processes. A parent who seeks adjustments in the child's educational program should notify the school of the requests in writing. Then, parents must know that they have the right—as appropriate—to all of the following:

◆ Diagnostic assessments to be made by the school at no expense to them.

◆ Notification of school decisions and the opportunity to provide consent before such assessments occur.

◆ Reviews of their child's official school records.

◆ Examinations of the results of assessments and appropriate explanations.

◆ Requests for reassessments.

If the school refuses to make adjustments by providing such services, the school must, by law, outline six different bits of information. They must explain:

◆ Exactly what they are unwilling to do.

◆ Their reasons for not wanting to do it.

◆ Any alternatives they discussed.

- ◆ If they rejected the alternatives, why they rejected them.
- ◆ The documentation they used to make their decisions.
- ◆ Other issues that might apply.

Adjustments in the student's educational program might range from requests for diagnostic testing to placement in special education to inclusion in mainstreamed classes. Parent concerns regarding any of these issues should be addressed in writing to the school, and responses from the school should be considered carefully before additional dialogue is requested. If further dialogue seems warranted, particularly if it might be adversarial, parents should be prepared to engage in due process procedures if the school continues to reject requests.

WHEN PLACEMENT IS A CONSIDERATION

When parental requests for adjustments are accommodated by the school and the student is declared eligible for special education placement, parents have additional rights. They must by law:

- ◆ Receive a copy of the Individualized Education Program (IEP) that will be in effect thirty days after their child is declared eligible.
- ◆ Be invited to attend all meetings that relate to the IEP.
- ◆ Be accompanied by an interpreter if they are hearing impaired or speak a language other than English.
- ◆ Give permission for the actual placement.
- ◆ Request new testing if the child's needs seem to change.
- ◆ Be informed of the child's progress in school.

Most of these procedural guidelines resulted from federal legislation designed to protect individuals with disabilities. Figure 9.1 provides a reproducible that explains the specifics of Section 504 of the Rehabilitation Act of 1973. It is appropriate for faculty in-service training activities, distribution to parents, or inclusion in handbooks for teachers in the special education department. The same is true of Figure 9.2, which explains a few of the specifics of the Individuals With Disabilities Act (IDEA), commonly known as PL 94-142.

Discussion of the child's progress in school also involves decisions to include him or her in mainstreamed classes. School personnel and parents must recognize that, based on these federal statutes, the burden of proof is on the school to provide services that are designed to benefit the student. For example, one woman recently objected to her son's placement in mainstreamed classes and was told by the school that she had to prove that the placement wasn't working. The reverse is true. The school had to prove that the placement *was* working—and then document it—or make changes that met the needs of the student.

9.1 – SECTION 504 OF THE REHABILITATION ACT OF 1973

No otherwise qualified individual with disabilities in the United States . . . shall, solely by reason of his/her disability, be excluded from the participation in, be denied the benefits of, or be subjected to discrimination under any program or activity receiving federal financial assistance

- It is a civil rights statute created to prevent discrimination against people with disabilities.

- Regulations apply to preschool, elementary, secondary, and adult education programs and activities that receive Federal financial assistance.

- Students are considered disabled if they: have a physical or mental impairment that substantially limits one or more major activity; have a record of such an impairment; or are regarded as having such an impairment.

- Students are considered "otherwise qualified" if they meet the academic and technical standards necessary for admission or participation in an institution's program or activity.

- An individual with a disability is a person who has a physical or mental impairment that *substantially limits a major life activity* such as: walking, learning, hearing, seeing, speaking, breathing, working, caring for oneself, performing manual tasks.

- Disabling conditions can include: emotional disturbances, learning disabilities, AIDS, past alcohol or drug addiction, cancer, environmental illness, attention deficit disorder, diabetes, asthma, physical disabilities, behavior disorders, mental retardation.

9.2 – INDIVIDUALS WITH DISABILITIES EDUCATION ACT (IDEA)

PL 94-142, The Education for All Handicapped Children Act

A free, appropriate public education for all handicapped children in the United States, 3 to 21 years of age, is required by federal legislation (PL 92-142). The education must be provided at public expense, either in a public school or a private or state school setting as determined by your child's needs.

- An education is a civil right.

- Students are eligible for special education services if they are: hearing impaired, learning disabled, speech/language impaired, sight impaired, mentally impaired, educationally impaired, behavior disordered, multihandicapped, health impaired, physically impaired.

- Public schools are responsible for identifying students with disabilities.

- Public schools must provide all necessary assessments to identify the disability.

- Special education services must be provided for the needs of every student with a handicap.

- Special education services must be agreed upon at a multidisciplinary conference.

- Special education services must be described in an Individualized Education Plan (IEP).

- Public schools must monitor the provision of special education services.

- Appendix C of PL 94-142: "The IEP meeting serves as a communication vehicle between parents and school personnel, and enables them, as equal participants, to jointly decide upon what the child's needs are, what will be provided, and what the anticipated outcomes may be."

- Students in need of special education services are entitled to the appropriate education regardless if the disability is mild or severe.

- The law requires that the education be appropriate and in the least restrictive environment.

- Local Education Authorities and State Education Authorities must provide services to students with attention deficit disorder. These students can be serviced under categories such as "specific learning disabilities," "other health impaired," and "seriously emotionally disturbed," if the student meets the necessary criteria.

Similarly, another mother indicated that her son, early in the school year, had adjusted successfully to placement in a mainstreamed class, primarily because the teacher was able to provide a great deal of individual help. The inclusion of another student with severe behavioral problems, however, altered the atmosphere in the classroom so dramatically that the former student was unable to receive the individualized help he required and had come to expect.

The mother had the right to request another meeting to determine the status of her child's IEP goals. The purposes of mainstreamed placement probably were still appropriate; the conditions for accomplishing them, however, had changed. Because of this change, the original mainstreamed placement was no longer appropriate, and adjustments had to be considered.

Figure 9.3 further explains parents' rights regarding the implementation of Section 504 of the Rehabilitation Act. It provides additional distinctions between Section 504 and PL 94-142. The reproducible is appropriate for teachers, counselors, and administrators as well as parents and special education personnel. Finally, Figure 9.4 explains some of the characteristics of the Americans With Disabilities Act (ADA). It is particularly important for parents and school personnel because of its explanations of enforcement guidelines.

TAKING ANOTHER LOOK AT STUDENT RIGHTS

Parents must be aware of the procedural safeguards that protect the individual rights of their children. The intransigence of some schools requires that parents understand processes for securing needed adjustments in a child's educational program. Sometimes, however, the reverse is true. The intransigence of some parents requires that schools understand the processes for securing the same adjustments.

Parents resist a child's placement in special education for a variety of reasons. Some are unable to admit that the child is somehow "different" from other children. Some fear the label "special education" that accompanies them and their children throughout the school and community. Some are justifiably concerned about the absence of positive role models in many of their children's special education classes. Many are concerned about the educational quality of special education placement, especially as it relates to college admission.

We have enumerated many of these fears elsewhere in this book. We need not go into them again here. The important thing is that schools—and parents—understand that everyone shares the responsibility of safeguarding the individual rights of students. Share Figure 9.5 with administrators, special education personnel, counselors, teachers, and parents, therefore, to inform them of the due process considerations that enable schools as well as parents to provide appropriate placement for students who may have learning disabilities.

9.3 – Public Schools and Section 504 of the Rehabilitation Act

- Section 504 is much broader in scope than IDEA.

- Students are not required to be in need of special education in order to be protected by 504.

- Section 504 requires notification, but no consent is required prior to an initial evaluation.

- Protects the civil and constitutional rights of students with disabilities.

- Prohibits institutions receiving federal funds from discriminating against "otherwise qualified" individuals solely on the basis of the disability.

- Public schools must address the needs of students considered "handicapped."

- Public schools must identify and serve students who are not receiving a public education.

- Students cannot be denied the right to participate in a program or benefit from a service that is offered to students who do not have any disabilities.

- Students with disabilities must be given services that will offer them an equal opportunity.

- Section 504 requires a written plan for placement and services.

- Decisions for placement must be made by people who know the student, understand the evaluation information, and are knowledgeable about the placement options.

- Students with disabilities cannot be forced to accept different services from those being offered to nondisabled students unless these services are necessary to be effective for the students.

- School must advise parents of their rights under federal law.

- Parents must be given notice as to the identification, evaluation or placement of their student.

- Parents have the right to examine all student records and receive copies.

- Pubic school must provide written assurance of nondiscrimination.

- Public schools must have a compliance coordinator.

- Public schools must provide a procedure for resolving complaints.

- Section 504 does not provide additional funds to the schools.

9.4 – The Americans With Disabilities Act (ADA)

- This act protects the rights of individuals with disabilities.

- The act prohibits discrimination on the basis of disability in employment, activities of state and local governments, public and private transportation, public accommodations, and telecommunications.

- This law mandates that these individuals have a right to participate in the mainstream of life.

- The Rehabilitation Act is an affirmative action law, but does not have guidelines for enforcement. The ADA does have enforcement guidelines.

- The ADA has five sections:

  Title I: Employment. Any employer with fifteen or more employees may not discriminate against an individual with a disability in hiring, promoting, providing benefits, or any activity related to employment, if the individual is qualified to perform the responsibilities of the job, with or without accommodations.

  Title II: Public Services, including state and local government transportation. This title is divided into Subparts A and B. Subpart A requires programs from the state and local government to be accessible to individuals with disabilities; it also requires institutions covered under #504 to undertake a self-evaluation plan to identify programs that are not accessible to individuals with disabilities and to set a time line for correcting this problem. Subpart B requires that buses and other vehicles leased or purchased be made accessible to individuals with disabilities.

  Title III: Accommodations in Pubic Facilities. All facilities must be made accessible to individuals with disabilities, or alternative locations must be made available to allow for full participation. Any new construction or alterations must include accessibility.

  Title IV: Telecommunications. Services must be available for individuals who are hearing or sight impaired.

  Title V: Miscellaneous Provision. Protects individuals with disabilities from the ADA's limiting or voiding other federal or state laws that provide similar or better protection for their rights.

9.5 – Due Process

PARENT'S ROLE	SCHOOL'S ROLE
1. May request referral for evaluation	May recommend evaluation
2. Must sign consent form for evaluation	Need parent signature for evaluation
3. Must sign consent for placement	Need parent signature for placement
4. May refuse to sign consent	May initiate a due process hearing to compel consent for evaluation and placement
5. May appeal decision of hearing officer	May evaluate without consent if hearing officer upholds the district, subject to parent appeal
6. Parent consent due in 10 days	May request due process hearing if no parent consent in 10 days
7. Right to an independent educational evaluation at public expense	May initiate a due process hearing to demonstrate evaluation is appropriate
8. If evaluation is appropriate, may still have independent educational evaluation at parent expense	Results must be considered by district in any decision
9. May initiate Level I due process hearing	May initiate Level I due process hearing
10. Make request in writing	Contact state board of education within five days
11. Select their choice for hearing officer	Select a choice for hearing officer
12. Have right to strike first name off list of hearing officers	State Board of Ed selects hearing officer
13. Final hearing decision within 45 days	Final decision within 45 days
14. May appeal within 30 days after decision	May appeal within 30 days after decision
15. May request a Level II review	May request a Level II review
16. May be advised by counsel	May be advised by counsel
17. May present evidence, confront, cross examine, and request attendance of witness	May present evidence, confront, cross examine, and request attendance of witness
18. Prohibit evidence that has not been disclosed at least 5 days prior to hearing	Prohibit evidence that has not been disclosed at least 5 days prior to hearing

	PARENT'S ROLE	SCHOOL'S ROLE
19.	Have record of the hearing	Have record of the hearing
20.	Have written findings of fact and decisions	Have written findings of fact and decisions
21.	Parents may bring the child to the hearing	May not refuse to have child at the hearing
22.	Set hearing for a convenient time	Allow parent to pick convenient time for hearing
23.	Receive a Level II decision	Receive a Level II decision
24.	May appeal Level II decision and bring a civil action in State & Federal court	May appeal Level II decision and bring a civil action in State & Federal court
25.	Child has right to remain in present placement until case is settled	Must allow child to remain in present placement until case is settled
26.	Right to review and inspect educational records	Must allow parents to review records
27.	May request that records be amended if information is inaccurate	Must respond to request to amend if information considered inaccurate by the parents
28.	May request hearing if district refuses to amend the records	Have 15 days to amend or refuse to amend the record—must defend refusal
29.	Must be informed of decision regarding amending the record, and this explanation remains part of the record	Must inform parents of decision and keep decision as part of record

REVISITING THE QUESTION OF ACCOMMODATIONS

Each of the statutes discussed thus far is designed to provide equality for individuals with disabilities. We discussed accommodations at some length in Section 4, Figures 4.14a & b and 4.15. Share these with students, parents, counselors, and teachers to inform them of the wide variety of accommodations that satisfy the expectations of federal statutes and that promote success for students who are placed in regular or special education classrooms.

Figure 9.6 explains to students, parents, and others the effects of Section 504 and ADA on the obligations of colleges and universities. College-bound students and their parents should be familiar with these obligations and should review them prior to interviews with college personnel or when filling out applications. An awareness of these obligations will enable them to avoid answering questions or volunteering information that may hurt their chances for admission.

It's also important that students and parents understand what colleges and universities are *not* required to do. As most of us have learned over the years, elementary and secondary schools are more flexible than colleges and universities.

Universities maintain the demands of their admissions standards and assure the integrity of their curricula and educational processes in order to challenge the intellectually best among us—not only to learn what is currently important but to generate new knowledge and to compel society to look at the world differently. Students accepted for admission must have the intellectual ability and training to compete successfully with other inquisitive, competent, and intellectually aggressive students.

To lower admissions standards for students with learning disabilities might permit more of them to enter college, but it would not help them compete successfully within such an academically challenging environment. In fact, if such students had not mastered academic fundamentals or developed the compensatory skills that would enable them to function successfully on the college level, they would probably reexperience the frustration and anger that characterized much of their lives as children.

Similarly, if universities "watered down" their curricula to accommodate students who, because of disability or incapacity, were unable to compete successfully, the fundamental purposes of universities would be changed to the point where they no longer would be able to realize their essential function. Admissions requirements and academic integrity, therefore, are important considerations and must be communicated to students and parents so that students not only choose college for the right reasons but enter college with an understanding of the challenges awaiting them.

Figure 9.7 lists what colleges and universities are not required to do, and provides important information for students and parents who are engaged in the college search and application processes. Discuss the information with the family to assure their understanding of each item. College expectations and requirements are substantively different from those of high school. To the extent that we help students and parents understand these differences, we enable them to plan more realistically for the future and, eventually, to realize their goals.

9.6 – College or University Obligations Under 504/ADA

- Institutions cannot discriminate against a person solely on the basis of a disability.
- Individuals cannot be discriminated against in college recruitment, admission, and treatment after admission to a college.
- Colleges and universities are required to make reasonable accommodations to allow students with disabilities to fulfill academic requirements.
- Accommodations must be individualized.
- Institutions must make modifications "as are necessary" to ensure that academic requirements are not discriminatory.
- Modifications may include extension of time to complete assignments, course substitution of specific courses required for completion of degrees, and modifications in instruction of courses.
- Academic requirements that are essential to a program of study or required for licensing are not considered discriminatory.
- Institutions may not make preadmission inquiries about a student's disability.
- Institutions may not use admission tests or criteria if special provisions were necessary and were not offered.
- Institutions may not limit the number of students with disabilities admitted to the college.
- Institutions may not limit the number of students majoring in specific areas based on a disability.
- Institutions may not prohibit a student with a disability from pursuing a specific course of study.
- Institutions cannot limit eligibility for financial assistance or scholarships based on a disability.
- Institutions are required to inform students of services, academic adjustments, and the name of the 504 coordinator.
- Colleges may not charge students for necessary accommodations.
- The law requires that part-time students with disabilities must have equal access to financial aid, academic programs, and services.
- The law protects students from harassment or retaliation.
- Colleges must provide written information on how to access services or request accommodations.
- Colleges covered by Section 504 must have a 504 coordinator.
- Colleges covered by ADA Title II must have a designated ADA coordinator responsible for coordinating compliance efforts.
- Colleges must have written procedures established for handling complaints.

9.7 – What Colleges Are Not Required to Do

- Colleges do not have to provide readers for personal use or study.

- Colleges do not have to provide any special tutorial services other than what is provided for the general student population.

- Students cannot demand specific auxiliary aids as long as colleges provide methods of assistance that allow for equal opportunity.

- Colleges do not have to provide academic adjustments if these adjustments would *fundamentally alter* the nature of the course or program of study.

- Colleges do not have to design special academic programs.

- Colleges do not have to provide course substitutions when the academic requirements are essential to a program of study or necessary to meet licensing prerequisites.

- Colleges do not have to provide academic adjustments if this would place an *undue burden* on the institution.

- Colleges are not required to lower admission criteria for applicants with disabilities.

WHAT ARE REASONABLE ACCOMMODATIONS IN COLLEGE?

Accommodations in college are not much different from accommodations in elementary and secondary school. They are implements that level the playing field and promote equal competition for everyone. History narrates countless stories of some people being "more equal" than others. Such was the case in this country until relatively recently for many students with learning disabilities. Unfortunately, inequality is still a reality for others—for some who fail to receive appropriate educational services and for many others who still experience the effects of society's disregard.

Figure 9.8 lists a variety of accommodations that assure equality of opportunity for students with learning disabilities. None of these accommodations compromises the integrity of the college's curriculum or the instructional techniques of professors. Each of them makes life easier for students only to the extent that they do not have to combat the limitations of their learning disabilities while they meet the challenges of the college classroom.

That students understand their disabilities and inform professors and other university personnel of their learning needs is essential if they hope to maintain the "level playing field" that is so important for academic success. Share the information in Figure 9.8 with all college-bound seniors and discuss it sometime prior to graduation. Such a discussion probably should be part of a meeting with the student and his or her parents near the end of the school year.

Such a meeting is also an excellent time to share the information in Figure 9.9. A knowledge of one's learning disability and of the kinds of accommodations needed is useless unless the student shares it with admissions personnel and, after matriculation, with instructors. Students who require accommodations during the admissions and instructional processes must provide appropriate documentation of the disability, its effects on learning, and the specific accommodations needed to compensate for it. Such documentation, including testing results, should be no more than three years old.

Finally, Figure 9.10 provides a list of resources and references that detail federal legislation and discuss ways for the school to provide, and for parents to secure, the rights guaranteed by this legislation. In addition to this book, one or more of these references might be helpful to parents and school personnel who desire additional information about legislation or who have questions regarding specific legal issues.

CHECKING FOR UNDERSTANDING

Checking for understanding has been an integral part of lesson design ever since Madeline Hunter, one of education's most prominent theorists, emphasized the need for teachers to include in lesson planning a way to determine student understanding of the material. Fortunately, she convinced most educators that students don't automatically understand everything teachers say in the classroom. Occasionally, we have to check their levels of understanding and either transition to more sophisticated concepts or reteach the original material.

9.8—REASONABLE ACCOMMODATIONS IN COLLEGE

- Additional time to complete tests, assignments, and coursework.

- Substitution of nonessential courses for degree requirements.

- Modification of course instruction such as extended time for assignments, availability of instructor's lecture notes, and papers in place of exams.

- Test modifications such as extended time, oral exam, taped exam.

- Use of tape recorders in lectures/classes.

- Use of computers/calculators in exams.

- Use of Spellcheck/Grammarcheck.

- Assistance with finding a note taker.

- A quiet place to take exams.

- Allowing students to clarify questions before answering.

- Providing alternative test formats to computer-scored answer sheets.

- Providing students with information on how to access tutors.

- Providing taped texts.

- Providing readers for exams.

- Rewording questions on exams.

9.9 — STUDENT OBLIGATIONS TO COLLEGES

- Be cognizant of the learning disability; be able to articulate it; identify areas of strength and challenge; provide suggestions on appropriate accommodations.

- Be organized in plans for transitioning to college; be aware of financial needs; be prepared to schedule time for studies; arrange for housing and transportation to college.

- Students who want to have their disability considered during the admission process must disclose the disability and document why it is an important factor in the admission decision.

- College students must disclose the disability and provide appropriate documentation if requesting services.

- Documentation should be within the last three years.

- Documentation should state that a disability exists, how it impacts on the student, and what accommodations are necessary.

- A student must show that he or she is otherwise qualified to take a course of study, and that a "reasonable accommodation" would allow the student appropriate opportunities for success.

- Communicate with the disabilities support staff prior to beginning college; identify needs.

- Students must request services and accommodations.

- Meet often with the disabilities support staff on the college campus; be consistent with these contacts and know what accommodations will still be needed.

- Communicate with instructors; self-disclose; identify the accommodations necessary; become familiar with the instructor's procedures and policies for receiving accommodations.

9.10 – Resources and References

- The United States Constitution, 14th Amendment

- The Individuals With Disabilities Education Act (IDEA)

- Public Law 94-142, The Education for All Handicapped Children Act

- Section 504 of the Rehabilitation Act of 1973

- Public Law 89-313, Title I, State-Operated Programs for Handicapped Children

- The United States Family Educational Rights and Privacy Act of 1974

- Public Law 99-372, The Handicapped Children's Protection Act

- *A Guide to Section 504: How It Applies to Students With Learning Disabilities and ADHD,* Learning Disabilities Association of America, 4156 Library Rd., Pittsburgh, PA 15234

- *Advocacy Manual: A Parents' How-to Guide for Special Education Services,* Learning Association of America, 4156 Library Rd., Pittsburgh, PA 15234

- *"The Civil Rights of Students With Hidden Disabilities Under Section 504 of The Rehabilitation Act of 1973."* US Department of Education, Office of Civil Rights, Washington, DC 20202-1328

- *Legal Considerations for Serving Students With Learning Disabilities in Institutions of Higher Education,* by Jeanne M. Kincaid, Esq., 101 Varney Road, Center Barnstead, NH 03225

- *National Center for Learning Disabilities,* 381 Park Avenue South, Suite 1420, NY, NY 10016

- *Federation for Children With Special Needs,* Technical Assistance for Parents Programs, 95 Berkley Street, Suite 104, Boston, MA 02116

- National Information Center for Children and Youth with Disabilities (NICHY), 1233 20th Street NW, Suite 504, Washington DC 20036

The same is true of parents and school personnel. School personnel are required by law to provide appropriate services to students with learning disabilities. A neglect of these responsibilities can result in unnecessary frustration and failure for students and their parents and in legal reprisals—sometimes resulting in shocking sums of money—for the school. The better teachers, counselors, and administrators understand the school's responsibilities, the more likely the school will not only avoid lawsuits but satisfy the needs of a very special segment of its student population.

Similarly, parents must understand their rights regarding special education procedures and services. The parents of students with learning disabilities must know how to secure services in elementary and secondary school and to assure fair treatment when applying to, and competing in, a college or university. Share the quiz in Figure 9.11, then, with parents and school personnel to check their understanding of the rights and responsibilities of students with learning disabilities.

Schools are bound by a natural contract with the communities they serve. A friend once told us that a contract is a legal agreement in which the big type gives you something and the small type takes it away. That may be true with business, but it cannot be true in education. Locke and Rousseau told us decades ago that the social contract we share in a democracy is essential if rights are to be guaranteed and a sense of fair play is to prevail.

Assuring that parents and teachers understand the legal responsibilities of schools and colleges, therefore, does not give parents ammunition they can use in future courtroom battles with the school system. Instead, it guarantees that we all are playing by the rules and that everyone has the same opportunities not only for more enjoyment but for more success. Use the quiz in large-group meetings with the entire staff or during departmental meetings to kick off discussions of federal legislation and student/parent rights.

You might also share it with students and parents to determine their understanding of federal and state legislation and to shape their expectations of such specifics as IEPs, multidisciplinary conferences, tutorial services in college, and the college application process. Notice that the second part of Figure 9.11 provides an explanation of the answers.

LET'S WRAP IT UP

The legal system in this country has affected the direction and purposes of education perhaps more than any other social institution. From *Brown* vs. *Topeka* to the scores of court decisions upholding Title IX and Public Law 94-142, the courts have consistently promoted equal opportunity for individuals in this country to realize the American dream. This section has discussed much of the legislation that has guaranteed equal educational and employment opportunities for persons with learning and other disabilities.

As complex as these laws may seem to some of us and as difficult as they may be to implement, they are, in large part, all that stands between a child with learning disabilities and a future dotted with frustration and failure. That school personnel and parents understand the purposes and processes of these laws is essential if students with learning disabilities are to receive the services and the accommodations they require to realize success in elementary and secondary school, and in college.

9.11a—Quiz On IDEA/504/ADA

1. Special education services are required for a student with a disability who lives at home.
   T   F

2. Services for public school students can be provided in a regular classroom setting.
   T   F

3. Prior to any placement in any special education program, the student must be provided with an Individualized Education Plan.
   T   F

4. Once a student has been referred for a comprehensive case study evaluation, the school may take as long as needed to complete the evaluation.
   T   F

5. State and federal laws through 1997 require that all students with handicaps be reevaluated every three years.
   T   F

6. Parents are not allowed to attend the multidisciplinary conference being held on behalf of their student.
   T   F

7. Placement must be in the most restrictive environment.
   T   F

8. An IEP is good for all four years in high school.
   T   F

9. Parents may not challenge the contents of the student record.
   T   F

10. No information in a student's record can be released without parent's written permission.
    T   F

11. The Handicapped Children's Protection Act of 1986 provides for the payment of all legal fees by the child's family.
    T   F

12. Colleges are obligated to test and identify students who may have a learning disability.
    T   F

13. Students do not have a fundamental right to course alterations in college.
    T   F

14. Students may be denied admission to college solely based on having a disability.
    T   F

15. Colleges must develop an IEP for all students identified as learning disabled.
    T   F

16. Attention deficit disorder is considered a disabling condition.
    T   F

17. Colleges may deny students with disabilities the right to participate in certain courses in college.
    T   F

18. Students are responsible for self-identifying the existence of a learning disability.
    T   F

19. Colleges are not required to provide tutorial services specifically for students with learning disabilities.
    T   F

20. Colleges may charge students for necessary accommodations.
    T   F

21. Colleges are required to provide academic adjustments that would fundamentally alter the nature of a program of study.
    T   F

22. Colleges may inquire on the application for admission about the existence of a learning disability.
    T   F

23. Colleges that offer specific programs for students with learning disabilities may ask students to voluntarily disclose.
    T   F

24. Students taking college entrance tests under nonstandardized conditions may be questioned about this.
    T   F

25. Colleges are under no obligation to waive the math or foreign language requirement for graduation.
    T   F

26. A public high school has no obligation to provide services for students who are over the age of 18.
    T   F

27. A college must provide services and accommodations to students who may have been identified while enrolled in elementary school.
    T   F

28. Colleges may limit the number of students admitted with learning disabilities.
    T   F

29. College professors may deny accommodations to students with documented learning disabilities.
    T   F

30. Students must provide recent documentation in order to receive accommodations in college.
    T   F

9.11b—Answers to Quiz on IDEA/504/ADA

1. ___TRUE: Special education services are required for students with a disability if they live at home or in a group home; if they live in a state institution; if they live in a private school with a residential program; if they attend a public school; if they attend a private or parochial school; if they are in a hospital; if they are home due to a handicap; or if they are placed in a private school by a state agency.

2. ___TRUE: Services can be provided in a regular class setting in a public school with resource services; in a special classroom setting in a public school; in a special education program in a private day school or residential program; or in a special education program in a state residential facility.

3. ___TRUE: Prior to placement in any special education program, students must be identified, referred, evaluated, determined eligible, and provided with an Individualized Education Plan.

4. ___FALSE: Once a student has been referred for a comprehensive case study evaluation, the local school district has 60 days to complete the evaluation and schedule a multidisciplinary conference.

5. ___TRUE: State and federal law through 1997 requires that students with handicaps be reevaluated every 3 years, or more frequently if warranted or requested by parent or teacher.

6. ___FALSE: When the case study evaluation has been completed, the school district will schedule a conference. Individuals invited to the conference are parents, the student, a representative of the local school district, the director of special education or a representative, any school personnel who evaluated the student, individuals who may provide services to the student, anyone having significant information about the student, others invited to attend by the district or the parents.

7. ___FALSE: Placement must be in the least restrictive environment. Placement may be in a variety of settings from least restrictive to most restrictive including: regular classroom setting with no accommodations; regular classroom setting with accommodations; regular classroom setting with supplemental instructional services; some special education classes; all special education classes; special day school; or homebound instruction in a hospital, residential, or total care setting.

8. ___FALSE: An IEP cannot be developed for longer than one calendar year. Prior to the end of the year of the current IEP, or sooner, another conference will be scheduled for an Annual Review. The Annual Review is used to review the educational status of the student and to review the IEP.

9. ___FALSE: Parents have the right to challenge the contents of the record (excluding grades), and may ask for a correction or deletion of any information that is incorrect, misleading, or inappropriate.

10. ___TRUE: No information can be released from a student's record without written permission from the parents or the student if over 18 years old. The exceptions to this rule include information released to: parents or designated representative; employees or officials of the school or school district or State Board of Education; official registrar at another school with student request; a court order; emergency to protect health or safety of student; specifically required by state or federal law; or information classified as "directory information."

11. ___FALSE: The Handicapped Children's Protection Act of 1986 provides for the recovery of attorney fees. Parents may request reasonable attorney fees with some limitations.

12. ___FALSE: Colleges are not required by law to test or identify students with learning disabilities or suspected of having learning disabilities. Students must self-identify and provide their own documentation.

13. ___TRUE: Students do not have a fundamental right to course alterations in college. Each college should have a written procedure for requesting course waiver or substitution, but is not required to grant these requests.

14. ___FALSE: Students may not be denied admission to a college solely based on having a disability. "No otherwise qualified individual with disabilities in the US…shall, solely by reason of his/her disability, be excluded from the participation in…any program receiving federal financial assistance." (504)

15. ___FALSE: Colleges do not have any obligation to develop an IEP for students identified as having learning disabilities. Students are responsible for developing their own IEPs to use in college.

16. ___TRUE: Attention deficit disorder is considered a disabling condition. Students with ADD/ADHD are served under "other health related disabilities."

17. FALSE: Colleges may not deny students with learning disabilities the right to participate in any courses open to nondisabled students.

18. ___TRUE: Students are responsible for self-disclosing the existence of a learning disability, and must provide appropriate documentation in order to receive services in college.

19. ___TRUE: Colleges are not obligated to provide tutorial services specifically for students with learning disabilities. If tutorial services are offered for students, in general, then students with learning disabilities must have access to the same tutoring services.

20. ___FALSE: Colleges may not charge students with learning disabilities for "reasonable accommodations." Colleges that offer a specific program or services for students with learning disabilities that goes beyond the mandated services may charge a fee for these nonmandated services.

21. ___FALSE: Colleges are not required to provide academic adjustments that would fundamentally alter the nature of a program of study.

22. ___FALSE: Colleges may not inquire on an application for admission about the existence of a learning disability. Colleges may offer students the opportunity to provide any additional information that may be helpful in the admission process or provide an explanation for certain difficulties in courses taken in high school.

23. ___TRUE: Colleges that offer specific programs for students with learning disabilities may require students to identify that they are applying to this program, and may require students to self-identify.

24. ___FALSE: Colleges may not use the information of a nonstandardized test to deny admission to a student. Nor may colleges inquire as to the reason the test was taken in a nonstandardized format. Students may provide information if they feel it is appropriate.

25. ___TRUE: Colleges are not required to waive or provide substitutions for math or foreign language courses required to graduate from the college. Colleges must have a written policy as to the procedure for students to request a waiver or substitution.

26. ___FALSE: Public high schools are required by law to provide a free education to students with handicaps until the age of 21 or the receipt of a high school diploma, whichever comes first. Special education services terminate following the granting of a high school diploma. Parents may request a review of the recommendation to graduate and termination of services if they feel that the student has not reached a satisfactory level of achievement.

27. ___FALSE: In order for students to receive services and accommodations in college, they must provide recent (within the last three years) documentation. Students who have not been evaluated since elementary school must secure current documentation.

28. ___FALSE: Colleges may not limit the number of students admitted with learning disabilities, providing these students meet the same general admission criteria as other admitted students. Colleges with specific programs for students with learning disabilities may limit the number of students admitted if the program is only designed for a specific number of students each year.

29. ___FALSE: College professors are required by law to provide any accommodations mandated by law and considered to be "reasonable accommodations." Students must provide the appropriate documentation with the necessary accommodations identified.

30. ___TRUE: Students must provide the college with current psychoeducational evaluations that identity the student as learning disabled. Most colleges will accept documentation within the previous three years. However, other colleges may require more current documentation.

Lawyers are the only persons for whom ignorance of the law is not punished! Others of us are less fortunate. Students with learning disabilities are punished every year—for problems they didn't create. Their parents are also punished, saddened by the frustrations and unhappiness of their children, resulting not from disregard but from ignorance of the law. Schools, too, are punished for many of the same reasons, but their punishments are usually deserved.

Ignorance of the law is inexcusable for schools. Equally inexcusable is the inclination of some schools to fail to inform parents and students of their rights. That we work together with parents by assuring them and their children of appropriate services inheres in our fundamental purposes and results in educational experiences that benefit them as well as us. Parents are not the enemies of school systems. They are allies who complement our efforts to provide everything their children require to realize educational and personal success.

Don't get us wrong. We know some parents who use the law as drunks use lampposts, more for support than for illumination. They use the law to support their misinterpretations of the facts and their unrealistic expectations of the school, not to illuminate reasonable requests for services. These parents constitute a minority in most schools. They do, however, underscore even further the need for schools to understand the law and its implications for education.

Teaching children, especially those with learning disabilities, without an understanding of relevant law is like leading your family through a jungle without a map. Like the law, maps avoid potential problems, safeguard not only children but the entire family, and save you a whole lot of embarrassment. Sharing the map with others further assures that everyone is going in the same direction and working together to guarantee a safe and successful journey.

That's what schools are all about—safe and successful journeys. Such journeys in most schools involve a lot of hard work. In-service training programs must be provided, legal updates must be shared with teachers and administrators, and consultants or others must inform school personnel of recent changes in the law and of their implications for school policy. Without such hard work, schools invariably engage in practices that are organized, comfortable, and wrong. Share the materials in this section, then, with everyone, including parents and students, to assure that the rights of all students are guaranteed.

LD PROGRAMS—THEIR LIKELY AND DESIRABLE FUTURES

First, a quick story . . .

Blake was a second-grader with enough energy to heat the school. Unfortunately, the school didn't need heating, neither did his teachers, all of whom got "fired up" after only a half hour in the room with him. One even complained that after just ten minutes with Blake, she began to experience motion sickness! He was a bundle of curiosity surrounded by noise, constantly under foot, aggressively inquisitive, and rarely able to focus on anything for longer than a minute—a loving but exhausting riddle to everyone in the school.

To all but one…The school counselor was convinced that Blake had attention deficit disorder (ADD). ADD had been receiving more than its share of professional and commercial press and was rapidly becoming the "disability du jour" in many of the schools in neighboring suburbs. The counselor shared her perceptions with others, and Blake was referred to the school psychologist for diagnosis. After a few meetings with Blake and his parents, the school psychologist indicated that Blake "probably had ADD."

The school recommended a local psychiatrist for additional diagnosis and treatment, but Blake's parents made an appointment with one suggested by their family doctor. Having already reviewed the school's materials, the psychiatrist asked more questions about family history, Blake's general behavior at home, and the relationships among family members. Just before the conclusion of their appointment, she indicated to the parents that she would like to administer some of "her own tests."

The parents gave permission, the tests were administered, and Blake and his parents had their final appointment with the psychiatrist. She told them that Blake did not have ADD. She indicated that her tests revealed normal development in all areas—with one rather startling exception. Blake was unusually bright. She suggested that the school-administered tests may have failed to reveal Blake's intelligence because large-group settings permit a "less than serious" approach to test taking.

Although the high-average IQ results in Blake's school file revealed a capable youngster, they obscured his superior range of abilities and resulted in placement that failed to challenge him. Blake's parents discovered subsequently that the same may have been true for at least one or two of the other four or five students in Blake's class who had been suspected of ADD—three of whom were medicated for their problems.

Blake's coursework was accelerated, and his parents and teachers elevated their academic as well as their behavioral expectations of him. His playground behavior remained a challenge to school personnel as well as some of his classmates, but his grades improved and his focus in the classroom improved dramatically. As important, his parents were pleased with the school's eventual response to the psychiatrist's recommendations.

STRIVING FOR ACCURACY OF DIAGNOSIS

This story suggests a couple of considerations for all teachers. Children deserve understanding the most—when they deserve it the least. This is especially true of children with learning disabilities, but it is similarly true of all students. Their honesty and candor send signals to parents and teachers every day, but many of them are routinely misinterpreted. Teachers misinterpret student behavior for a variety of reasons, most of which are valid.

Most teachers require daily levels of psychic energy that would leave Freud slack-jawed. Their job responsibilities include everything from attendance reports to lesson plans to phone calls to parents. They deal with children who are shooting spitballs, crying from falls, running through halls, and climbing the walls. Then they have to attend meetings with special education teachers and counselors to identify possible reasons for student behavior. They depend on the specialists—you and me—to come up with the right answers.

Sometimes we don't. Misdiagnoses will continue to be made in the future. If they are made arbitrarily, however, they will continue to alienate parents and teachers from special education considerations and will reinforce the assertions of many mainstreamed teachers that special education departments are populated by charlatans. We can be certain, then, that the future of special education departments will be influenced largely by parents and teachers who misunderstand our purposes and who use stories like the one above—no matter how infrequent—to support their opposition to our programs.

Programs dealing with learning disabilities are especially vulnerable to such opposition. Their "hidden" characteristics will continue to mislead many parents and teachers, some of whom are still too imbued with the "pick-yourself-up-by-your-bootstraps" mentality to acknowledge the crippling effects of learning disabilities. We combat such thinking when we validate their legitimacy by diagnosing them correctly and avoiding capricious interpretations of student behaviors.

TAKING A CAREFUL LOOK AT OURSELVES

The future of learning disabilities programs is, to a very large extent, in our own hands. We may not agree with everything W. Edwards Deming said a few years ago, but we do accept his assertion that 95 percent of the problems in organizations are systemic. That is, such problems do not reflect the resistance or intransigence of people in the organization as much as they signal the dysfunction of the organization itself.

Schools, like the rest of us, have to look in the nearest mirror when children have problems. The first question they must ask is "What are we doing to provoke or contribute to this student behavior?" We discussed this question extensively in Section 1. It warrants additional consideration now, because the future success of school systems is so dependent on the answer.

The same is true of programs for learning disabilities. Special education departments must ask fundamentally the same question of themselves. "What are we doing to damage the lines of communication that are so vital to parent and teacher understanding of learning disabilities and their treatment?" If we accept the premise that most problems are systemic, we must ask ourselves how we might be contributing to the alienation or the misunderstanding that sometimes characterizes our relationships with others in the building or the community.

Because special education departments are powerful but remote forces in most schools, we inadvertently threaten teachers and students who don't understand our purposes and practices. We often occupy large areas of the building, teach smaller classes than mainstreamed teachers, and speak a language that is foreign to most other teachers and administrators. We exert a level of influence that is at times bothersome but generally unquestioned because of federal and state mandates.

Such favored status and obvious power can provoke jealousy or misunderstanding throughout the school and community. We must ask ourselves, therefore, what we are doing to contribute to it and how we might remedy it.

THE VALUE OF COLLABORATION

Collaboration is one answer. It is education's most recent catchword because it works. Collaboration is the organizational equivalent of sandbagging the river at flood stage. It involves several people coordinating their efforts to keep their heads above water. It promotes positive synergy in organizations, a phenomenon that makes the total greater than the sum of its individual parts. Collaboration is coalesced power that can cause 2+2 to equal 5 or 6.

Organizations realize such synergy only when antagonisms are virtually eliminated and mutual cooperation is guaranteed. Cooperation is the catalyst that creates and releases such organizational energy. It is effective only when the organization develops clearly defined goals and keeps them in focus. Such goals must relate to the mission statement and general philosophy of the organization and must be not only acceptable but preeminent in the minds of everyone who shares a responsibility to achieve them.

Without a continuing focus on such goals, teachers find themselves expected to "cooperate" with other organizational purposes: eliminating "waves," deferring to administrators, satisfying unreasonable parent requests, even placing students in mainstreamed classes to save money. In effect, they are expected to fall in line with purposes that have little to do with what the organization claims to stand for.

When this happens, the organization is determining the goals; that is, the needs of the school itself are determining its purposes—randomly, usually selfishly, and only incidentally to the needs of students. To assure synergy, however, the reverse must be true. Mutually acceptable goals must determine the organization. Goals must come first. They must drive the school system, and they must promote levels of cooperation that coalesce the skills and conceptual input of everyone who works with students.

This means that special education programs must:

◆ Help mainstreamed teachers understand the special needs of students with learning disabilities and assist them with the organization and delivery of the curriculum.

◆ Help mainstreamed teachers understand the purposes of inclusion and work on their behalf to accommodate the time and energy demands of working with students with learning disabilities and attending the several meetings to which they will be invited.

◆ Promote interesting and informative in-service training programs to update mainstreamed teachers and administrators on federal and state law, the purposes of special education services, learning research, curriculum revision, and relevant instructional technique.

◆ Work closely with teacher groups to develop and refine curriculum and promote instructional improvement that is in line with established practice and current learning research.

◆ Be available to teachers and administrators as consultants to promote the purposes of special education and to improve the quality of education for all students, especially those with diagnosed learning or behavioral problems.

◆ Be sensitive to the winds of discontent within the building and community, then establish dialogue with teachers and parents to explain legislative mandates and promote consensus among them.

Only when we align our purposes with the goals of the school, keep them in focus, and work closely with colleagues and parents to share and promote them do we guarantee a place in the school that recognizes the importance of our contributions and that complements the work of others.

THE DANGERS OF PROVINCIALISM

Let's admit it—some special education programs are peripheral rather than central to the school's instructional program. They are considered ancillary, subordinate, auxiliary to the people in the building who do the real work. They may be one of the school's support services—expected to operate outside the instructional arena, approached only when someone feels a need for them.

Such a perception may be consistent with the organizational flowcharts of many schools, but it fails to reflect special education's profound influence on schools within the past few decades. The research focusing on the instructional needs of students with learning disabilities and the profound questions being asked by psychologists and special education personnel are anything but ancillary and have resulted in significant new knowledge about classroom instruction.

Such research and a growing knowledge of the learning process have helped instruction evolve to the point in this country where modality learning and higher order thought process have become commonplace in many schools. Many teachers also have learned to accommodate the developmental milestones of adolescents that influence their levels of abstract reasoning and their ability to handle conceptually sophisticated material.

Little of special education is ancillary. Its influence has become so profound and the skills of special education have become so pronounced that it can no longer be allowed to operate on the periphery of the school's educational program. This move into the mainstream of education may be special education's most desirable future. Once accepted as central within the school's instructional program, the influence of special education may affect the learning of all students and promote a total school response to the needs of students with learning disabilities.

To accomplish this task, programs for learning disabilities must reexamine education's big picture and identify areas where it is appropriate to "color outside the lines." We must rethink our purposes and creatively redesign processes and programs to accomplish them. The relative isolation of special education is no longer tolerable in schools that are desperately seeking ways to accommodate the learning needs of disenfranchised, disadvantaged, or disabled students.

MESSAGES FROM THE MEDIA

Provincialism may be quaint in rural America, but it's self-destructive in schools and other organizations. Special educators who avoid the hustle and bustle of mainstream education are well advised to tap their reserves of psychic energy to make the move from bit player to box-office attraction. The supporting cast may contribute to the success of the movie, but when compared to the headliners, they are usually dispensable.

The dispensability of programs for students with learning disabilities seems to be a constant issue in the media. Many university undergraduate programs are reported to be questioning the validity of accommodations for students with learning disabilities. Graduate schools are imposing rigorous testing procedures on all students, including those with learning disabilities. In fact, it seems that the further students advance in school—as well as in life—the harder it is for them to find accommodations for disabilities.

Educators across the country are claiming that Public Law 94-142 has imposed regulatory as well as financial burdens on schools and communities. We need not name them, but influential groups nationwide are challenging the growing costs of required special education programs and are encouraging the federal government to eliminate the prescriptive mandates that affect local school decision making.

Many favor a return to the pre-1975, pre-Public Law 94-142 time when schools and local communities determined what was in the best interests of students with learning or behavioral disabilities. Some students benefited from local support. Unfortunately, many others were forced to adjust to the regular classroom or were placed in isolated rooms where they rarely received the specialized instruction they needed to learn at levels commensurate with their intellectual abilities. Many eased the burden on schools simply by dropping out. Then they became burdens on society—and themselves.

A recent article in the Boston *Globe* quoted a state representative as saying, "This is a system that allows those who are more aggressive or ambitious to beat the daylights out of those who are playing by the rules." Now is the time, he said, "...to inject a little common sense and equity into this rather than having advocates and aggressive parents just send us the bill." He went on to indicate that he wanted to change the portion of the law that allowed parents to challenge schools regarding the identification as well as the treatment of their children's learning disabilities.

This quote represents the thinking of a significant number of people in society who question the logic of tolerating disruptive students because of alleged behavioral disabilities. Many of these same people challenge the need to provide accommodations for students with learning disabilities who are otherwise intellectually capable. Said another state representative: "If you have above-average IQ, it ought to be an absolute bar to special education."

Like the many people who fail to understand that average and above-average students are the ones most affected by learning disabilities, such politicians are missing the educational boat. Unfortunately, they have the power and the wherewithal to change our futures. To transform them into allies in the fight against learning disabilities, we must educate them. As emphasized already in this section, the education of these people is in our hands.

TOOTING A FEW HORNS

A part of this responsibility is to share a knowledge of our several successes with friends as well as foes. Special education is always in need of good public relations. We are wise to remember, therefore, that good PR is a four-step process. One, do something good. Two, tell everybody. Three, tell everybody. Four, tell everybody. Tooting one's own horn is not always bad, especially when those aggressively misinformed critics out there keep taking potshots at us.

The Mortenson Research Seminar on Public Policy Analysis indicates that postsecondary opportunities for students with learning disabilities have improved significantly within the past fifteen to twenty years. They indicate that in 1978, only 2.6 percent of all first-time, full-time freshmen reported one or more disabilities. Sixteen years later, that figure rose to 9.2 percent—most of whom were students with learning disabilities.

In addition, between 1977 and 1993, the percentage of students served by federal programs has increased from 8.33 percent to just under 12 percent. The distribution of K-12 students with disabilities has changed as well. The number of students diagnosed with specific learning disabilities has grown from 21.6 percent of the total disabled population in 1977 to just under 50 percent by 1993.

Contrary to the opinions of some critics, the increase of students being diagnosed with specific learning disabilities has little to do with the predispositions of special education personnel to create jobs for themselves. Certainly, some special educators may be a bit overzealous in that regard. Stories like the one in the beginning of this section do happen in schools across the country.

What is more likely is the refinement of the diagnostic process and the increased sensitivity and willingness of classroom teachers to refer students for testing and possible eligibility for special education services. Growing numbers of mainstreamed teachers recognize the signs of learning disabilities in their students and are responding to the requests of special education departments to refer them for appropriate diagnosis and treatment. This, too, is a credit to special education teachers.

But the critics persist. They resent federal and state regulations, the costs of special education programs, the appearance of increased permissiveness in schools, and the apparent growth of special education programs. Consider the idea that critics are people who knock without entering. If such is the case, we have to open the door for them to promote their understanding of the purposes and value of programs for students with learning disabilities.

LET'S WRAP IT UP

As one of history's great insights suggests, "We have met the enemy, and he is us!" O.K., "enemy" is a bit strong, considering the sensitive and competent people who fill our ranks. Reconsider the notion, however, that we may be contributing to our own problems. We are well advised to heed Deming's observation that 95 percent of any organization's problems are systemic. At one time or another, every system must use the nearest mirror to reflect on what it is doing to cause some of its own problems.

Controversy touches almost everything we do. As a result, we find ourselves in criticism's cross hairs more than does any other educational system. We survive the occasional potshot when we ask ourselves, "What is it about the operation of programs for students with learning disabilities that is furthering the confusion and resistance of many teachers and parents, and provoking blatant threats from politicians?"

Each school must answer this question in its own way, but, above all, each must establish partnerships with its various constituencies to improve the general understanding of learning disabilities as well as the quality of special education services. Otherwise, misinformation and misunderstanding will continue to influence legislative decision making, and PL 92-142 will remain a periodic provocation rather than a continuing opportunity for all students.

Special educators must spearhead aggressive awareness campaigns throughout the country, particularly in local schools and communities. We must join forces with other professionals and parents to assure the reauthorization of needed federal legislation—and we must promote a general sensitivity to, and acceptance of, diagnostic and treatment programs for students with learning disabilities.